Nursing Research II

Nursing Research I

Edited by Phyllis J. Verhonick, R.N., Ed.D.

Professor of Nursing and Director of Research
School of Nursing, University of Virginia
Charlottesville

With 8 Contributing Authors

LITTLE, BROWN AND COMPANY, BOSTON

Nursing Research II

Contributing Authors

FAYE G. ABDELLAH, R.N., Ed.D., LL.D.
Assistant Surgeon General and Chief Nurse Officer
U.S. Public Health Service
Department of Health, Education, and Welfare
Washington, D.C.

VIRGINIA S. CLELAND, R.N., Ph.D.
Professor of Nursing
Center for Health Research
Wayne State University
Detroit, Michigan

DONNA KAYE DIERS, R.N., M.S.N.
Dean and Associate Professor
Yale University School of Nursing
New Haven, Connecticut

DANIEL HOWLAND, Ph.D.
Professor of Management
College of Administrative Sciences
Ohio State University
Columbus, Ohio

JANELLE C. KRUEGER, R.N., Ph.D.
Co-Principal Investigator
Regional Program for Nursing Research Development
Western Interstate Commission for Higher Education (WICHE)
Boulder, Colorado

RUTH LITFIN SCHMIDT, R.N., M.S.N.
Assistant Professor
Yale University School of Nursing
New Haven, Connecticut

ALTON L. TAYLOR, M.Ed., Ed.D.
Associate Professor of Education and Assistant Director
Office of Institutional Analysis
University of Virginia
Charlottesville

JOHN P. YOUNG, D. Eng.
Professor of Public Health Administration
School of Hygiene and Public Health
The Johns Hopkins University
Baltimore, Maryland

Preface

THE purpose of *Nursing Research II* is basically the same as
that of the first volume in this series. The material is aimed at the
beginning researcher, who has a master's or doctoral degree. The
subject is specific clinically oriented researches in nursing. Selected
investigations exemplify the scientific method or research process
in clinical settings.

Each contributing author is either a nurse researcher or a scientist who has worked very closely with nurses in research. Because
nursing research is still in its infancy compared with other disciplines, nursing must rely on other professions to assist with its
beginning investigations.

As in the earlier volume, the collaborative approach attempts
to bridge the gap between nursing and other areas of scientific
endeavor.

To build a solid foundation of research for a growing profession
is a long, slow process, and contributions will be required from a
broad range of disciplines.

P. J. V.

Charlottesville

Contents

Nursing Research in a Clinical Setting

I

THE conduct of research in nursing related to patient care has been plagued with multiple problems. There are few precise measurements for investigating nursing care to patients. Also it is difficult to maintain tight controls in a patient setting, the clinical laboratory of the nurse-researcher. Some investigators in nursing have been able to overcome successfully these difficult barriers to carrying out clinical research. It is their examples in Part I of this volume that will assist the beginning nurse researcher, for it includes contributions by three outstanding nurse-researchers. The problems that they study are directly related to the improvement of patient care.

The first chapter, by Dr. Faye Abdellah, deals specifically with the development of criterion measures for research in nursing. Specific sources and types of criterion measures are listed and the extension of their application in the study of nursing phenomena is described in detail. Dr. Abdellah has pulled measures together from a wide variety of sources as well as from her own experience.

Dr. Virginia Cleland, the author of Chapter 2, discusses general research in the clinical setting. Dr. Cleland also presents in detail two researches in which she has been involved. One is the study of the effect of stress on performance, and the other is the prevention of bacteriuria in female patients with indwelling catheters. Clinical investigations in nursing leading to the prevention of complications or illnesses are truly pioneering efforts. The study of preventing urinary infections is an excellent blueprint for nurses interested in clinical research pursuits.

In the final chapter of Part I Donna Diers and Ruth Litfin Schmidt present their work on interaction analysis in nursing research. Direct and systematic observation in the clinical setting produces data that may serve as a basis for developing a theoretical framework. The problems encountered in clinical research are realistically outlined, and excellent guidelines are presented for nurse researchers.

The combination of the three chapters in Part I is a relatively comprehensive guide for nurse-investigators by four nurse-authors who have had first-hand experience in patient-oriented research.

Criterion Measures for Research in Nursing
Faye G. Abdellah

I

IN the face of the complex problems associated with the organization, financing, administration, and delivery of health services,
there is a growing consensus concerning the need for innovation
and experimentation if the United States is to succeed in fulfilling
goals declared by Congress, which call for making available to all
persons the optimum level of quality health care economically
feasible.

One of the more promising approaches for resolving the complicated issues involved in the management and delivery of health
services appears to lie in research and the application of interdisciplinary skills not commonly represented in the health field,
e.g., systems management and operations research, computer and
information sciences, mathematics and quantitative methods,
managerial economics, political science, and other relevant disciplines. The introduction of such interdisciplinary skills into health-
services research, although necessary, is not sufficient. Of equal
importance is the need for nurse-researchers who can deal with
some of the real problems important to nursing practice. What is
important to nursing practice or nursing education, or both, is
determined by criterion measures.

NEED FOR DEVELOPING CRITERION MEASURES

The failure of the nursing profession to formulate agreed-on goals and health priorities reflects one of the key problems encountered in trying to define criterion measures against which to evaluate the effects of services provided. Nurses themselves cannot agree on measurable criteria for effective nursing care. First, let us define a criterion measure. It is a comparison, object, rule, standard, or test for making a judgment, especially a qualitative judgment, and it may serve as the basis for assignment to a class or category. It is also the behavior goal by which progress is judged. Thus a criterion is an external basis for judgment. The criterion variable is sometimes referred to as the dependent variable. A *criterion measure* is a score or a value in the dependent variable or in the variable to be predicted.

Unlike the use of criterion measures in controlled laboratory research, in which the organism being studied is in a controlled environment, such as in a test tube or cage, in nursing these measures must be employed in the framework of the patient's complex environment. Since there are so many extraneous variables in the situation, both organismic and environmental, it is exceedingly difficult to keep the variables under sufficient control. There is a recognized lag in the development of studies in clinical nursing practice. This lag is attributable to the large number of methodological problems that are very difficult to solve. One of the most important problems is the development of criterion measures of nursing effectiveness.

Assessment of quality of care must rest on a conceptual and operational definition. The definition of quality nursing care is very elusive and very difficult to describe. Some investigators feel that criteria of quality are nothing more than value judgments that are applied to several aspects, properties, ingredients, or dimensions of a process called nursing care. As such, the definition of quality may be almost anything anyone wishes it to be, although it is a reflection of the values and goals apparent in the nursing-care system and in the society of which nursing is a part.

The difficulties in identifying criterion measures in nursing have directed much of the research in nursing into areas that are more amenable to research, e.g., the study of the nurse — what she does, how much time she spends on patient care, and so forth. This knowledge has value in that it helps to identify problem areas that need to be studied in more depth. Ultimately, however, the nurse as she practices must be measured against the effects (criterion measures) of nursing practice on the patient or client. Likewise, studies of the role of the nurse have value in giving direction to the nursing profession but lack specific information on the effect of practice on patient care. These studies will have little decisive impact on the improvement of nursing practice if there are no adequate criterion measures to evaluate the effects of changed practice on patient care.

Measurements of patient care, in terms of valid and reliable criterion measures, are a crucial part of research in nursing. That the measurement of the effects of nursing practice on patient care continues to be identified as the number one priority for nursing research reflects the difficulties being encountered in finding valid and reliable measures. Measurement of the effectiveness of patient care can be approached by evaluating the adequacy of the facilities in which patient care is provided, the operating policies of the administrative and organizational structure of the agency providing patient care, the professional qualifications and competency of personnel providing the care, and the evaluation of the consumer of the care, namely, the patient or client and the larger public.

EVALUATION OF QUALITY OF CARE

An important question to be raised is: "What is to be measured?" One might develop a list of qualities to be measured and then look at the presence or absence of each quality listed. One might also attach a weight to the qualities, reflecting the importance of each quality. One might also select the qualities that are so important that if they were absent, the quality of care would assuredly be low. One might also select only those qualities that have experimentally determined measurability, validity, and reliability. Evaluation of the quality of care has sometimes been developed to such a degree of mathematical sophistication that those who first attempted to apply it have had to bypass it and have found that it could not be applied on a day-to-day basis.

The nurse-researcher can take some initial steps to assure that the development of the evaluation of the quality of care is being carried out properly. One must first choose the qualities that comprise the criterion measure or dependent variable. Weights must be attached to these in terms of priorities. There must also be specified measures of degrees of presence of these qualities. The researcher then combines this array in some functional form or forms. Figure 1 depicts the principles and sequence for utilizing criterion measures.

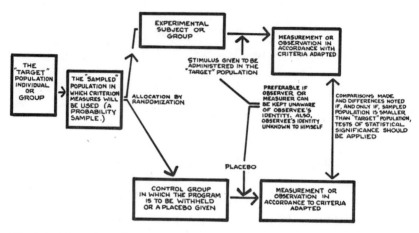

Fig. 1-1. Flow chart showing principles and sequence to follow in using criterion measures.

Nurse-researchers become discouraged in accomplishing goals of the research design. Frequently the measures are too complex, or the day-to-day documentation is either too tedious or not visibly relevant to what is going on in the real-world setting. As a result substitute measures are used or approximated and become lost in the data acquisition. This results in the consumption of so much time and so many resources that judgments are made that the documentation is not worth the effort.

RECOGNITION OF SIGNIFICANT CRITERIA

The major achievements or breakthroughs in nursing need to be defined in terms of the following characteristics: First, they have to involve a new perception of relationships or they have to result in new operations, including scientific ones. Specifically they have to help people to see something not perceived before as represented by new discoveries or new verifiable propositions. A second essential condition, whether perceptual or operational, is that they should prove fruitful in producing a substantial impact that leads to further knowledge. Important advances typically will define combined theory, methods, and results. Scientific advances usually cut across at least two of these aspects and often across all three of them.

SELECTION OF CRITERION MEASURES

The criterion measure(s) selected will be influenced by the research problem and the hypotheses that were developed to explore the problem. After defining these variables as concretely and operationally as possible, the researcher must decide how the dependent variable will be measured, i.e., whether it will be a direct or an indirect measurement. This decision will be influenced by the ease with which the variable can be directly measured and the extent to which a subtler measure might yield more meaningful data. In most studies the researcher has available a variety of criterion measures to assess the dependent variable. If the variable can be measured in terms of a physiological response, there are available many scientific measuring instruments, yielding highly refined numerical measurements, that might serve as criterion measures. For example, useful physiological criterion measures include, among others: urinary specific gravity, pH, hematocrit, hemoglobin, arterial pressure, blood and plasma volume, temperature, cardiac output, clotting time, prothrombin time, osmolarity (blood and urine), and nitrogen balance.

If the variable is within a psychological or sociological phenomenon, satisfactory testing scales can also be employed. Such variables as personality, motivation, perception, creativity, abilities of all types, intellectual mechanical aptitudes as well as a variety of social attitudes can be measured by using ordinal scales and standard pencil and paper instruments. If this research has already been completed, the researcher has to accept the measures of the variables as developed by others since these data were originally designed for another purpose. Hospital records, e.g., provide a source of retrospective data but may be limiting in their value particularly because definitions of terms may be markedly different.

Most researchers have to develop their own explanatory or dependent variables. For highly complex variables, measurement can be a difficult task, requiring consultation with experts in the field of measurement.

There are specific criteria that are useful in evaluating the efficiency of criterion measures. Very often a criterion is quite sound as a statement of sufficient conditions to confirm the testing of a hypothesis but is too narrow to serve as a general definition of confirmation.

Criterion measures must meet certain tests in order to be acceptable. Four of the most important criteria for evaluating the adequacy of criterion measures are validity, reliability, sensitivity, and meaningfulness.

Validity

Validity is the most important of the four criteria mentioned. If a measure is not valid, it does not really matter that it meets the conditions of the other tests. Validity is sometimes referred to as relevance. Validity of a measure must be assessed independently on its own merits. It is highly desirable to validate a measure empirically by correlating it with some independent behavioral criterion — a criterion that describes some meaningful objective and observable action.

Before instruments can be selected and developed, it is essential that the researcher have an understanding of the concepts that are basic to measurement. Historically the concept of validity has been given many different definitions that can be ranked from the very empirical to the very theoretical.

The validity of a measure in nursing is simply an empirical matter because it can be defined as the magnitude of its correlation with the patient-change outcome criterion. The patient-change outcome criterion represents the consensus of nursing representatives about an acceptable solution to a given patient's problem. The patient-change outcome criterion is the only valid criterion measure as far as nursing is concerned. Accordingly the validity of any other measure obtained during an experiment can be ascertained by determining its correlation with this criterion. An empirical correlative approach becomes necessary not only to discover the relationship of the variables with the patient-change outcome criterion (validity) but also to determine the dimensionality of the measures themselves. The validity of any measure used in an innovative-patient experiment can be determined by its correlation with the patient-change outcome criterion, and the same set of computed correlation coefficients (together with the other intercorrelations) can be used by the researcher to determine the empirical dimensions of all experimental measures. This can be accomplished through factor or cluster analysis.

Reliability

This criterion is sometimes referred to as the reproducibility or repeatability of a measure. It refers to the consistency or precision of the measure. A measure is considered to be reliable if it is consistently reproducible. The concept of reliability has a somewhat different meaning when applied to certain patient-subsystem measures because of the nature of the measures of the patient situation in which measurement occurs. When the measure is tested for reliability, the first step is to determine if the measure is reproducible.

Frequently the measure is a behavior rating obtained in the real-world setting where the behavior itself occurs only once. In these circumstances the researcher cannot repeat the measure, hence he or she has to use the second method — a consensus about the behavior that occurred in lieu of the usual correlation. In such cases the reliability of the instruments is more appropriately considered a consensus among judges.

Sensitivity

This test refers to the ability of the measure to detect fine differences among the subjects being studied. For example, a scale consisting of only two categories — improved or not improved — to measure the effects on patients of a specific nursing practice may result in grouping together in the improved category patients whose conditions actually vary widely, some showing more improvement than others. Dividing the scale, however, into too many categories may not increase the sensitivity, since some of the categories may represent distinctions that are too fine for the measure to detect accurately. Sensitivity of a measure by itself is not sufficient without reliability. As a scale is subdivided to increase its sensitivity, specifications for each of the scale values must also be of sufficient clarity and distinction to permit the use of the scale with a high degree of reliability. The measurements on a thermometer represent an example of a true numerical scale with a high degree of sensitivity.

Meaningfulness

The meaningfulness of a measure can also be called the pragmatic test of the measure as a whole, i.e., does the measure have any practical, real-world meaning and application? Meaningfulness of a measure is related to validity, reliability, and sensitivity. If a measure of a variable is not valid, it cannot be meaningful. If the measure is not reliable, it cannot yield meaningful results and if it is insensitive, it loses some of its meaningfulness.

SOURCES OF CRITERION MEASURES

Criterion measures come from many sources. The researcher explores the literature as one source because many measures pertinent to patient-care problems have been developed for laboratory studies or other different but related situations. Other sources are the nurse-practitioner, the clinical nurse specialist, and the family nurse-practitioner working in the community setting and the home as well as in the hospital. In institutional settings, personnel who have daily contact with patients can often suggest important variables in the patient situation.

Discussions with other health workers also provide a fruitful source of potential criterion measures. Most important is the observation of the daily participant in a living situation, which gives the researcher a pertinent source of information for the selection of criterion measures.

USE OF CRITERIA TO MEASURE OUTCOMES

The patient-change outcome criterion is typically a real-world behavior directly related to the solution of the problem being studied. Since the choice of items is, to a large extent, dependent on the patient problem under consideration, the researcher needs to choose criteria that nurses judge and agree on as appropriate solutions to the problem. For example, the patient-change outcome criterion needs to be considered on the basis of whether it is designed for the individual who is acutely or chronically ill or physically and/or mentally handicapped.

In nursing education the student-change outcome criteria are usually skills, grades, or other measures of academic achievement. Measures such as student-participant satisfaction with one's role and expectations are also important outcomes in some experiments. It should be noted that outcome criteria are specific participant- and social-situation variables that have been selected by nurses as a solution to the problem.

Most important are the observation of the participants and an intimate acquaintance with daily living situations that give the researcher his most pertinent source of information for the selection or creation of criterion measures. It is from all of these sources that criterion measures evolve (Table 1-1).

HISTORICAL DEVELOPMENT OF CRITERION MEASURES IN NURSING

Industrial engineers and nurse-researchers have joined forces to develop measures to evaluate patient care. Howland recognized the need for systems models designed to provide organized information to assist in the management decision-making process related to patient care [1]. Descriptions of man-machine systems in task performance and resource utilization variables were developed.

Table 1-1. Selection and Creation of Criterion Measures

Sources	Types
Personal History	History of patient as member of sub-system
Physiological Readings	Measures of, e.g., blood pressure, respiration, nitrogen balance, urine pH, and cardiac output
Behavioral Ratings	Checklist of symptoms and behaviors; measures of behavioral performance
Psychological Tests	Social adjustment measures (personality and academic achievement tests)
Essay and Open-ended Questions	Measures of satisfaction, morale, and self-regard
Attitude and Expectancy Scales	Measures of personal attitudes and expectancies, morale and cohesiveness measures, attitudes of community toward subsystem
Economic Records	Records both of financial productivity of subsystem and of cost to community of maintaining subsystem
Administrative Records	Academic records of participants while in subsystem
Research Journal	Narrative accounts of events related to any outcome criteria of the experiment

Howland and his research team specified certain characteristics of a systems research model:

1. It is designed to provide descriptive rather than prescriptive models of man-machine systems.
2. It specifies relationships between levels of task performance and resource utilization.
3. It is based on empirical methods rather than on formal mathematical systems.
4. It is problem-oriented rather than technique-oriented.

The nurse-patient-physician triad was developed by Howland and McDowell. The investigators conceptualized the triad as a servosystem in which the patient generates signals to the monitor. The monitor may respond to the patient signals at one of three levels. The first provides information about patient condition; at the second level the monitor determines the difference between actual and desired patient performance, and makes this information available to the regulator; at the third level the nurse serves as a monitor and takes necessary action for the regulation of the patient's condition. The progressive thinking of this research team has brought together the concepts of homeostasis first envisioned by Cannon and later developed by Wiener and Ashby.

The rationale basic to the nurse-patient-physician triad is that it is viewed as a self-regulating mechanism that constantly compares actual and desired patient conditions and takes action to minimize the difference between the two. This action (which might be nurse action or physician action) is taken to reestablish and maintain the state of the patient within specified limits or an error bandwidth.

Wolfe conducted an exploratory study to identify the factors contributing to the quality of nursing care and to determine the feasibility of measuring these factors [2]. He attempted to develop tools and criteria to measure patient care, but his design and procedures were not adequate to achieve these aims.

Jelinek first published an activity model in 1964 the purpose of which was to demonstrate the feasibility of characterizing the nursing function as a complete system [3]. The model proved to be useful in describing the "real-world" behavior of a nursing unit. In addition it showed that the quantitative aspects of nursing care, measured by the time devoted to various nursing activities by the nursing staff, are closely related to various predetermined and measurable characteristics of the unit that are thought to be predictable. The major thrust of Jelinek's research is in evaluation and development of instruments for measuring both performance and organization characteristics of the patient-care operation.

Direct measurement of patient care was undertaken by Leventhal and Sharp when they conducted an exploratory study to test several hypotheses relating to the independent variable of stress as evidenced by change in facial expressions [4]. Much of this research was based on the earlier work of Birdwhistell (1952). The investigators were successful in developing a complete system of symbols that permitted the observer to record changes in facial expressions.

McLemore adapted the predictive model proposed by House to conduct a study of the organizational effects of nurse-management workshops [5]. It was thought that the extent of success in management-training programs in nursing might be determined by selecting criteria of desired outcomes, ranging from the favorable reactions of workshop participants to the more effective functioning of hospitals. A major problem encountered in this study was one of criterion. Success is defined differently by different people. Even if agreement was reached on which criteria should be examined, there was disagreement on the level that must be attained.

Ingmire attempted to ascertain the extent to which learning opportunities provided in the continuing education program improved leadership skills [6]. A unique contribution of this research was the development of situational exercises that were used to measure overt, manifest behavior, both before and after training, and thus they gave an indication of whether or not actual behavior was changed by participation in the continuing education program.

Johnson [7] also moved into the area of direct measurement and conducted an extensive study of the Palmar Sweat Index (PSI) that resulted in the identification of psychological and behavioral factors associated with it. Theories of psychological stress were basic to the research and were used to evaluate the data produced by the measuring techniques being evaluated.

Measurement of patient care stimulated Dorothy Smith to approach this problem by the development of a nursing-analysis tool (Nursing History Form) to be used as a basis for hospital nursing and programming [8]. The tool provides a beginning step for the evaluation of nursing care by organizing information from patients to permit the development of an effective nursing-care plan.

White extended the earlier work of the development of a progressive patient-care system by constructing a simplified checklist of five nursing criteria to classify patients into intensive, intermediate, or self-care [9]. Bath (by nurse or assistant; or tub-shower) was found to be the most discriminating criterion.

Smith developed a checklist to record interruptions while giving nursing care [10]. The checklist needs further validations. It should prove useful in additional studies of greater depth that attempt to uncover the causes of interruptions.

Wandelt explored the problem of uninterrupted patient care and nursing requirements [11]. This was a descriptive study to determine whether or not the patient's requirements as assessed by a competent nurse could be modified if provided by the same nurse for an uninterrupted interval. The hypothesis was substantiated. Nursing-care requirements of chronically ill adults were modified by periods of uninterrupted care administered on five successive days. Two measurements of nursing-care requirements were not substantiated because of insufficient data. These were the number of requests made by patients and activities judged by competent nurses to be required for comprehensive care, and attitudes of personnel. This study needs to be replicated and extended to other patient-care milieus.

Still another approach was used by Klaus in which an investigation was made of the contribution of clinical experience to nursing proficiency and of how it might be accomplished more efficiently and effectively [12]. A variety of techniques (task analysis, critical incident, and so on) were applied to the definition of instructional objectives concerned with adequate patient care. Information was provided to show how the nurse's time is divided. Proficiency performance was defined and the problems of finding effective criterion measures were spelled out. This research should be particularly useful in measuring on-the-job performance.

If criterion measures that deal with direct measurement of patient care are to be identified, appropriate clinical laboratories have to be developed. Beland (1966) set up such an experimental unit that proved to be successful in providing a setting in which interdisciplinary research could take place.

Research in nursing can produce new knowledge, better methods of caring for people, and sounder rationales for testing nursing practices. Nurses may undertake studies that throw light on patient problems or reveal characteristics of the community setting of health problems.

The first significant early attempt to measure quality nursing care was made by Reiter and Kakosh in 1950 [13]. They identified

12 components of nursing care to define some standards for appraising observed nursing care. These components are:

1. Control of environment
2. Mental adjustment
3. Condition of skin and mucous membranes
4. Elimination
5. Posture, position, and exercise
6. Rest and sleep
7. Nutrition
8. Observation of signs and symptoms
9. Administration of laboratory tests
10. Administration of medicines
11. Administration of treatments
12. Teaching health

Each component was defined in operational terms and an observation guide was developed to record these observations.

Six qualitative categories were next developed and defined to form criterion measures that might be quantitatively scaled. They are:

Dangerous. The patient's health or welfare is endangered by the nursing care that he received.

Safe. No harm comes to the patient from having had nursing care; patient's life and values were protected.

Adequate. To the extent that it is possible, the patient's standards and customary way of living are kept normal so that he recovers to the greatest extent his former state of health at his own rate of recovery.

Optimum. The patient's integrity is respected and he is helped to improve his state of health and is better able to care for himself.

Maximum. The design of patient care is based on the best known scientific advances to date.

Ideal. Patient care is examined and evaluated for the purpose of improvement through controlled research in nursing.

Quality nursing practice is based on scientific findings that emerge from a study of nursing practice itself. Quality nursing practice was defined by Reiter and Kakosh as follows:

For the patient it means that the best present nursing practice is not good enough and for the nurse it means incorporating research in nursing into the practice of nursing. The components of such care not only include the conscious and continuous search for the reasons underlying the nursing care but also the creation of new ways of care.

Several other direct attempts have been made to measure quality nursing practice. A long-range study was initiated by Aydelotte and Simon at Iowa [14]. Four experiments were conducted in an ongoing hospital setting to test the hypothesis that increasing the amounts and quality of nursing care would produce improvements in patient welfare. Changes introduced on the experimental wards consisted of increasing the size of the nursing staff, conducting in-service education programs, and combining increased staffing and in-service education. With the exception of a reduction in patient complaints during the first experiment, no improvement in patient welfare was produced. The results suggest that there is a limit to the contribution that nursing care can make to patient welfare and that this limit is much closer to the existing level of care than was formerly thought.

Patient welfare as a criterion measure for evaluating changes differentiates this study from other types of research in nursing. Researchers recognize that the welfare of the patient is the most relevant criterion for evaluating changes in nursing practice. However, patient welfare is a complex phenomenon containing multiple criterion measures, making it difficult to define and even more difficult to measure.

Simon continued the work by studying activity patterns of hospitalized medical and urological patients with the aim of deriving patient-activity indices that might be used as measures of patient welfare [15]. Sampling was carried out by nurse-observers who used a special code to record what each patient was doing at the moment of observation. Twenty-eight different indices were computed for each patient, each representing the proportion of time that the patient spent in a given category of activity. These indices were correlated with other patient-welfare measures and were found to be significant.

Bryant and New undertook an experiment with staffing patterns focused on two independent variables: the ratio of staff nurses to auxiliary personnel and the ratio of all nursing personnel to patients [16]. The study was designed to answer two questions: (1) When the total nursing hours/patient are varied, how does the proportion of nursing time spent with the patient vary, and what happens to the attitudes of both patients and nurses concerning the new situation? (2) When the composition of a nursing team is varied, how does the proportion of nursing time spent with the patient vary, and what happens to the attitudes of both patients and nurses concerning the new situation?

Answers to these questions were sought by staffing two units in each of two hospitals for nine consecutive weeks with nine different combinations of nursing personnel. The proportion of staff nurses varied from 25 to 75 percent of the total number of personnel, and the average hours of nursing care provided each patient ranged from 2.1 to 5.1. Each variable had three possible alternatives, resulting in nine possible combinations. The research thus employed a factorial design. Each combination of staffing was tried out for one week and evaluated. The procedure used for observing nurse activities was adapted from time-sampling methods developed by the Public Health Services' Division of Nursing. Attitudes of patients and personnel were evaluated from questionnaire and interviews. The study was a logical sequel to the nurse-utilization studies that had been done previously.

Questions have been raised about the validity and practicability of subdividing the independent variables into so many different subgroups and then making an assessment of change in one week's time. Despite the weaknesses in the research design, valuable clues are provided about nurse-staffing patterns that need to be tested further. For example, in experimental "situation 8," which was a high total hours nursing-staff combination, many of the nurses felt uneasy and tired because there was insufficient work for them. In other words, high levels of nurse staffing could have negative consequences or as the investigators conclude, too many nurses may be worse than too few.

An important replication of some aspects of the Iowa study was conducted by Bryant (1964), testing the effects of minimal nursing care. In essence the study was conducted to explore the effect on patient welfare, varying the staffing pattern when nursing hours/

patient-day are at minimal levels or less than two hours, using the tools and techniques developed by Aydelotte and New. A significant finding was that as hours/patient-day and kinds of nursing hours were varied, no major changes in patients' reactions were detected except at very high levels of hours.

The pioneering work of Aydelotte and Simon stimulated several other studies of attempts to measure the quality of nursing care [14].

A four-year study of nursing care of the hospitalized patient with a diagnosis of myocardial infarction was undertaken by Nite and Willis at Community Studies, Inc., Kansas City [17]. A nurse and a social scientist participated in giving direct care to patients and were able to identify some of the "measuring rods" that could be used in evaluating a special type of care given to these patients. The conceptualization underlying this research is that nursing practice can be therapeutic when it is directed toward correctly identified problems of specific patients, and when administered to the patient will give evidence of resolution of these problems.

The researchers were able to identify specific criteria of improvement to measure the progress of the cardiac patient. Examples of such criteria vis-à-vis the patient were that: He will gradually show less apprehension as he is given an understanding of the physiological process causing pain; he will permit the nurse to perform necessary activities for him; and he will tend to sleep during the day after major activities and during the entire night without medication.

Attempts to measure quality nursing by the nurse's performance have had limited use in measuring the effect of nursing care on patient recovery. A small but significant study was conducted by Dumas in which she showed that clinical experiments in nursing practice are feasible and can be used to measure quality nursing [18]. The aim of this research was to observe the effect of an experimental nursing process on the incidence of vomiting during recovery from anesthesia. One experiment included the study of a sample of patients who were scheduled for surgical intervention. Patients assigned to the experimental group were given nursing care by research nurses who used the experimental nursing process. This is a process directed toward helping the patient obtain a suitable psychological state for surgery. Specific steps are described in this process: (1) the nurse observes the patient's behavior and explores with him whether or not he is experiencing distress; (2) the nurse explores further to find out what is causing the distress and what is needed to relieve it; (3) an appropriate course of action is next undertaken to relieve the stress; and (4) the nurse follows through on her action(s) to see if the distress is relieved. This experimental nursing process proved to be successful in reducing postoperative vomiting. An important theoretical basis for this study is that emotional reactions of surgical patients to their illness and treatment have important consequences for their postoperative course. The study demonstrated further that the relief of emotional distress is a part of the nurse's professional role.

Elms extended the work of Dumas and developed a measurement index for predicting patient responses to surgical recovery that can assess the need for specified nursing intervention [19]. Criteria were developed for judging specific nursing needs postoperatively, testing the hypothesis that it is possible to predict a patient's response to surgery on the basis of immediate postoperative behavior patterns correlated with previously assessed personality traits. Instruments included: the Edwards Personal Preference Schedule (EPPS), an interview, and a questionnaire. The investigator might have strengthened her research had she used the EPPS in combination with the Minnesota Multiphasic Personality Inventory (MMPI). Further testing of the instruments is necessary. The value of Elms' study is that it provides a way to examine immediate postoperative behavior as an indicator of the patient's adaptation to surgery. Such a determination may provide a scientific basis for nursing intervention.

There are many dimensions to the measurement of quality care. Feyerherm proposed a mathematical model to study changes in activity patterns for nurses and aides [20]. Time spent in various activities was assumed to be related to staff composition and patient mixtures. The model was fitted to data from the day shift on two medicosurgical units and one obstetrical unit. Variables were related to patient mixtures based on total patient census, numbers of patients in care-level categories, and the number of patients in hospital-day categories.

Investigators have also adapted methodologies from the behavioral sciences to measure the quality of care.

Nurses' notes were selected for analysis as a way of studying ritualistic behavior. Walker and Selmanoff [21] defined ritualistic behavior operationally as repetitive acts that were judged by nursing services in the university hospital to be dysfunctional, e.g., unnecessary, useless, undesirable, or harmful in achieving adequate patient care. Not all ritualistic behaviors are harmful; some can serve useful purposes.

Nurses' notes were selected, since they represent the recorded, professional judgment of the nurse and are an important aspect of the special contribution of the professional nurse in the determination of the patients' mediconursing diagnosis and therapy. Data were obtained through interviews with professional nurses, practical nurses, and interns. Observations were also made by members of the research team of the time spent in writing, and the incidence of referral to the nurses' notes was studied by observing patient care actually given on several wards of the university hospital.

Nurses' notes were found to be relatively unimportant by the majority of the mediconursing personnel interviewed. Doctors and supervisory nurses made minimal use of nurses' notes. Nurses spent little time in writing notes, and an analysis of the content of these notes showed a high incidence of omission of essential information. However, the chart was still recognized as the primary means of communication of those aspects of a patient's condition and progress not recorded elsewhere. The investigators concluded that, in the confusion of change, rituals had apparently been discarded but had not been replaced with pertinent goal-oriented behavior.

Flitter and Tate developed a nursing-performance evaluation instrument for use by hospitals for evaluation and guidance related to the general staff nurse, and a manual was also prepared for its use [22]. The form has merit but needs further testing.

Griffin and Perlmutter conducted an exploratory study using closed-circuit television for data collection and identification of criteria for nursing practice [23]. This study extended the earlier work by Matheney, Griffin, and Kinsinger that successfully tested the feasibility of using closed-circuit television to enable an existing number of nursing instructors to teach an increased number of students. The study provides an objective tool to document what actually happens in a nursing situation. The finding of this study shows that videotapes and closed-circuit television offer promising tools to provide objective documentation and may be a major break-through in the measurement of the quality of nursing care.

An exploratory study conducted by Hall (1968) that has great potential in providing clues to the measurement of the effects of nursing practice was carried out at Loeb Center for Nursing and Rehabilitation. Hypotheses and methodology were later tested by Alfano in a larger study and provide definitive results about the therapeutic effects of nursing care on patients in this unique environment. Since only professional nurses provide care at the Loeb Center, it is hoped that new concepts can be identified in the measurement of patient welfare directly related to nursing care.

Professional Standards Review Organizations (PSRO)

In 1972 (P.L. 92-603, Title XI), Congress amended the Social Security Act to mandate professional review of health care delivered to those individuals participating in Medicare (Title XVIII), Medicaid (Title XIX) and Maternal and Child Health Programs (Title V). The PSRO provides the organizational structure and system for evaluating the quality of health care. This is a commitment on the part of the Federal Government to assure that all health care is necessary, meets professional standards, and is economical and appropriate. An underlying concept of PSRO is that health care is provided by practitioners and review of care provided should be performed by peers. The present legislation emphasizes review by doctors but increased pressure by the nursing profession on Congress in time will lead to greater involvement of nonphysician health-care practitioners in PSRO review.

The American Nurses' Association in a contract from the Department of Health, Education, and Welfare 1974-1976 has undertaken a major step in developing guidelines for review of nursing care at the local level. This is the first major national effort on the part of the nursing profession to define specific criteria of practice and outcome measures [24].

Another recent milestone effort directed at identifying standards of practice (criterion measures) is the work of Ruth Bryce of the

Veterans Administration in which she and her colleagues developed standards and educational guidelines for spinal cord injury in nursing care [25].

BARRIERS TO BE OVERCOME

Failures in the Measurement of Quality Nursing Care

The critical variable that nurses seek to measure is the efficiency of nursing practice in hospitals or in health agencies as judged by standards set by peer-group panels, and audit or quality-control type committees. Failure to measure efficiency stems from such practices as overreliance on nursing and medical records that are incomplete; the setting of standards of poor practice by peer groups; the difficulty of transferring standards from one setting to another; emphasis on patient care, ignoring environmental and other factors that are also important; and problems of different observer reactions, since quality is measured as a continuous variable.

Measurement presents failures in measuring patient care. The assessment of the outcomes of patient care also presents difficulties in that the health of an individual or group of individuals is altered during the process. There is also overattention given to measures that do not include valid and reliable measures of patient satisfaction and that do not give indications of any component effects other than those in the total. Also used are mortality and morbidity rates rather than precise measurements of the effect care has on patients. The process also includes a lack of a comprehensive conceptual framework in which to measure the impact of the care on patients.

Lacking valid and reliable instruments for measurement of the end results of the effect of nursing care on patients, we must make measurements in terms of intermediate goals. Direct measurement of patient care, which is clinical evaluation, is recognized as being more valid. However, it is less precise than other less direct but more specific forms of measurement. It is important to test the reliability of the method used by arranging for independent review of the individual situations being studied.

A major problem with physiological measures of nursing effectiveness is that factors other than nursing care can affect these measures [26].

A major problem in measuring quality nursing is the lack of instrumentation to measure it directly. Measurement of the nursing care of "patient as a whole" may not be possible. Measurement of quality nursing might be made on the basis of the "scientific rightness" of our assessment of the patient's nursing problems and our management of them.

The nursing problems that professional nurses are called on to assess and manage daily may form the basis for evaluating quality nursing care. Quality nursing may be measured indirectly by examining the system or organization provided for dealing with these nursing problems. The degree to which communications are systematized, e.g., may be one of the most important criterion measures that can be used in assessing quality nursing practice.

The identification of criterion measures of nursing practice poses many problems because of its complexity. Multiple studies will have to be undertaken before measures of quality nursing can be identified. Measurement of quality care will have to be more direct and indirect before a complete assessment of the effect of nursing practice on patient welfare can be made.

PATIENT-CARE CRITERIA

It is generally agreed that criteria of quality are value judgments that are applied to several aspects, properties, ingredients, or dimensions of a process called medical care of which nursing is an integral part. Measurement depends on the development of standards that may be empirical or normative. The former derives from actual nursing practice, the latter from "experts" in the field who serve as judges.

Patient care in hospitals is being appraised by four techniques. First is the examination of the prerequisites for adequate care, such as the minimum and optimum levels of facilities, equipment, professional training and distribution of personnel, and the organizational structure of the institution. Nursing has yet to define the prerequisites for adequate nursing care for groups of patients with common diagnoses and for patients of different age groups and in different situations.

Second is the evaluation of performance, particularly of tasks related to patient care. Here such observable quantitative measures can be used as the time that nursing personnel spend on activities with patients, utilization rates for specific procedures, length of patient stay, use of chest x-rays, laboratory and other diagnostic procedures, autopsy rates, pathological reports on surgical specimens, and correlations between preoperative and postoperative diagnosis. Researchers have been preoccupied with the quantitative aspects of this approach and have placed undue emphasis on the value of such studies. Such quantitative measures can provide little other than baseline measures.

Development of rating scales to measure levels of adequacy of patient care is the third way of measuring the quality of care. Scales need to be developed that provide appropriate yardsticks to estimate qualitative levels of care. As nursing research moves in the direction of clinical research, direct measurement of patient care becomes highly relevant and is the most difficult parameter to achieve.

Criterion measures of patient care and precise instrumentation to measure the effects of nursing practice on patient care are clearly the major gaps in nursing research.

Criterion measures of nursing practice must derive from the dependent variables that indicate the effects of practice on patient care. The criterion measures of patient care may be categorized into four main groups, including [27]:

Group I. Criterion measures of patient care related to preventive care needs
These measures are observable in all patients/clients in the patient's ability to:

1. maintain adequate hygiene and physical comfort
2. achieve optimal activity, exercise, rest, and sleep
3. prevent accident, injury, other trauma and the spread of infection
4. maintain proper body mechanics and prevent and correct deformities.

Group II. Criterion measures of patient care related to normal and disturbed physiological body processes that are vital to sustaining life, the patient's ability to:

5. facilitate the maintenance of a supply of oxygen and nutrition to all body cells
6. facilitate the maintenance of elimination, fluid and electrolyte balance, regulatory mechanisms, and sensory functions
7. recognize the physiological responses of the body to disease conditions — pathological, physiological, and compensatory

Group III. Criterion measures of patient care related to rehabilitative needs, particularly those involving emotional and interpersonal difficulties, the patient's ability to:

8. identify and accept positive and negative expressions and reactions and the interrelatedness of emotions and organic illness
9. facilitate the maintenance of effective verbal and nonverbal communication; progress toward achievement of personal spiritual goals; and awareness of self as an individual with varying physical, emotional, and developmental needs
10. promote the development of productive interpersonal relationships
11. create or maintain a therapeutic environment, or both
12. accept the optimum possible goals in light of limitations, physical and emotional.

Group IV. Criteria of patient care related to sociological and community problems affecting patient care, the patient's ability to:

13. use community resources as an aid in resolving problems arising from illness
14. understand the role of social problems as influencing factors in the cause of illness

The type of criterion measure used is influenced by the research problem and the hypotheses that have developed to explore the problem. Once the variables have been defined, the researcher must then decide how the dependent variable — the criterion measure — will be measured. The decision to select a direct or indirect measure will be influenced by the ease with which the variable can be directly measured.

The investigator seeking to measure physiological responses has available a number of scientific measuring instruments, yielding highly refined numerical measurements, that may serve as criterion measures. There are also many tests and scales available to measure psychological or sociological phenomenon.

Because of the lack of descriptive research about patient behaviors, judgments of quality are often incomplete and based on partial evidence. Measurement scales need to be developed that discriminate different levels of patient response. A problem in scaling that must be solved is the way in which different components on the measurement scale are to be weighed in the process of arriving at a total.

Ordinal scales that relate the different categories in the scale in terms of graded order are available. Grading or ranking may be according to some underlying continuum of intensity. Ordinal scales developed by behavioral scientists such as Thurston, Likert, Guttman, Edwards, and Stevens have been readily adopted and in many instances used inappropriately in nursing research. Before scales developed by other disciplines are used for measurement of patient care, they need to be pretested thoroughly to see if the scale is still reliable and valid in the new setting. Attention must be given to the validation of these scales in patient-care settings, and those studies that have used such scales previously need to be replicated to validate the findings. Whether the method for measuring the variables has been designed by others or developed by the researcher, the measures that are used must meet certain tests to be considered acceptable. Four of the most important criteria for evaluating the adequacy of the measures are validity, reliability, sensitivity, and meaningfulness in terms of the "real world" of patient care.

REFERENCES

1. Howland, D., and McDowell, E. E. Measurement of patient care; a conceptual framework. *Nursing Research* (New York) 13:4–7, Winter, 1964.
2. Wolfe, H., and Breslin, P. *Factors Affecting Quality of Nursing Care.* Pittsburgh: University of Pittsburgh, 1968.
3. Jelinek, R. C. An operational analysis of the patient care functions. *Inquiry* 6:53–58, June, 1969.
4. Leventhal, H., and Sharp, E. Facial expressions as indicators of distress. In S. S. Tompkins and C. E. Izard (Eds.), *Affect, Cognition, and Personality; Empirical Studies.* New York: Springer Verlag, 1965, pp. 296–318.
5. McLemore, S. D., and Hill, R. J. *Management-Training Effectiveness; A Study of Nurse Managers.* (Studies in Personnel and Management Number 16), Austin, Texas: Bureau of Business Research, University of Texas, 1965.
6. Western Interstate Commission for Higher Education. *Follow-up Performance of the Experimental Group; Effectiveness of a Leadership Program in Nursing.* Ingmire, A. E., principal investigator. Boulder, Colorado: The Commission, 1967.
7. Johnson, J. E. Influence of purposeful nurse-patient interaction on patient's postoperative course. In *Exploring Progress in Medical-Surgical Nursing Practice.* (A series of papers presented at the 1965 Regional Clinical Conferences sponsored by the American Nurses' Association in Washington, D.C. and Chicago, Ill., 1965.) New York: American Nurses' Association 2:16–22, 1966.
8. Smith, D. M. Clinical nursing too! *American Journal of Nursing* 68:2384–2388, Nov., 1968.
9. White, R. P., *et al. Patient Care Classification: Methods and Application.* Baltimore: Department of Medical Care and Hospitals, School of Hygiene and Public Health, Johns Hopkins University, 1967.
10. Smith, J. What stops you? *American Journal of Nursing* 59:848–851, June 1959.
11. Wandelt, M. A. *Uninterrupted Patient Care and Nursing Requirements.* Detroit, Mich: Wayne State University, 1963.
12. Klaus, D. J., *et al. Controlling Experience to Improve Nursing Proficiency; Background and Study Plan Report.* Reports No. 1–4. Pittsburgh: American Institutes for Research, 1966–1968.
13. Reiter, F., and Kakosh, M. E. *Quality of Nursing Care; A Report of A Field Study to Establish Criteria.* Conducted at Institute of Research and Studies in Nursing Education, Division of Nursing Education, Teachers College, Columbia University, 1950–1954. New York: Graduate School of Nursing, New York Medical College, 1963.
14. Aydelotte, M. K. Use of patient welfare as a criterion measure. *Nursing Research* 11:10–14, Winter, 1962.
15. Simon, R. J., and Hudson, W. R. Experimental study of the relation between nursing care and patient welfare. *Journal of Applied Psychology* (Washington) 48:268–274, August, 1964.
16. Bryant, W. D., and New, P. *Nursing Resources on the Ward and Nurse-*

Patient Relationships. Kansas City: Community Studies, 1957.

17. Nite, G., and Willis, R. N., Jr. *Coronary Patient: Hospital Care and Rehabilitation.* New York: Macmillan, 1964.

18. Dumas, R. G., and Leonard, R. C. Effects of nursing on the incidence of postoperative vomiting. *Nursing Research* 12:12–15, Winter, 1963.

19. Elms, F. R. *Prediction of Post-Surgical Nursing Needs.* Fort Worth: Harris College of Nursing, Texas Christian University, 1967.

20. Feyerherm, A. M. Nursing activity patterns; a guide to staffing. *Nursing Research* 15:124–133, Spring, 1966.

21. Walker, V. H. *Nursing and Ritualistic Practice.* New York: Macmillan, 1967.

22. National League for Nursing, Research, and Studies Service. Method Rating the Proficiency of the Hospital General Staff Nurse. New York: The League, 1964.

23. Griffin, G. J., *et al.* New dimension for the improvement of clinical nursing. *Nursing Research* 15:292–302, Fall, 1966.

24. American Nurses' Association. *Guidelines for Review of Nursing Care at the Local Level.* Kansas City, Missouri: American Nurses' Association, 1976.

25. Veterans Administration. Standards and Educational Guidelines for Spinal Cord Injury Nursing Care. In *Program Guide, Nursing Services.* Department of Medicine and Surgery, Veterans Administration. Washington, D.C.: Publication G-12, M-2, Part V, March 15, 1976.

26. Johnson, B. A., *et al.* Research in nursing practice; the problems of uncontrolled variables. *Nursing Research* 19:341, July–August, 1970.

27. Abdellah, F. G., and Levine, E. *Better Patient Care Through Nursing Research.* New York: Macmillan, 1965.

SELECTED READINGS ON CRITERION MEASURES

Abdellah, F., and Levine, E. *Better Patient Care Through Nursing Research.* New York: Macmillan, 1965.

Anderson, A. J., and Altman, I. *Methodology in Evaluating the Quality of Medical Care.* Pittsburgh: University of Pittsburgh Press, 1962.

Beland, I. L. *Clinical Nursing. Pathophysiological and Psychosocial Approaches* (2nd ed.). New York: Macmillan, 1970.

Chow, R. Postoperative cardiac nursing research; a method for identifying and categorizing nursing action. *Nursing Research* 18:4–13, January–February, 1969.

Chow, Rita K. *Cardiosurgical Nursing Care.* New York: Springer, 1976.

Daily, E. F., and Morehead, M. A. A method of evaluating and improving the quality of medical care. *American Journal of Public Health* 46:848–854, July, 1956.

Denson, P. J. The quality of medical care. *Yale Journal of Biology and Medicine* 37:523–536, June, 1965.

Denson, P. M., *et al.* Studies in cardiovascular syphilis II: Methodologic problems in evaluation of therapy. *American Journal of Syphilis, Gonorrhea and Venereal Disease* 36:64–76, Jan., 1952.

Denton, J. C., *et al.* Predicting judged quality of patient care in general hospitals. *Health Services Research* 2:26–33, Spring, 1967.

Donabedian, A. Evaluating the quality of medical care. *Milbank Memorial Fund Quarterly* 44:166–206, Part 2, July, 1966.

Donabedian, A. Promoting quality through evaluating the process of patient care. *Medical Care* 6:181–201, May–June, 1968.

Flagle, C. D. Prospects for research in long-term care. *Gerontologist* (St. Louis) 4:No. 2, Part II, June, 1964.

Fleishman, E. A. Performance assessment based on an empirically derived task taxonomy. *Human Factors* 9(4):349–366, August, 1967.

Gersten, J. W., *et al.* Evaluation of rehabilitation in home or clinic setting: Problems and methods. *Archives of Physical Medicine and Rehabilitation* (Chicago) 47:199, 1966.

Glasser, J. H. Conceptual issues in the analysis of medical care utilization behavior. The selection of statistical techniques. In M. R. Greenlick (Ed.), *Proceedings of a Conference on Conceptual Issues in the Analysis of Medical Care Utilization Behavior.* Washington: Department of Health Education, and Welfare, 1969.

Hill, B. A. Observation and Experiment. *New England Journal of Medicine* 248:995–1001, June 11, 1953.

Howland, D. *The Development of a Methodology for the Evaluation of Patient Care.* Columbus: Ohio State University, 1960.

Hutchinson, G. B. Evaluation of preventive services. *Journal of Chronic Diseases* (St. Louis) 11(5):497–507, May, 1960.

Kelman, H. R., and Willer, A. Problems in measurement and evaluation of rehabilitation. *Archives of Physical Medicine and Rehabilitation* (Chicago) 43:172–181, April, 1962.

King, I. M. *Toward a Theory of Nursing. General Concepts of Human Behavior.* New York: Wiley and Sons, 1971.

MacMahon, B., *et al.* Principles in the evaluation of community mental health programs. *American Journal of Public Health* 51(7):963–968, July, 1961.

Makover, H. B. The quality of medical care: Methodology of survey of the medical groups associated with the health insurance plan of New York. *American Journal of Public Health* 41:824–832, July, 1951.

O'Malley, M., and Kossack, C. F. A statistical study of factors influencing the quality of patient care in hospitals. *American Journal of Public Health* 40:1428–1436, Nov., 1950.

Polansky, N. A. (Ed.). *Social Work Research.* Chicago: University of Chicago Press, 1960.

Proceedings of a Conference on Conceptual Issues in the Analysis of Medical Care Utilization Behavior. Washington: Department of Health, Education, and Welfare, 1969.

Rosenfeld, L. S. Quality of medical care in hospitals. *American Journal of Public Health* 47:856–865, July, 1957.

Selltiz, C., *et al.* Research Methods in Social Relations. Revised in One Volume.

New York: Holt, Rinehart, and Winston, 1966.

Sheps, M. C. Approaches to the quality of hospital care. *Public Health Reports,* 70:877–866, Sept., 1955.

Solon, J. A., *et al.* Delineating episodes of medical care. *American Journal of Public Health* 57:401–408, March, 1967.

Stauffer, S., *et al.* Measurement and Prediction. Princeton: Princeton Univ. Press, 1950.

Suchman, E. A. *Evaluative Research.* New York: Russell Sage Foundation, 1967.

Weckwerth, V. E. A Conceptual model versus the real world of health care service delivery. In C. E. Hopkins (Ed.), *Conference Series.* Outcomes Conference I-II. Methodology of Identifying, Measuring and Evaluating Outcomes of Health Service Programs, Systems and Subsystems. Washington: Department of Health, Education, and Welfare, 1969.

Investigations in the Clinical Setting
Virginia S. Cleland

2

THE aim of clinical nursing research, as with all research, is to enlarge and refine existing knowledge. This task involves obtaining systematic and controlled observations to describe or explain phenomena. Use of the scientific method leads to valid generalizations which then become the source of new knowledge to be incorporated into nursing practice.

The nursing literature abounds with exhortations about individualized nursing care. Individualized care can be derived only from the generalizations that can be made about the nursing care of groups of patients who share common problems. The nurse-researcher looks for generalizations and the skilled nurse-clinician decides which generalizations should be used in the care of a particular patient.

Research in a basic discipline may have as its sole purpose to increase knowledge with no thought as to the use of that knowledge. Research in a profession has as its ultimate aim to improve the practice of that profession. Thus nurses, as researchers, seek knowledge of relationships that will guide action and modify the methods or the very nature of that professional practice.

Research on which this chapter was based was conducted while the author was a PHS predoctoral fellow in nursing research and the recipient of a grant from the U.S. Public Health Service, Division of Nursing (NU00248). Portions of this chapter appeared, in slightly different form, in *Nurs. Res.* 14(4):292–298, 1965, and *Nurs. Res.* 20(4):309–318, 1971. Used by permission.

For a research topic this author prefers to start with a nursing problem or a question of personal interest and of empirical significance to nursing. Then a search of the literature commonly reveals relevant concepts for developing a scientific rationale for exploring the problem. Because many nurse-researchers obtain doctoral preparation in basic disciplines, there is danger that nursing will be used merely as a testing ground for theories that are of no great interest or pertinence to nursing. By starting with a health or nursing problem and then moving on to a possible theoretical explanation, we may avoid this pitfall of irrelevance. Typical of these studies, generally unimportant to nursing, have been those published in psychology journals in which nursing students have served as research subjects. These studies commonly reflect the clinical psychologist's need for study subjects for his own research and the availability of nursing students on psychiatric affiliations.

In this chapter the author will describe two studies which represent very different research problems. One pertains to the effect of situational stressors on the cognitive performance of general-duty nurses. (This study was first published in *Nursing Research* 14:292–298, Fall, 1965.) The other is a study of the relative effectiveness of different types of perineal care in preventing bacteriuria in female patients with indwelling catheters. Although both studies were conducted in the clinical setting, in the former, nurses were the research subjects, and in the latter, female patients were the subjects. Both studies involved random assignment of subjects. In the study of environmental stressors the investigator waited until each subject could be found in the ward environment representative of the stressor condition to which she had been randomly assigned. In the catheter study the experimental variable could be actively manipulated.

In the stressor study use was made of a 3 X 4 factorial design. There were four levels of one independent variable, e.g., X_1, X_2, X_3, X_4, and three levels of the other, Y_1, Y_2, Y_3. With this type of design a control group is not necessary since each level acts as a comparative group for the other. However, Stressor Condition I was regarded as a control group since it represented the lowest level of environmental stressors for the general-duty nurses. Similarly in the catheter study (a 2 × 5 design), Treatment Condition A_1 (no perineal care by the nursing staff) could be regarded as a control group. Actually these treatment groups provide baseline data against which graduated treatment effects can be compared.

The two studies will now be reviewed. To assist the reader, tables, figures, and references for the first study are identified by the letter A and for the second study, by the letter B.

EFFECT OF STRESS ON PERFORMANCE

The author first became interested in the effect of environmental stressors on cognitive performance from reading reports of research in which it could be questioned whether the stressor agent was really so perceived by the subject or whether it was only an annoyance. It seemed that the stressor should have personal significance to the subject, which is unlikely in the typical experiments conducted with college sophomores in introductory psychology classes. At the same time, the author believed that this problem had significance for nursing because in a clinical setting nurses must do their thinking in an environment filled with stressful and interfering activity. If such activity decreases cognitive performance, surely this is reflected in the quality of nursing care. These relationships should provide worthwhile content for a field experiment.

An understanding of the variables that affect skilled performance when subjects are confronted by situational stressors is meaningful for motivational theory, personality theory, and sociopsychological theory. Investigations of the effect of psychological stress on skilled performance have often culminated in contradictory results, with the stressor sometimes improving performance and sometimes producing a decrement. When these results are examined in detail, it becomes evident that the definition of "stressor" differs from experiment to experiment. In this study a field experiment was conducted using registered nurses as subjects and measuring their nursing test performance under conditions of graduated levels of situational stressors. Because these stressors were a part of the usual work environment, they were of personal significance to the subjects.

General Theory

The theoretical formulation for this paper is essentially that of the Yerkes-Dodson Law which, although first described in 1908, was long ignored and only in recent years has reappeared in the literature [17]. Broadhurst has written an excellent statement on the history and theoretical importance of the principle [3]. The Yerkes-Dodson Law states that there is a curvilinear relationship between level of motivation and level of performance and that, with an increase in the difficulty of the task, there is a decrease in the level of motivation for optimum performance of that task.

As possible explanation for the Yerkes-Dodson Law, Easterbrook has advanced the concept of "range of cue utilization" which he defines as "the total number of environmental cues in any situation that an organism observes, maintains an orientation toward, responds to, or associates with a response [7]." Cues can be separated by definition into two general classes including: (1) peripheral, which are occasionally or partially relevant and (2) central, which are immediately relevant to the principal task at hand.

After an extensive review of research, Easterbrook concludes that motivation may be either facilitating or disruptive to performance, depending on the range of cues optimum for the task. As motivation level increases, some cues lose their effectiveness for guiding action. If these cues are irrelevant to the task, performance will be improved but if they are relevant, performance will be impaired. When the level of motivation is low, the organism, while giving vacillating responses to many surrounding stimuli, will respond to few task-oriented cues of any kind. In fact the subject will fail to remember associations and relationships and may be on the one hand, incapable of organized task performance. On the other hand, increases in motivation can be said to reduce the range of cues utilized by the subject in all cases.

Independent Variables

The independent variables studies included: (1) need for social approval and (2) situational stressors.

The work of Crowne and Marlowe led them to believe that their Scale of Social Desirability is a measure of the motivational variables [6]. The scale was developed by using true and false items which were "based upon culturally sanctioned and approved behavior, but which are improbable in occurrence [10]." A sample item is: "Before voting I thoroughly investigate the qualifications of all the candidates." Subjects who attribute to themselves a high proportion of culturally approved statements and who deny culturally unacceptable traits are inferred to have a high need for social approval. Marlowe and Crowne obtained a Pearson product-moment correlation of —.54 between their test and the Barron Independence of Judgment Scale.

Strickland and Crowne reported that subjects who endorse socially desirable statements about themselves also are more likely to yield to group pressure in the conforming situation [14]. Horton, Marlowe, and Crowne used the scale as a measure of "social sensitivity [8]." They predicted that subjects showing a high need for social approval would be more sensitive and responsive to situational demands, defensive in test situations, and prone to give guarded (common) responses as compared to subjects with low need for social approval. They also predicted that these differences would be apparent when the test was given under relaxed conditions but would disappear under speed conditions in which personal stimulus variables are less likely to be operative. Their predictions were supported.

Because this scale was developed on college students, its use was appropriate for nursing graduates of the same age range. The reliability of the test, based on the Kuder Richardson formula 20, measure of internal consistency, was .88. A test-retest correlation of .89 has also been reported [6]. The scores earned by the nurses in this study were very similar to the scores originally reported by Crowne and Marlowe (nurses: N = 60, Mean = 14.05, SD = 5.15; college students: N = 120, Mean = 13.72, SD = 5.78).

SITUATIONAL STRESSORS (MANIPULATED VARIABLE)

For our present purposes the term psychological will be used as an intervening variable that exists secondary to threatened or blocked goal-seeking behavior. Stress per se cannot be defined in terms of either the stimulus or the response but rather occurs as an interaction of the individual's motivation and the field situation. Lazarus, Deese, and Osler have pointed out the similarities of this concept to the physiological stress defined by Selye [9, 13]. Paralleling the Selye tradition, all types of situational stimuli that produce psychological stress within the individual will be referred to as stressors.

This definition of stress is also in general agreement with a conclusion drawn by Basowitz, et al., in their study *Anxiety and Stress,* wherein they state: "In future research, therefore, we should not consider stress as *imposed* upon the organism, but as its *response* to internal or external processes which reach those threshold levels that strain its physiological and psychological integrative capacities close to or beyond their limits [1]."

Broverman and Lazarus have grouped situations producing stress into two principal classes, including (1) ego-threatening stressors and (2) cognitive-interference stressors [4]. Ego-threatening stress may be produced by presenting the subject with an unsolvable task or a set of false norms with which to compare his performance or by berating his performance while he is engaged in the task.

Cognitive-interference stress refers to the effects of techniques that create conflicting demands on the subject's intellectual processes such as distractions, interruptions, time pressure, or requirements to do too many things simultaneously. In the experiment reported in this paper the situational stressors were of the type that would be expected to produce cognitive interference.

It is believed that the two independent variables — (1) the need for social approval (a motivational variable) and (2) the stressors of the situation in which the subject is functioning (an environmental variable) — may interact in an additive manner. The motivational variable is considered to be both energizing and directional. Vogel, Baker, and Lazarus view this as intrinsic motivation and presume it to be an enduring characteristic of the individual [15]. In addition the environmental situation provides cues that may arouse in the individual an induced motivation which is transitory. The intrinsic motivation and the induced motivation combine to provide the total strength of motive in a particular situation.

In measuring situational stressors, no attempt was made to separate physical and mental stressors, and it is probable that a heavy assignment for the general-duty nurse includes both. After considerable observation in the field-setting, the author concluded that the situational stressors could best be measured by a combination of four factors, including: level of dependency of patients, nursing staff available, work assignment, and time of testing. These components were measured independently and combined to form the four gradations of situational stressors. Because it was impossible to control directly the degree of dependency of the patients on a ward unit, this was adjusted by the use of a ratio between patient dependency and nursing staff available. Thus two units could be regarded as equal in the quantity of situational stressors on the nurse if the greater number of dependent patients on one unit was offset by the availability of a larger staff.

LEVEL OF PATIENT DEPENDENCY

This is a quantitative measure (3, 2, 1 scale) of the level of physical dependency of each patient on the unit. Highly dependent patients require more assistance with the activities of daily living and also usually receive more treatments, medications, and diagnostic and evaluative procedures than less dependent patients. These levels of dependency have been shown to correlate closely with the workload to be performed by the nursing staff. Connor et al., found that total-care patients required five times more care than did self-care patients (137 vs 27 minutes) [5].

Level 3. These patients have two or more of the following problems present; they: (1) are confined to bed, (2) have to be fed, (3) receive daily IV administration, (4) are incontinent, (5) are on isolation, (6) exhibit marked emotional disturbances, (7) require help with ambulation, or (8) are receiving oxygen therapy.

Level 2. These patients require help with one of the preceding problems.

Level 1. This group includes ambulatory patients who need no assistance with the activities of daily living.

By classifying each patient in the unit, it was possible to determine the percentage of patients at each level of dependency as described above to define the gradations of situational stressors.

This was obtained by classifying the nursing staff according to the following scale of job titles and multiplying by the number of persons on duty in each category:

Head Nurse	5 points
General-Duty Nurse	4
Senior Nursing Student	3
Junior Nursing Student	2
Freshman Nursing Student	1
Practical Nurse	2
Practical Nursing Students	1
Ward Aide	1
Ward Clerk	2

Thus a staff of 20 points might consist of one general-duty nurse, one senior student, two junior students, two practical nurses, three ward aides, and one ward clerk. It is recognized, however, that these points when added together do not measure quality. For example, although five practical nurses add up to 10 points, their work is not equal to that of two head nurses.

The general effect of size of assignment and the time of testing are obvious to nurse-readers. The four factors influencing the quantity of stressors were then combined to define the ordinal segments on the situational stressor continuum.

Condition 1. Lowest Level of Stressors (Control Group). Testing done immediately on reporting for duty but before receiving an assignment. The subject was told that her nursing activities would be performed by other staff members until she would be free to assume them herself. Testing was done at 7:00 A.M. in a quiet room.

Condition 2. Moderately Low Level of Stressors. The subject functioned as a team-leader for half of a 40- to 42-bed unit with a total ward unit staffing of at least 25 points. No more than 40 percent of the patients were classified at a 2 or 3 level of dependency. Testing was done at 11:00 A.M. in the nursing station.

Condition 3. Moderately High Level of Stressors. The subject functioned as a team-leader for the entire 40- to 42-bed unit with total ward unit staffing of no more than 20 points. At least 50 percent of all patients were classified at a 2 or 3 level of dependency. Testing was done at 9:00 A.M. in the nursing station.

Condition 4. Highest Level of Stressors. The subject functioned as nurse-in-charge of a 40- to 42-bed unit either on the head nurse's day off or on the evening tour of duty. At least 50 percent of all patients were classified at a 2 or 3 level of dependency, and total ward staffing was no more than 20 points. Testing was done at 10:00 A.M. or 4:30 P.M. in the nursing station.

Dependent Variables

Two measures of the dependent variable, nursing performance, were obtained through the scores earned by the subject on the two nursing tests developed specifically for this study. Both tests were based on medicosurgical nursing content since these clinical areas were represented by the patients in the hospital units used for the study. The test-development sample consisted of 144 senior nursing students in five hospital schools of nursing. Measures of validity, reliability, item difficulty, and item discriminative value were obtained for each test.

NURSING ACHIEVEMENT TEST (NAT)

The NAT was designed to evaluate cognitive behavior (knowledge, understanding, application, and critical thinking). A summary of the pretest data on the final form of the NAT reveals: possible score = 36; mean = 25.62; SD = 3.5; difficulty range = 27 to 89 percent; coefficient of internal consistency $r = .72$; and standard error of measurement = 2.31.

SOCIAL INTERACTION TEST (SIT)

The SIT was developed by using items which were written from descriptions of actual nursing incidents and represented stressful and difficult interactions for the nurse. In its final form the test had 19 items, 14 of which were drawn from a 30-item Social Interaction Inventory developed by Methven and Schlotfeldt [12].

Further, the SIT was developed as a measure of a complex type of performance that requires a broad range of cues. The assumption was made that in order to "take the role of the other" the nurse subject would have to go outside of herself to perceive the best solution from the point of view of the person in the test item and that this type of cognitive process, because of the wide range of cues involved, would be more susceptible to the untoward influences of a high stressor environment than would the cognitive processes involved in a more typical achievement type test [11]. Berlew used interpersonal sensitivity as a special case of complex problem solving in a study of the relationship between motive strength and problem-solving efficiency and supported his hypothesis that the Yerkes-Dodson Law was applicable [2].

A summary of the pretest data on the final form of the SIT shows: possible score = 19; mean = 9.27; SD = 3.13; difficulty range = 27 to 83 percent; coefficient of internal consistency r = .65; correlation with psychiatric nursing–field practice grades r = .72; standard error of measurement = 1.98.

Hypotheses

Four hypotheses were selected as a basis for the study:

1. There is a curvilinear relationship between quality of performance on the combined nursing tests and quality of situational stressors.
2. The quality of performance as measured on the more difficult items of the NAT will reach maximum level on a lower stressor condition than will the quality of performance on the less difficult items of the same test.
3. The quality of performance as measured by the NAT will show less deterioration as a function of situational stressor than will the SIT score.
4. Subjects scoring high on need for social approval will demonstrate greater deterioration on the NAT with increased stress than subjects showing low need for social approval.

Method

The experiment was planned as a 3 X 4 analysis of variance design. On the ordinate were three categories of subjects representing high, medium, or low need for social approval, as measured by the Marlowe-Crowne Scale of Social Desirability and on the abscissa, four graduated conditions of environmental stressor. Since two tests were used as measures of the dependent variable, nursing performance, the analysis of the data was carried out twice. Level of significance acceptable was set at $p < .05$.

SUBJECTS AND PROCEDURE

The 60 nurses who served as subjects were all graduates of the same hospital-school of nursing and were employed as general-duty nurses on medicosurgical units in the hospital where the school was located. Each subject had spent three to six years in this work environment. They were female, 20 to 23 years of age, and three of them had about one year of general college education.

The Marlowe-Crowne Social Desirability Scale was administered to each nurse, the scores being placed on a continuum from high to low. By use of a table of random numbers, the subjects with the four highest scores were assigned, one to each stressor condition, and then the next four, and so on, until all of them had been assigned. Of the 15 subjects assigned to each stressor condition, there were five with a high need for social approval (mean = 19.65), five with a low need (mean = 8.8), and five who represented the middle range (mean = 13.70).

After the nurses had been assigned to their respective treatment conditions, two statistical tests were conducted as a further check that the ability of nurses in each group was the same. From school records it was possible to obtain each nurse's NLN and state-board test scores. Analysis of variance was computed using (1) the NLN Achievement test scores in medicosurgical nursing and then repeated using (2) the medicosurgical test scores from the state-board examinations. In both instances there was no statistical difference in the scores earned by the nurses in the various treatment groups.

By means of the weekly timesheets in the nursing office it was possible to anticipate which subjects might meet the prescribed experimental conditions on a particular day. On the appropriate day the experimenter, using the Nursing Cardex and the Nursing Care Guide, classified the patients according to their dependency and calculated the ratio between level of dependency and nursing staff available. If the experimental conditions were met, the test was administered to the subject at the appropriate time. The nurse was asked to delegate or postpone her nursing activities while taking the test but was told that if the safety or comfort of a patient was involved, she could leave the test while she attended to the nursing task.

Results

Examination of the data indicated that the assumptions underlying the analysis of variance technique, namely, independence of the scores, normal distribution, and homogeneity of variance had not been violated. The findings will be reported in the same order in which the research hypotheses were originally listed.

Hypothesis 1. In order to test the null hypothesis, it was necessary to convert the raw scores of each subject on the NAT and the SIT to Z scores (mean = 50, SD = 10) and then to add the two Z scores. Figure 2-1 shows the rather commonly described curvilinear relationships between motivation and performance, and a simple analysis of variance supported the belief that the effect of the situational stressors upon performance was significant (Table 2-1).

Hypothesis 2. To test this hypothesis it was necessary to divide the NAT into two equal groups of "difficult" and "less difficult" items. In order that the measure be independent, the items were categorized according to the difficulty index obtained from the right and wrong responses of the 144 nursing students in the pretest sample. Figure 2-2 reveals that the subjects reached a maximum level of performance with a lower stressor condition on the more difficult than on the less difficult items. On the more difficult items the peak performance was reached at Condition 2 but on the less difficult items, the peak came at Condition 3.

Hypothesis 3. A comparison, using Z scores, of the performance levels on the two tests over the four situational stressor conditions can be made by examining Figure 2-3. For Condition 1 (control groups) there was no difference in the level of performance. The remaining three conditions were analyzed statistically by a "split-plot" design in which the effect of stressors was confounded

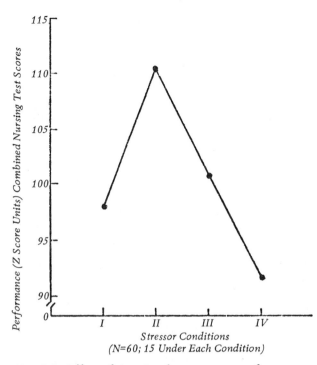

Fig. 2-1. Effect of situational stressors on performance on combined nursing test scores.

Table 2-1. Analysis of Variance of Scores on the Combined Nursing Tests for Four Situational Stressor Conditions

Source of Variation	d.f.	Mean Square	F
Between stressor conditions	3	937.800	3.29[a]
Within groups	56	285.300	
Total	59		

[a]$F_{.95}$ (3,55) = 2.78.

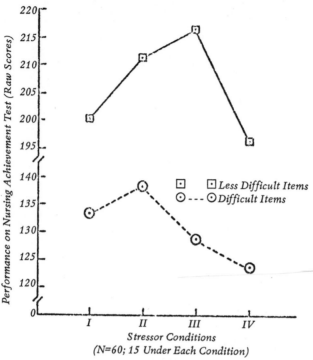

Fig. 2-2. Relationship of performance on two levels of item difficulty to increasing quantity of situational stressors. *Key:* ▣——▣, Less difficult items; ⊙---⊙, more difficult items.

"between subjects" and the effect of the tests was a "within subjects" factor [16]. This design permitted a more precise analysis of the effects of the tests. A significance of interaction between stressors and tests in effect indicates that the influence of situational stressors on the NAT was different from their effect on the SIT. The interaction was found to be significant (Table 2-2). Thus the patterns of performance on the two tests are different, and visually it can be seen that performance on the SIT had the greater deterioration.

Hypothesis 4. Figure 2-4 reveals that the need for social approval has very different effects on performance, depending in part on the level of situational stressors. As one would hypothesize from viewing this graph, the interaction of the two independent variables was significant (Table 2-3). The interaction between the two variables tended to hide the main effect of each and neither was significant.

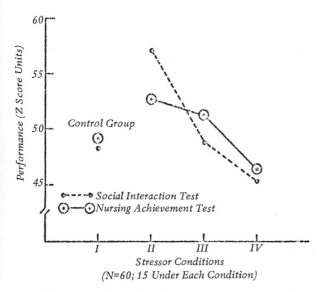

Fig. 2-3. Comparison of effects of stressors on performance on each nursing test. *Key:* ⊙ and ●, Control groups; ●---●, SIT; ⊙—⊙, NAT.

Table 2-2. Analysis of Variance of Interaction Between Stressor Condition and NAT and Stressor Condition and SIT

Source of Variation	d.f.	Mean Square	F
Between subjects	44		
Stressors	2	54.6777	
Subjects/groups	42	11.3317	
Within subjects	45		
Tests	1	3050.8444	
Tests X stressor	2	6.8112	3.35[a]
Tests X subjects within groups	42	2.0365	
Total	89		

NOTE: Stressor condition 1 the control group, omitted.

[a]$F_{.95} (2,42) = 3.22.$

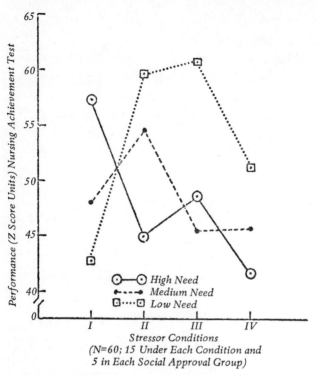

Fig. 2-4. Effect of stressors on performance on NAT by nurses with high, medium, or low need for social approval. *Key:* ⊙——⊙, High need; ●---●, Medium need; and ⊡ · · · ⊡, Low need.

Table 2-3. Analysis of Variance on the NAT of Interaction of Stressor Condition and Need for Social Approval

Source of Variation	d.f.	Mean Square	F
Stressor conditions	3	12.3780	1.75
Need for approval	2	18.8166	2.67
S X N	6	25.5277	3.62[a]
Within cells	48	7.0583	
Total	56		

[a]$F_{.95}$ (6,48) = 2.30.

Thus it was necessary to analyze the simple effect of each variable at each level.

Table 2-4 shows that the need for social approval had a significant effect at the first three stressor conditions. Under the very high stressor of Condition 4, the effect of need for social approval was not of sufficient magnitude to be significant. When the data were submitted to trend analysis, a significant linear trend was found. Thus it is apparent that, as the need for social approval increased, performance on the NAT decreased.

Table 2-4. Analysis of Variance on the NAT for Simple Effects of Need for Social Approval

Source of Variation	d.f.	Mean Square	F
Need for social approval for			
Stressor condition 1	2	24.8000	3.51[a]
Stressor condition 2	2	27.2667	3.86[a]
Stressor condition 3	2	32.0667	4.54[a]
Stressor condition 4	2	11.2667	1.60
Within cells	48	7.0583	

[a]$F_{.95}$ (2,48) = 3.19.

The effect of situational stressors was similarly analyzed at each of the three need-for-approval levels (Table 2-5). It was found that stressor conditions had a significant effect with high and low need-for-approval subjects, but the effect was not significant with the nurses who displayed a medium need for approval. This effect of the stressors was found to characterize a significant quadratic trend.

Discussion

Hypotheses 1 and 2 duplicated the original findings of Yerkes and Dodson, but used human subjects and a normal work environment with the common stressors of hospital-nursing employment.

Table 2-5. Analysis of Variance on the NAT of Simple Effects of Stressor Conditions

Source of Variation	d.f.	Mean Square	F
Stressor conditions at			
high need	3	21.4666	3.0413[a]
medium need	3	8.1833	1.1594
low need	3	33.7833	4.7863[a]
Within cells	48	7.0583	

[a]$F_{.95}$ (3,48) = 2.80.

(The original study was done with white mice and electric shock.) It was found that there is a curvilinear relationship between motivation and performance. It was also determined that subjects reach maximum performance on difficult test items at a lower stressor condition than for the less difficult items.

With the third hypothesis, that the quality of performance on the NAT will deteriorate less under stress than that of the SIT, the author was attempting to distinguish between tasks that are difficult and tasks that require a wide range of cue utilization for their solution. It was inferred that the SIT involved a wider range of cue utilization than the NAT because the former required the subject to "take the role of the particular other." The raw scores of each test were converted to Z scores. That there was no difference in the scores earned on the two tests under Condition 1 (control condition) was interpreted as a control for differences in the two tests with respect to level of difficulty. If, then, there was no difference in the level of difficulty of the two tests, the greater deterioration found for the SIT in Conditions 3 and 4 would support the presumption that this test involved a wider range of cues and that the increased stress (attributable to the situational stressors) interfered with the process of cue utilization. Thus corroboration is found for Easterbrook's hypothesis that an increase in motivation reduces the range of cues utilized by the subject, which in turn produces deterioration if the task requires responding to a wider range of cues than that which the subject can utilize.

The fourth hypothesis pertained to the interaction of need for social approval and situational stressors. On Condition 1 (lowest stressors) the order from highest to lowest performance was high, medium, and finally low need-for-approval subjects. On Condition 4 (highest stressors) the rank order was low, medium, and then high need-for-approval subjects. This reversal was interpreted as support for the view of motivation as having an intrinsic component (measured here as the need for social approval) and an induced component (the situational stressor conditions) which interact to form a motivational effect. Thus subjects with a high need for social approval perform best under conditions of lowest situational stressors. As the environmental stressors are increased, these subjects quickly pass their optimum level of motivation, and performance begins to deteriorate. On the other hand, subjects with a low need for social approval require moderate situational stressors to bring their motivational level up to the optimum for maximum performance.

Although comparisons have been made here in the extreme Conditions 1 and 4, a word of caution is in order. Although the low need-for-approval subjects performed better under the high stressor level of Condition 4 than did either of the other need-for-approval groups, this performance was considerably below the maximum performance achieved on lower stressor conditions. All need-for-approval groups deteriorated markedly on Condition 4 for both tests.

The study showed, then, that thinking quality deteriorates as the quantity of environmental stressors increases; that deterioration is greater when the type of thinking is more difficult; and that, if the factor of difficulty is held constant, deterioration is greater when the task involves using the broader range of cues present in social interaction.

Implications for Practice

One interpretation of the poor test performance of the control group is that with Condition 1 (7:00 A.M.) the nurses apparently lacked sufficient stimulation for maximum performance [4a]. Evidently their thinking was not focused sharply enough on the task. The best nursing performance was achieved under Condition 2 (good staffing). Performance deteriorated rapidly for Conditions 3 and 4. Because these last two assignments represented comparable situations with regard to patient dependency and staffing (weekend staffing), the increased responsibility of being either a team-leader (Condition 3) or the nurse-in-charge (Condition 4) seems to have added appreciably to the perception of environmental stressors.

The gravity of these findings is illustrated by the drop in performance between Conditions 2 and 4, which is just slightly less than two standard deviations. Comparing this with the scale of common IQ tests, one could say that a difference of two standard deviations represents the difference between thinking based on an IQ score of 115 and that based on an IQ of 85.

It was also found that with the increased stressors of larger assignments, quality of performance deteriorated more rapidly for the difficult test items than for less difficult items. It is common to see the staff nurse, in an attempt to escape environmental stress, hunting for a quiet place and time to teach a patient or retreating to the linen closet or an examining room to plan her team's assignment.

One must not, however, overlook the less sympathetic interpretation of the data. Although deterioration was faster when the type of thinking was more difficult, the reverse was also true, i.e., when the quality of thinking was simpler, more stressors were needed to attain maximum performance. Staff members appear to perform less efficiently by distributing their lighter assignment over the usual interval.

Another finding was that performance on test items based on social interaction deteriorated in the presence of increased environmental stressors at a much greater rate than did performance on general factual items. This finding supported the hypothesis that stressors decrease the range of cues utilized. Initially, peripheral cues — those that are occasionally or partially relevant to a task — are lost. This loss may improve performance by focusing attention on the central task. However, with greater stress some central cues — those immediately relevant to the task — also will not be perceived. Then the central task may be dealt with inappropriately.

This finding, that social interaction deteriorates under mounting situational stress, has great significance for nursing. To interact effectively with patients or staff, a nurse must perceive the cues necessary to distinguish the common and the uncommon elements regarding any given problem or request. If she is deluged by peripheral cues about other tasks to be performed, she may fail to perceive the cues that are most relevant to the patient with whom she interacts. Only when nurses have time to distinguish the cues related to patients' welfare can they be expected to plan individualized care.

This suggests important cognitive reasons for separating the functions of nurses. There is a need for nurses who, utilizing narrow ranges of cues, can complete many prescribed tasks effectively and in minimal time. There is also need for nurses who, utilizing broad ranges of cues, can determine patient needs, plan appropriate nursing care, and evaluate the care received. When all types of activities are assumed by the same nurse, quality of performance decreases or the cost of the service becomes prohibitive because of the excessive time consumed.

PREVENTION OF BACTERIURIA IN FEMALE PATIENTS WITH INDWELLING CATHETERS

This next study was designed to answer questions relative to the prevention of bacteriuria in female patients who are abacteriuric at the time that an indwelling catheter is inserted. Urinary-tract infections associated with indwelling catheters are a significant health problem in hospitals and nursing homes. It has been estimated by Dr. C. K. Himmelsbach of Georgetown University that each year about 300,000 patients are victims of hospital-acquired urinary tract infection [21]. Martin et al. [26] extrapolated from their studies at Jersey City Medical Center and estimated that 31,000 patients in the United States die each year from gram-negative bacteremia occurring within 10 days of indwelling catheterization.

Nurses seem unaware of the gravity of the problem because the recurring bouts of infection usually occur after the patient has been discharged. Turck et al. [28] summarized studies on the treatment of bacteriuria and reported "Only about 20% of patients with chronic infections of the urinary tract remain free from significant bacteriuria after cessation of treatment, regardless of the type or duration of chemotherapy." Thus bacteriuria is prevalent, serious, and very difficult to treat and is often acquired in the hospital while the patient is being treated for some other condition. When it develops as an iatrogenic disease, health professionals are doubly responsible for learning how to prevent it.

The author became interested in this problem because of the existence of a criterion measure for "bacteriuria" which could be measured independently of the medical diagnosis "symptomatic urinary tract infection." The lack of precise, quantifiable criterion measures has been a great deterrent to nursing research, particularly to clinical nursing research. In this instance Kass [22] has so conclusively demonstrated the relationship of bacteriuria to symptomatic urinary-tract infection that most physicians today believe that diagnosis should be based on the status of urine cultures rather than on waiting for a diagnosis that can be based on symptoms. For this reason the presence or absence of bacteriuria (100,000 colonies of one pathogenic organism/cc of urine obtained by catheterized specimen) could be determined independently of the physician.

For a few brief days the thought existed that this study could be done independently of physicians. Two medicoclinical researchers were sought initially, primarily for the purpose of gaining access to patients. Today the author would say that the dream of independent research is a false value. It may meet a personal need but rarely a research goal. Clinical research is so complex and so multifaceted that there is a chance for success only by providing members of every relevant discipline opportunities to make their maximum contributions. Investigators must listen carefully to those who view the problem from a different perspective. This may include workers with greater or less preparation than their own but always with different knowledge. The working goal must be interdependence, like the relationships within a healthy family, wherein each member is permitted maximum growth and contribution. Very quickly this study developed into a project of an uncommon type of scientific cooperation between nursing and medicine in the study of a clinical problem of mutual concern. There was collaboration in the development of the design, in the conduct of the study, and in the interpretation of the findings.

Rationale

Nursing's greatest contribution can be in developing better methods to prevent bacteria from gaining access to the bladder when a catheter is being used. There are three means by which bacteria may ascend the lower urinary tract. They can: be pushed in by the catheter, move up the lumen of the catheter, and, finally, move up the space between the urethral wall and the catheter. The first route was excluded as a concern of this study.

Sterile closed-drainage systems have been shown by Kunin and McCormack [23] to be an effective deterrent in preventing movement of bacteria up the lumen of the tube. The closed-drainage systems are almost always disposable, but most important they provide a closed tube from bladder to collection bag which greatly reduces the possibility of contamination by airborne bacteria and by bacteria on the hands of the hospital workers. Modeled after some work of Desautels et al. [18], the possible effectiveness of an intravenous-type drip chamber molded into the collecting tube was explored as another deterrent to the upward movement of bacteria.

As a nurse, the author was primarily interested in preventing entrance of bacteria from the space between urethral wall and catheter. The exudate that collects between catheter and urethral mucosa after the catheter is in place 12 to 24 hours is an excellent culture medium and also links the vaginorectal flora of the perineum to the bladder. This is probably relevant to the fact that lower urinary tract infections are so much more common among women than among men. The male has a distinct health advantage in having a longer and curved urethra.

There were three articles in the literature which reported studies aimed at preventing entrance of bacteria by the periurethral route. Two were so poor methodologically that they need not be commented on here. The third was done by Linton and Gillespie [24] and involved the use of a doughnut-shaped plastic foam pad, containing an antimicrobial agent, that was placed around the catheter and pushed up against the urinary meatus. Their work showed promise, but it involved only a small number of patients during a relatively brief interval (less than four days). It seemed appropriate to examine the use of the polyurethane pad in conjunction with perineal care.

Throughout the literature it has been shown time and again that antimicrobial agents were ineffective in preventing bacteriuria when they were administered systemically. Martin and Bookrajian [25] summarized these studies and concluded that the prophylactic use of antimicrobial agents merely shapes the character of the resultant bacteriuria. However, there were also two recent exceptions reported in the literature. Plorde et al. [27] described some success through the use of kanamycin in preventing bacteriuria in male patients who had prostatectomies. Kunin and McCormack [23] reported data that suggested medication with antimicrobial agents might be beneficial in preventing bacteriuria during the first seven days of catheterization after which it probably loses its effectiveness. Kunin suggested that this might be related to closed-drainage systems, i.e., perhaps the new closed systems prevent entrance of such large numbers of bacteria that the antimicrobial agents can effectively prevent multiplication of the smaller numbers. Here is an example of an accepted scientific generalization (the ineffectiveness of antimicrobial agents in preventing bacteriuria) that has to be restudied because the accompanying conditions of the original fact gathering have changed, namely, the advent of closed-drainage systems.

This study then had three purposes, including to compare and examine

1. the relative effectiveness of specific types of perineal care in preventing bacteriuria.
2. the effectiveness of a collection tube containing a drip chamber vs another set without such a mechanism.
3. the effect of systemic antimicrobial agents in preventing bacteriuria.

The third purpose is a medical research goal, since any findings would not materially affect nursing actions. The design for this study was experimental in that there were random assignment of subjects and manipulated independent variables [4b].

Independent Variables

VARIABLE A, PERINEAL CARE

The five types of care were as follows:

1. No perineal care was given by project nurses and the hospital staff was instructed not to give perineal care; no attempt was made to prevent patients from administering self-care.
2. Twice daily perineal care was given by project nurses. This involved a thorough mechanical cleansing of the perineum including the periurethral area and the proximal few inches of the visible catheter to remove mucoid secretions and exudate. The equipment for this procedure consisted of a sterile disposable irrigating set, sterile sponges, and foil packets containing 3 percent hexachlorophene soap solution (pHisoHex). Equipment was discarded after being used once. The procedure was carried out using clean gloves or no gloves after thorough hand washing.
3. The same procedure as in 20 but with sterile gloves.
4. A sterile polyurethane doughnut-shaped pad to which was applied a bacitracin-neomycin ointment was placed around the catheter at the meatus. The slit ends of the pad were held together by a 14-mm Michel wound clip. After the pad ends were clipped together, the pad was pushed up against the meatus. Both pad and ointment were changed twice daily using sterile gloves.
5. The pad and ointment procedure was used together with the perineal care described under A3 as previously described.

VARIABLE B, CLOSED DRAINAGE SYSTEM

The two types of sterile, closed-drainage, disposable systems were as follows:

1. A heavy-duty plastic bag with 2000 cc capacity, with a drainage tube of 9/32-inch internal diameter bonded to bag, and with a horizontal mounted discharge spigot at the bottom of bag with a clamp and cap fitting over the end of the drainage spigot. (B-D Asepto Set by Becton Dickinson and Co., Rutherford, N.J. 07070.)

2. Same as in 1. except that the discharge spigot was mounted in the center at the bottom of the bag, and there was a protective pocket into which the spigot end was slipped. There was a drip chamber which formed an air barrier between bag and tubing, and the air vent was protected against accidental wetting. (Curity System by Kendall Hospital Products, 309 W. Jackson Blvd., Chicago, Ill. 60606.)

VARIABLE C, SYSTEMIC ANTIMICROBIAL AGENTS

This variable was not controlled by the investigators and thus will be reported and discussed as survey rather than as experimental data.

Dependent Variable, Definition of Terms, and Hypotheses

The incidence of bacteriuria was associated with the use of indwelling catheters in patients whose initial urine or second-day specimen was abacteriuric and whose catheter was in place for at least 60 hours. Thus, although quantitative counts were made each day, the patients were divided into two categories, namely, bacteriuric or nonbacteriuric.

The following definitions were established:

Bacteriuria. The presence on culture of 100,000 or more colonies of one pathogenic species/ml of urine obtained by catheterized specimen. When two catheter specimens were so obtained, patient was classified as being bacteriuric.

Abacteriuria. The absence upon culture of any colonies of pathogenic bacteria in 1 ml of urine obtained by catheterized specimen.

Nonbacteriuria. The presence on culture of less than 100,000 colonies/ml of catheterized urine of one type of pathogenic organism.

Incidence of Bacteriuria. Number of patients who became bacteriuric during a prescribed interval (bacteriuric patients/patients at risk).

Three hypotheses guided the study:

The incidence of bacteriuria will be greatest in condition A_1 and least in A_5, with the other conditions ranking between them: $A_1 > A_2 > A_3 > A_4 > A_5$.

The incidence of bacteriuria will be less with the use of drainage system B_2: $B_1 > B_2$.

Patients receiving systemic antibiotics, in contrast to those who do not, will have a lower incidence of bacteriuria (retrospective survey).

Method

EXPERIMENTAL SUBJECTS

The study was limited to adult female patients in whom a catheter was in place for at least 60 hours. Patients in the psychiatric, obstetrical, gynecological, and urological services were omitted. The investigators believed that the questions being asked could best be answered using a patient sample in which anatomicophysiological complications of the urological system could be avoided. To be admitted to the study, either the first or second specimen had to be negative on culture, i.e., abacteriuric. Also it was necessary for the patient to give oral consent to be a member of the study. No patients refused consent and most of them seemed to enjoy the regular and repeated contact with project staff. Two patients admitted to the study were later dropped, one at the patient's own request and one by the family's request (the latter patient was terminally ill). Physician-consent was granted by the heads of the services involved and it was not necessary to obtain medical consent for individual patients.

Patients were randomly assigned to the experimental condition. If the catheter was removed in less than 60 hours or if the patient was found to be already bacteriuric, she was dropped and her place in the study reassigned. A total of 184 patients were included in the study.

PROCEDURE

Since the catheterization was not a part of this study, it was planned that as soon as an order for catheterization of a female patient was written, the nurse who noted the physician's order would notify the Nursing Office secretary. The secretary, after referring to the randomized assignment sheet, told the nurse which type of drainage system to use and reminded her to put a sterile urine specimen in the ward refrigerator. The research-project nurses were responsible for all nursing care related to the urinary system after that point. The project staff-members (who worked from 8 A.M. to 8 P.M., seven days a week) marked the Kardex, patient's record, and door and bed cards; instructed the patient; gave the specific perineal care; emptied the collection bag; collected daily urine specimens from the catheter and from the bag; and maintained protocol records of relevant information taken from the patient's health history and record of treatment. The investigators had planned that project nurses would empty the drainage bags every 12 hours. Hospital staff felt that this was unsatisfactory and a return to the eight-hour schedule became necessary. This meant that bag emptying could not be done by project staff-members, and therefore the emphasis shifted to staff education in the proper emptying of the bags.

The method for reporting new patients to the project staff did not work out as planned. After three months a change was made wherein project nurses surveyed the hospital daily to find any female patients who had had indwelling catheters inserted since the last survey. This procedural change meant that it was not possible to assign the drainage systems in a strictly random pattern. The solution to this problem was to stock the hospital with "B_1" drainage systems for four weeks and then change to "B_2" systems for four weeks. The random assignment of patients to the five types of perineal care was not affected. With the change it was also impossible to obtain a specimen at the time of catheterization. Rather the first specimen might be drawn 1 to 24 hours after catheterization. With either method the second specimen was obtained the morning following catheterization.

SPECIMEN COLLECTION

Urine specimens were obtained each morning aseptically as follows: (1) from the lumen of the catheter by a syringe and needle and (2) from the spigot of the bag. Collection continued until bladder urine was bacteriuric for two consecutive specimens or until patient was discharged or catheter removed. If urine from the collection bag became bacteriuric while the bladder urine was still clean, a new sterile collection system was connected to the catheter in an attempt to prevent contamination from the bag. If the catheter had to be changed, the patient was dropped from the study. Specimens were carried in an ice chest during collection rounds and until the cultures could be prepared.

LABORATORY METHODS

A laboratory technician assigned to this project was responsible for plating and reading all differential cultures. The nurse members of the project staff used a miniature culture technique (Testuria by Ayerst Laboratories, New York, N.Y., 10017) as a screening device to make the initial separation of abacteriuric from bacteriuric patients. This simplified culture method has a reported incidence of 1 percent false negatives which was considered tolerable for this study [20]. If any colonies appeared on the Testuria plate, a traditional plate culture was prepared from the refrigerated urine specimen.

Results

PATIENT SAMPLE

As a pretrial sample to test procedures, 12 patients were used but were not included in any tabulations. Excluding them, the project staff had contact with a total of 492 female patients of whom only 184 are included in the final data analysis. The total breakdown is shown in Table 2-6. Those patients labeled as "incomplete" were those in whom only one positive specimen was obtained before the catheter was removed. If there were no other data on which to base a decision, the patient was considered to be incomplete. However, if there had been two positive bag specimens or a positive midstream specimen of the same organism, or both, as in the catheter specimen, the patient was classified as bacteriuric and remained in the study sample. The eight patients excluded from the study as "indeterminant" were those in whom the cultures fluctuated in so bizarre a fashion, bouncing between positive and negative and showing

Table 2-6. Patients Seen by Project Staff

Patient Description	Number
Admitted to study	184
Not admitted — bacteria in initial specimen	165
Not admitted — catheter in place < 60 hrs	126
Admitted but incomplete	9
Admitted but indeterminate	8
Total	492

unusual shifts in predominant organism, that there could be no professional agreement (two physicians and one medical technologist) on the disposition.

The high incidence of bacteriuria (31.5 percent) found in the initial specimen was similar to that reported by Kunin and McCormack [23]. They found that 25.2 percent of their sample of 941 patients had greater than 10 colonies. Their percentage would have been greater had they excluded all patients with any initial evidence of bacteria as was done here. As previously mentioned the patients in this study were all females; they ranged in age from 20 to 98 with a mean age of 60.3 years.

The acquisition of bacteriuria among patients with various clinical conditions can be seen in Table 2-7. In order to determine which of them might be significant clinically, an attempt was made to define the patient groups in whom the risk of developing bacteriuria was above average. Since the overall infection rate was 53.3 percent (Table 2-8), the criteria for empirically defining "high risk" became those diseases wherein a bacteriuric rate exceeding 53 percent was found. The validity of the criteria was tested using a cross-validation technique. To accomplish this the 184 patients were divided into two random subgroups each of which contained 92 patients, of whom 43 had remained nonbacteriuric throughout the study and the other 49 had become bacteriuric. Looking at the first subsample, it was found that patients with heart disease, renal disease, and medically treated neoplasms all had rates higher than 53 percent.

Table 2-7. Bacteriuric Rates for Patients by Disease Types, Age Groups, and Hospital Room Types[a]

Characteristic	Number of Patients	Incidence	Percentage
Surgical procedure	84	35	41.7
Diabetes mellitus	21	8	38.1
Hypertension	21	11	52.4[b]
Renal disease	24	14	58.3[b]
Liver disease	15	6	40.0[b]
Heart disease	27	16	59.3[c]
Medical neoplasm	30	24	80.0[c]
Surgical neoplasm	34	10	29.4
< 59 years	87	50	57.5[c]
> 60 years	95	47	49.5
> 70 years	30	60	50.0
Single room	28	16	57.1[c]
Multiple unit	157	82	52.2

[a] Bacteriuria = development of two positive specimens and/or positive mid-stream specimen of same organism as in catheter specimen.

[b] Criteria for defining "high-risk" patients.

[c] Assumed to be spuriously high because of other factors.

Table 2-8. Cross-Validation Subsample Showing the Test of the Criteria Defining High Risk

	High Risk	Non-High Risk	Total	X^8
Non-bacteriuric	14	29	43	2/m
Bacteriuric	27	22	49	2/m
Totals	41	51	92	3.84[a]
% Bacteriuric	65.9	43.1	53.3	2/m

NOTE: 2/m = not relevant.

[a] $p < .025$.

Using the other subsample, all patients who had one or more of these three conditions were placed in a high-risk group. The remaining patients were considered to be non-high-risk patients. Using a chi-square test of independence, it was found that the probability was less than .025 that such differences could have occurred by chance (Table 2-8). In the same table it can be seen that among the "high-risk" patients the incidence of bacteriuria was 65.9 percent, and among the "non-high-risk" patients the rate was 43.1 percent. For these three clinical conditions (heart disease, renal disease, and medically treated neoplasms), a high level of stability was demonstrated since it was possible to develop the criteria on subsample A and to test them successfully on subsample B. Likewise the criteria could be developed on subsample B and tested successfully on subsample A.

From Table 2-7 it can be seen that there were two other situations associated with high incidence of bacteriuria, namely, age of 60 or less and the occupancy of a single room in the hospital. These were assumed to be spurious conditions, i.e., associated with high incidence of bacteriuria because of some unidentified third factor. This experience provides the author an opportunity to comment on a general problem in nursing research. It has been too common a practice among nurse-researchers and particularly nurse-faculty advisors to engage in studies of any nursing phenomena. Nurses must learn to focus on preferably one, maybe two, areas of research and become masters of them. It is only when the researcher knows considerably about the phenomena being studied that it is possible to discern a spurious relationship and not be led astray. In this case the use of single rooms by patients with more acute and complicated diseases (example: use of anticarcinogenic drugs for non-operable patients) produced the higher incidence of bacteriuria.

TREATMENT EFFECTS

Table 2-9 shows the incidence of bacteriuria for each treatment condition and drainage system. Tables 2-10 and 2-11 report the same data but are separated to show only one variable at a time. Since the data are nominal, analysis was by the chi-square test of independence. Table 2-12 shows the comparisons which were made: none was statistically significant.

Table 2-9. Relative Effectiveness of Treatment Conditions and Drainage Systems

Treatment Conditions	A_1		A_2		A_3		A_4		A_5		Totals
Drainage Systems	B_1	B_2	B_1	B_2	B_1	B_2	B_1	B_2	B_1	B_2	
Non-bacteriuric	12	7	8	7	11	9	8	3	9	12	86
Bacteriuric	10	10	10	10	10	8	6	9	13	12	98
Totals	22	17	18	17	21	17	14	12	22	24	184
% Bacteriuric	45.5	58.8	55.6	58.8	47.6	47.1	42.9	75.0	59.1	50.0	53.3

Table 2-10. Relative Effectiveness of Treatment Conditions

Treatment Conditions	A_1	A_2	A_3	A_4	A_5	Totals
Non-bacteriuric	19	15	20	11	21	86
Bacteriuric	20	20	18	15	25	98
Totals	39	35	38	26	46	184
% Bacteriuric	51.3	57.1	47.4	57.7	54.3	53.3

Table 2-11. Relative Effectiveness of Drainage Systems

Drainage Systems	B_1	B_2	Totals
Non-bacteriuric	48	38	86
Bacteriuric	49	49	98
Totals	97	87	184
% Bacteriuric	50.5	56.3	53.3

Table 2-12. Chi-square Tests for Significant Differences by Treatment and by Drainage System

Variables	N	d.f.	X_2	Result
Treatment (variable A)				
A_1 vs A_2 vs A_3 vs A_4 vs A_5	184	4	1.0298	NS
A_1 vs A_2	74	1	.0735	NS
A_1 vs A_3	77	1	.0131	NS
A_1 vs A_4	65	1	.0642	NS
A_1 vs A_5	85	1	.0040	NS
A_2 vs A_3	73	1	.3607	NS
A_1 vs $A_2 + A_3$	112	1	.0144	NS
A_4 vs A_5	72	1	.0005	NS
A_1 vs $A_4 + A_5$	111	1	.0536	NS
Drainage system (variable B)				
B_1 vs B_2 (confounded with A)	184	1	.4096	NS
B_1A_1 vs B_1A_2 vs B_1A_3 vs B_1A_4 vs B_1A_5	97	4	1.4540	NS
B_2A_1 vs B_2A_2 vs B_2A_3 vs B_2A_4 vs B_2A_5	87	4	2.7705	NS

Thus it is concluded that the four treatment conditions consisting of various types of perineal care had no effect on the incidence of bacteriuria which was any different from patient administered self-care. We concur with Kunin and McCormack: "The proper method to avoid periurethral contamination remains to be determined [23]." Similarly the inclusion of a drip chamber in the collecting tube of the drainage system had no differing effect. Thus it is concluded that Hypotheses 1 and 2 (see section on "Dependent Variables . . ." in this chapter) were not supported.

Whereas the use of the drip chamber was not found to be effective, a word of caution should be added. Three products were tried initially and the one that we judged to be best was used in the study. However, none of the systems was mechanically adequate in the hospital environment to test the hypotheses accurately.

ANTIBIOTICS

On the patient protocols a record was kept of all antimicrobial agents administered. This was an independent variable uncontrolled by the investigators. After all data collection had been completed, patients who had received no antibiotic agents during the period in which the indwelling catheter was in place became the control group for this retrospective analysis. Those patients who received 1, 2, or 3 antibiotics each for 100 percent of the time that the catheter was in place were included in this analysis. Any patient who received any antibiotic for less than 100 percent of the time was excluded. The antibiotic agents were classified into three groups according to type of action, namely, bacteriostatic, broad-spectrum bactericidal, and finally the narrow-spectrum bactericidal agents (Table 2-13).

A comparison of the incidence of bacteriuria among patients receiving various types of antibiotics is shown in Table 2-14. Here the probability is less than .001 that such differences could occur on the basis of chance alone. Because the broad-spectrum bactericidal agents had been expected to be the most effective, this group was compared against the control group. Here the difference was significant at the level of $p < .0001$. The strength of the relationship is expressed by Cramer's phi prime statistic ϕ' as described by Hays [19]:

$$\phi' = \sqrt{\frac{x^2}{N(L-1)}} \quad \text{where L = smaller of R (number of rows) or}$$
$$\text{C (number of columns)}$$

This statistic has an advantage over the more familiar contingency coefficient in that the former has a maximum possible correlation

Table 2-13. Classification of Antibiotics

A. Bacteriostatic:
  Nitrofurantoin (Furadantin, Macrodantin)
  Tetracycline (Achromycin)
  Sulfonamide (Gantonal)
  Chloramphenicol (Chloromycetin)
  Chloramphenicol and tetracycline
  Lincomycin (Lincocin)
  Sulfonamide and lincomycin

B. Broad-spectrum bactericidal:
  Ampicillin
  Cephalothin (Keflin)
  Cephaloridine (Loridine)
  Streptomycin
  Kanamycin
  Gentamicin
  Ampicillin and kanamycin
  Ampicillin and streptomycin
  Ampicillin and cephaloridine
  Ampicillin, kanamycin, and cephaloridine
  Streptomycin and methicillin
  Kanamycin and penicillin

C. Narrow-spectrum bactericidal:
  Procaine penicillin
  Cloxacillin
  Aqueous penicillin
  Penicillin V (Vi Cellin K)
  Methicillin

---

of 1.0, which means that it can be interpreted in a manner similar to a Pearson product-moment correlation (r). Cramer's phi prime was .4731 when broad-spectrum antibacterial agents were compared with the control group. This means that the former accounted for 22.4 percent of the variance in the incidence of bacteriuria in the four groups of patients. Thus hypothesis 3 (see Dependent Variable, Definition of Terms, and Hypotheses, on p. 58) is supported. The use of broad-spectrum bactericidal agents is statistically and empirically significant. Among patients receiving broad-spectrum antibiotics the incidence

Table 2-14. Relative Effectiveness of Various Types of Antibiotic Prophylaxis

Effectiveness	None	Bacteriostatic	Broad-Spectrum Bactericidal	Narrow-Spectrum Bactericidal	Totals	X_2
Non-bacteriuric	20	11	29	4	64	
Bacteriuric	62	10	9	7	88	
Totals	82	21	38	11	152	29.86[a]
% Bacteriuric	75.6	47.6	23.7	63.6	57.9	

[a] $p < .001$; $\phi' = .4432$.

of bacteriuria was 23.7 percent and among those not receiving antibiotics, the incidence was 75.6 percent.

Because the concept of "high-risk" as used in this paper was defined on the basis of these data, it would not be legitimate to compare the effectiveness of broad-spectrum bactericidal agents on "high-risk" and "non-high risk" patients. However, one can compare the effect of absence of antibiotics and the use of broad-spectrum bactericidal agents on high-risk patients and then again on non-high-risk patients. This is shown in Table 2-15. On both groups of patients the incidence of bacteriuria is markedly lower among patients receiving broad-spectrum antibiotics, and these differences are statistically significant with $p < .001$.

Length of Time Catheter Is in Place. Attempts to analyze the data giving attention to the factor of time can be made only after warning the nurse-reader of the danger involved. These data are included because of the empirically known relevance of the time factor. Of the 98 patients in this study whose urine became bacteriuric, 26.17 percent became so by the second day, 45.3 percent by the third day, 75.5 percent by the fourth day, 92.8 percent by the eighth day, and 98.9 percent by the 12th day. Two outstanding successes were instances when catheters were removed, one at 16 days, another at 20 days, without the patients' having developed bacteriuria. This predilection to eventual development of bacteriuria is well enough accepted that the author of this paper is unaware of any investigator ever claiming that bacteriuria could be prevented in continued use of the indwelling catheter. Rather it is in short-term cases that effort is directed at trying to prevent bacteriuria until the catheter is no longer needed.

In order to observe the effect of time, the patients were divided into two groups, including those whose bacteriuric status was determined within the first four days (either they became bacteriuric or the catheter was removed nonbacteriuric) and those patients whose outcome was determined after four days. This method is conceptually weak. Patients who remain nonbacteriuric for four days after insertion of an indwelling catheter probably are somehow different

Table 2-15. Comparison of Effectiveness of Broad-spectrum Bactericidal Agents and Absence of Antibiotics on High-risk and Non-high-risk Patients

Effectiveness	No Antibiotics	Broad-spectrum Bactericidal	Totals	X_2
High-risk patients				
Non-bacteriuric	4	9	13	
Bacteriuric	29	6	35	
Totals	33	15	48	9.67[a]
% Bacteriuric	87.9	40.0	72.9	
Non-high-risk patients				
Non-bacteriuric	16	20	36	
Bacteriuric	33	3	36	
Totals	49	23	72	16.36[a]
% Bacteriuric	67.3	13.0	50.0	

NOTE: ϕ' = .4487; .4765.

[a] < .001.

than patients who become bacteriuric during these first four days. Thus one cannot claim that the two groups of patients are comparable and thus the data are impossible to interpret with any degree of confidence. To examine validly the effect of the factor of time, it would be necessary to use a different type of experimental design. Patients would have to be admitted to a study and then randomly assigned to short-term (< 4 days) or long-term (> 4 days) catheterization.

Seasonal Pattern of Bacteriuria. Data were analyzed three different ways in an attempt to determine if any seasonal pattern could be found. First, the data were grouped November through April and May through October; second, December through February, March through May, June through August, and September through November; third, January through March, April through June, July through September, and October through December. No differences were found, and it was concluded that there were no seasonal variations in the incidence of bacteriuria accompanying the use of indwelling catheters.

Hour of Catheterization. Here the data were analyzed into day and night patterns (7 A.M.–6 P.M. and 7 P.M.–6 A.M.) and by tour of duty of the nursing staff (7 A.M.–2 P.M., 3 P.M.–10 P.M., 11 P.M.–6 A.M.). Again no differences were found. The fact that no seasonal or hourly differences were found is not surprising since there were no reasons (other than possibly spurious ones) to expect differences. The findings are reported, however, in that this information may be very helpful to other researchers who may wish to limit (for economic reasons) their sampling and will be able to assume that a seasonal or daytime sample was representative of the total population.

IMPLICATIONS FOR PRACTICE

We therefore conclude from this study and from previously reported research that until other data possibly change the conclusions, the care of patients with indwelling catheters should involve consideration of the following factors:

1. Indwelling catheters should be avoided whenever possible.
2. Catheters should be removed as soon as possible.

3. Catheters should be irrigated only if the passage is blocked.
4. Catheter and drainage tube should not be disconnected in order to obtain urine specimens; a needle and syringe should be used and urine withdrawn from the catheter lumen or specimen removed from the bag spigot.
5. Perineal care should be based on the patient's hygienic and comfort needs.
6. Drip chambers in collecting tubes are not yet technically operational; their merit cannot be tested clinically until a satisfactory model is available.
7. Broad-spectrum antibiotic agents are effective in helping to prevent bacteriuria.

Since the nursing hypotheses in this study were not supported, a question can be raised on the reason this paper should be published. Earlier in this chapter the author commented on the differences in the goal of research in a basic discipline and in a profession. Since the hypotheses were not supported, this study did not contribute anything new to the body of positive knowledge. However, the goal of research within a profession is to guide professional practice. Since thousands of nursing hours are consumed in administering perineal care, it is important to say publicly that in this study there was no evidence that this practice has any effect in preventing bacteriuria in female patients with indwelling catheters. To develop a scientific basis for nursing practice, it is as important to exclude from practice that which is unnecessary and perhaps merely ritualistic as it is to add to the practice that which has been scientifically documented.

REFERENCES

A. *Effect of Stress on Performance*

1. Basowitz, H., et al. *Anxiety and Stress.* New York: McGraw-Hill, 1955, p. 289.
2. Berlew, D. E. Interpersonal sensitivity and motive strength. *Journal of Abnormal Psychology* (Washington) 63:390–394, September, 1961.

3. Broadhurst, P. L. The interaction of task difficulty and motivation; the Yerkes-Dodson Law revived. *Acta Psychologica* (Amsterdam) 16:321–338, 1959.

4. Broverman, D. M., and Lazarus, R. S. Individual differences in task performance under conditions of cognitive interference. *Journal of Personality* (Durham, N.C.) 26:94–105, March, 1958.

4a. Cleland, V. S. Effects of stress on thinking. *American Journal of Nursing* 67:108–111, 1967.

4b. Cleland, V. S., et al. Prevention of bacteriuria in female patients with indwelling catheters. *Nursing Research* 20:309–318, 1971.

5. Connor, R. J., et al. Effective use of nursing resources; a research report. *Hospitals* 35:30–39, May 1, 1961.

6. Crowne, D. F., and Marlowe, D. A new scale of social desirability independent of psychopathology. *Journal of Consulting and Clinical Psychology* (Washington) 24:349–354, August, 1960.

7. Easterbrook, J. A. The effect of emotion on cue utilization and the organization of behavior. *Psychological Review* (Washington) 66:183–201, May, 1959.

8. Horton, D. L., Marlowe, D., and Crowne, D. F. The effect of instructional set and need for social approval on commonality of word association responses. *Journal of Abnormal Social Psychology* (Washington) 66:67–72, January, 1963.

9. Lazarus, R. S., Deese, J., and Osler, S. F. The effects of psychological stress upon performance. *Psychological Bulletin* 49(4):293–317, 1952.

10. Marlowe, D., and Crowne, D. F. Social desirability and response to perceived situational demands. *Journal of Consulting and Clinical Psychology* (Washington) 25:109–115, April 1, 1961.

11. Mead, G. H. *Mind, Self, and Society,* edited by C. M. Morris. Chicago, Ill.: University of Chicago Press, 1934.

12. Methven, D, and Schlotfeldt, R. M. The social interaction inventory. *Nursing Research* (New York) 11:83–88, Spring, 1962.

13. Selye, H. (Ed.). *Annual Reports on Stress* (Vol. 1). Montreal: Acta, 1951.

14. Strickland, B. R., and Crowne, D. F. Conformity under conditions of simulated group pressure as a function of the need for social approval. *Journal of Social Psychology* (Provincetown) 58(1):171–181, 1962.

15. Vogel, W., Baker, R., and Lazarus, R. S. The role of motivation in psychological stress. *Journal of Abnormal and Social Psychology* (Washington) 56:105–112, January, 1958.

16. Winer, B. J. *Statistical Principles in Experimental Design.* New York: McGraw-Hill, 1962.

17. Yerkes, R. M., and Dodson, J. D. The relation of strength of stimulus to rapidity of habit-formation. *Journal of Comparative Neurology and Psychology* 18:459–482, 1908.

B. *Prevention of Bacteriuria in Female Patients with Indwelling Catheters*

18. Desautels, R. E., et al. Technical advances in the prevention of urinary tract infections. *Journal of Urology* (Baltimore) 87:487–490, March, 1962.

19. Hays, W. L. *Statistics for Psychologists.* New York: Holt, Reinhart and Winston, 1963, pp. 604–606.
20. Heinze, E. G., et al. Simple methods for detection of bacteriuria in the physician's office. *Henry Ford Hospital Medical Journal* 16:279–282, 1968.
21. Himmelsbach, C. K. "News." *American Journal of Nursing* 69:2206–2207, October, 1969.
22. Kass, E. M. Asymptomatic infections of urinary tract. *Transactions of the Association of American Physicians* (Philadelphia) 69:56–64, 1956.
23. Kunin, C. M., and McCormack, R. O. Prevention of catheter-induced urinary-tract infections by sterile closed drainage. *New England Journal of Medicine* 274:1151–1161, May 26, 1966.
24. Linton, K. B., and Gillespie, W. A. Causes and prevention of postoperative urinary infection in female patients. *Journal of Obstetrics and Gynaecology of the British Commonwealth* (London) 69:845–849, October, 1962.
25. Martin, C. M., and Bookrajian, E. N. Bacteriuria prevention after indwelling urinary catheterization. *Archives of Internal Medicine* (Chicago) 110:709, November, 1962.
26. Martin, C. M., et al. Prevention of gram-negative rod bacteremia associated with indwelling urinary-tract catheterization. In J. C. Sylvester (Ed.), *Antimicrobiological Agents Chemotherapy.* Proceedings of the Second Interscience Conference on Antimicrobial Agents and Chemotherapy held in Chicago, 1962. Ann Arbor, Mich.: American Society for Microbiology, 1963, pp. 617–623.
27. Plorde, J. J., et al. Course and prognosis of prostatectomy. *New England Journal of Medicine* 272:269–277, February 11, 1965.
28. Turck, M., et al. Relapse and reinfection in chronic bacteriuria. *New England Journal of Medicine* 275:70–73, July 14, 1966.

Interaction Analysis in Nursing Research
Donna Kaye Diers
Ruth Litfin Schmidt

3

FOR nursing research to make its most effective contribution to the development of nursing theory, both the problems selected for study and the methods used must be relevant to the practice of nursing. Much nursing research has focused on educational or administrative questions. Even that which has focused on the nurse's activities has often lumped all activity with the patient under one large category of "direct patient care" [87].

An important part of research in nursing practice is concerned with what goes on between the nurse and the patient and the consequences that this relationship has for the patient. The research hypothesis can be stated as a causal relationship between two variables: the effect of interaction between nurse and patient on the patient. To test such hypotheses, we must be able to make operational "nurse-patient interaction," the causal relationship, and "patient condition." The controlled experiment is the most widely accepted way to define operationally the "cause" [37, 51].

Measuring "patient condition" has received considerable attention as a problem in measuring "patient welfare" [72]. The independent variable, nurse-patient interaction, presents some especially difficult measurement problems and is the focus of concern in this chapter.

INTERACTION AS TREATMENT

A broad concept of nursing that includes the totality of the patient's experience views the nurse-patient conversation as an important part of the nursing treatment or even as a treatment in itself [8]. This focus calls for a significant shift in thinking about the sciences relevant to nursing — a shift from sole emphasis on the physical sciences to a concern with the social sciences. To move toward patient-centered practice guided by explicit theory requires the research identification and testing of components of interaction that have important effects on the patient.

Considerable evidence from experimental studies indicates that nursing interaction can have an effect on patient behavior. Most current operational definitions of the independent variable — nursing — fall into two major categories. Nursing is defined by a script which the nursing follows [62, 65] or is loosely defined, making replication or implementation of findings difficult [1, 27, 28, 55, 70, 71]. If the nurse-patient interaction is to be regarded as a treatment in itself, directions for its use must be specific enough to guide practice, yet general enough to allow for the "art" of application.

There have been numerous attempts to provide such directions. Studies of interaction have taken three approaches: (1) descriptive or correlational studies of interaction [5, 9, 32, 33, 36, 39, 40, 42, 44, 54, 74, 75, 84, 86, 88]; (2) studies that use responses to hypothetical interactions as indices of nursing [16, 17, 25, 34, 38, 52, 61, 68, 73, 81]; and (3) studies that use interaction analysis tools developed in other disciplines and applied to nursing situations [12, 43, 64, 80]. All of these approaches have limited usefulness for nursing practice, either because the measurement of nursing is not clinically relevant or because the hypothetical situation does not necessarily accurately reflect reality. In addition descriptive studies have not often been carried to the point of experimental testing. Many descriptive studies of interaction end with the invention of categories that may never be seen again. The Nurse Orientation System (NOS) and the research which ensued using this content analysis tool represent an attempt to circumvent some of the problems in previous work. As it developed, the NOS has become a useful tool for the measurement of nurse-patient interaction.

As a treatment, any nursing approach to the patient must meet the criteria for any other treatment, i.e., it must be specific to the patient's condition, its effects must be measurable, and it must be teachable. It may be possible, to effect change in a patient's condition with a "personalized" style of interaction and even to demonstrate the effectiveness of such an approach in a clinical experiment. But to identify or teach the elements in the nurse's approach, one must be able to describe the interaction that produced the effect. Interaction analysis — the description of the content and structure of communication between people — provides the means of specifying, quantifying, and hence communicating to others the components of different kinds of nursing processes.

INTERACTION ANALYSIS

Content analysis or interaction analysis is a technique developed during World War II by political scientists for the analysis of German propaganda in the mass media [18]. The method has been picked up in sociology and psychology and applied to the study of small groups [2, 63], psychotherapy [24, 30, 49], and more generally to the analysis of interview data of any kind.

As the term is herein used, "interaction" is taken to mean verbal interchange. The analysis of such communication is difficult and complex because usually several messages are conveyed simultaneously — affective as well as cognitive. Furthermore the message received is not exactly that which was intended. This probably explains why communication science is new and communication theory and research largely descriptive. "Interaction analysis" or "content analysis" has sometimes been used to denote the study of non-verbal movement [7, 77], the vocal but not verbal qualities of speech [67], or some temporal variables [56, 76, 89]. Sometimes only one-half of the interaction is studied — only the nurse's verbalizations.

Interaction is behavior as opposed to attitudes (although interaction data have sometimes been taken as evidence of attitude) [61]. In some studies verbal behavior is taken as indicative of other things such as diagnosis of personality traits [24, 31, 47, 48] or of psychopathy [53]. Problems of validity multiply with increasing inferential distance from the interaction categories to the concept.

Sources of Data

There are both direct and indirect methods of data collection for interaction analysis. The direct method is used by Bales [2] and Conant [13]. Non-participant observers classify the interaction while it is happening. Sometimes the interaction is tape recorded too, but the primary data collection is "live." The direct method is especially useful in working with small groups when an individual member's conversation might be obscured or lost on a tape recording. It also affords the opportunity to include non-verbal behavior such as head nodding and body positioning.

This method has some important disadvantages. First it may require complicated equipment and facilities not usually available to nurses or appropriate to the clinical setting. Second the original event can never be duplicated with the same participants using the same words, facial expressions, emphasis, and so on. The action cannot be stopped by the observer, and he is forced to keep up with every word or unit, a nearly impossible task in some cases. Observers may miss units by trying to hear, see, and record everything.

There are several indirect methods for obtaining interaction data. Television or videotape recording, audiotape alone or in combination with FM transmitting-receiving equipment, shorthand recording by non-participant observers, and memory reconstruction are all possible methods.

Tape recording the interaction, then classifying the units while listening to the tape is perhaps the most popular and widely used method. The accuracy of the coding depends to a great extent on the fidelity of the electronic equipment and the investigator's skill in manipulating the equipment. In the clinical-nursing setting, recorders pick up all of the extraneous noises present unless care is taken to place the microphones so that distortion of voice and sounds is minimized. This generally means at least consultation with an electronics expert, investing in high-quality microphones, and testing the equipment in the setting so that the best placement can be determined. Nurse-researchers are usually not familiar enough with efficient recording techniques to know how to obtain the best possible recordings from the equipment on hand.[1] Unless a hospital room is already equipped for sound production, we usually depend on movable recorders.

Most commercial recorders are too heavy to be easily moved into a patient's room, and those that are not too heavy are sometimes inadequate for very accurate reproduction. If it is possible to move only the microphone into the room (as with radio transmitters) and leave the recorder elsewhere, this problem is diminished. However, we have found that the physical structure of many clinical settings nearly eliminates the possibility of using wireless sender-receiver equipment. The steel and concrete buildings interfere with sound unless the microphone and receiver are in the same line of sight.

If one is interested in inconspicuous or concealed sound recording equipment, an FM system is ideal when combined with a commercial recorder. The technical problems can be worked out.

Sound film, television, or videotape recording are also ideal methods because not only do they furnish a permanent record of the interaction but visual data is not lost as it is with other indirect methods [14, 35, 91]. In the clinical-nursing setting this kind of data collection is complicated since it requires special facilities with which most hospitals are not equipped. It is also expensive.

The question of invading the patient's privacy to tape record or videotape the interaction is often raised. The question is sometimes framed as a conflict of interests: the researcher's desire to obtain spontaneous, complete recordings (which suggests that the subjects are unaware of being recorded) and the practitioner's concern that nothing be done to harm the patient (which suggests that the patient be told of the recording and offered the option of declining). Stating the issue this way seems to assume that there is something about tape recording that is inherently harmful to patients or that most people would object violently, or both, and deliberately change their interaction patterns if they knew they were being recorded.

Actually experience indicates that with the proper precautions to guard the patient's (and nurse's) identity, very few objections are raised by either patients or nurses to being recorded. If the researcher is acting as a participant observer, her own comfort with the technique is likely to be the most important factor. Nurse-researchers may be more comfortable when they tell the patient he is being recorded and ask his permission than when they are concealing the equipment. Several conflicting reasons may be offered for the ease with which patient permission to record is obtained. For some patients it may be the desire not to upset the system and suffer the consequences or a hesitation to say "no" to a nurse who presents him with a choice but represents those on whom he is independent. For others, participation in research may represent an opportunity to contribute rather than merely take from the system, and so allows a rare small measure of independence. It seems that patients, particularly in a teaching and research institution, come to expect some unusual treatment and if they are told that by allowing themselves to be recorded they may be contributing to the betterment of care, they do not object. We have found that the most comfortable introduction to the patient is to say, "I'd like to use this tape recorder so I can remember what we've said and so I won't have to interrupt by taking notes. Is that okay with you?"

Another part of the argument against using tape recorders (or informing the participants) is that such methods distort the interaction so that the findings are meaningless. Experience suggests, however, that patients and nurses very quickly forget that they are being recorded as the relationship develops. We have data that include some very intimate conversations with no apparent efforts on the part of the participants to censor their talk. Of course some people may simply wish to "disclose" and, given the opportunity, will do so. The most important point, however, seems to be the nurse's skill in assuring the patient that the data are confidential and the nurse's own comfort in herself being recorded. One way to increase the researcher's comfort with the recorder in addition to training in operation of the equipment, is to use inconspicuous recorders. Even if the researcher makes it clear to the patient that he is being recorded, she can maintain the illusion that nothing unusual is going on by having the recorder out of sight in a pocket or drawer, with only the microphone showing.

Non-participant observation and tape recording have been discussed earlier.

Whether tape recording has an effect on patients has been systematically studied. In one study, patients were asked to give their permission to be recorded during labor and were again interviewed postpartum concerning their feelings about, among other things, being recorded [83]. Without exception the patients said that they had other things on their minds during labor and were not conscious of the tape recorder or sometimes even of the observer, beyond a mild curiosity about the purpose of the research.

In two much more tightly controlled studies a random sample of patients was tape recorded in each of several treatment groups and the outcome of the interaction compared with patients who were not recorded [50]. The first study was an experiment testing the effect of eliciting the patient's participation in decision making on the outcome of the predelivery enema. Patients were randomly assigned to two treatment groups and the presence of the recorder was assigned by a strictly random method. The measurements were fecal return, retention of fluid, and fluid return. There were no significant differences attributable to the presence of the recorder.

A second experiment tested the effect of nursing during admission to the hospital on various indicators of patient welfare, including postoperative vomiting and the patient's subjective impression of the admission experience. Patients were randomly assigned to each of three treatment groups, and the presence of the recorder was determined by a strictly random method. In this study only a random third of the patients were tape recorded.

It was predicted that if the presence of the tape recorder had any effect on the outcome of the interactions, it would be to increase the distress of the patient and thereby contribute to post-operative vomiting. The difference between the taped and non-taped groups was not significant.

Patients were interviewed the evening after admission by a paid interviewer and asked, among other things, if concerning nursing care they had received more, as much as, or less than they expected during admission. It would be expected that if the presence of the recorder were distressing to the patient, she would report that she received less nursing care than she expected during admission. This pattern did not occur.

The major justification for using the tape recorder to collect data on nursing interactions is that the recording is likely to be more complete and "accurate" than any other method of collecting verbal data. Other methods that have been used in interaction studies include memory reconstructions and stenographic recordings in shorthand.

The principal advantages of using memory reconstructions as the primary source of interaction data are that they are easily accessible and that information about what the nurse saw and what she thought and felt, as well as what she and the patient said is contained on the forms. The main disadvantage is the questionable accuracy of reconstructing a participant observation from memory. The observer is always subject to unconscious editing of the reconstructions as well as to selective perception and recording. When an interview with a patient is particularly tense, the observer may be more likely to distort the reconstruction. "Ghost recording," i.e., recording as said something that the nurse merely wished she had said, may be a problem. When the researcher knows that the reconstruction will be analyzed with respect to its outcome, she may be more likely unconsciously to distort the data in the direction that she knows to be "better" [46].

Stenographic recording of interactions is not used frequently, probably because it means adding another person to the setting and taking a chance on the observer's ability not only to record but also to hear accurately. The stenographer must also be able to work very rapidly and record even the "uh-huh," "umm," and "huh?" that are left out of usual dictation. If a non-participant stenographer is used, she should probably be trained to take down all of the data. She may also need an orientation to the clinical setting and to the kinds of topics and scenes that she will hear and see. Queasiness probably affects accuracy.

Given that tape recording is already an indirect method of data collection, some studies may require an even more indirect representation of interaction—transcribed tape recordings. Generally the further one moves from the original event (e.g., from "live" data to tape to transcript) the more probable that data are lost.

THE NURSE ORIENTATION SYSTEM (NOS)

Content analysis, or as we later called it, "interaction analysis," involves classifying units of verbal behavior into categories.

Categories can be constructed from data or derived from theory and applied to data, or a combination of both; indeed, a combination approach was used in developing the Nurse Orientation System.

The idea for studying nursing interaction grew out of the observation that nurses seemed to ignore emotional needs in conversations with patients. It was suspected that this was not because nurses were ignorant of the possibility of psychological needs, but rather that they did not know how to approach patients or to handle what might happen if they did. It was felt that some kind of in-service educational program geared toward helping nurses deal with the emotional needs of patients might be productive. But to test whether it was or not, a measurement of nurse and patient verbal behavior was needed.

At the time the study began, there was some work being done in nursing using Bales' *Interaction Process Analysis* [12]. The principal investigator was trained in the use of IPA but had some doubts about its application to clinical data. The assumptions of group movement toward a task accomplishment underlying IPA did not necessarily fit the nursing situation. Still, some of the IPA categories, particularly the so-called social emotional ones — showing and releasing tension, agreement and disagreement, and showing hostility or solidarity — and the concept of "evaluation" that Bales uses seemed valuable.

A review of interaction studies in nursing revealed a number of possible ways of classifying nursing data, but none of them seemed exactly right for this study. Because the eventual application of the system was going to be "normal" nursing interactions, it was decided to collect some such data to see what the range of verbal behavior was in nurses with no special training or commitment to interaction as a treatment.

Data Collection

Arrangements were made with a Veterans Administration hospital to monitor 7 nurses on one ward with a tape recorder and record everything they said. The nurse-investigator accompanied each staff nurse about the ward as she did her daily routine duties. The researcher carried a small portable tape recorder and kept running notes of non-verbal behavior, subjective impressions of the inter-actions, and so on.

The researcher first met in a small group with the staff people who were to be involved in the data collection. She introduced her-self as a graduate student in nursing and outlined her interest in using that particular setting. She told the nurses that she was interested in what kinds of conversation normally took place between nurses and patients in a long-term relationship. She emphasized that working with patients who have been sick a long time can be very trying for the nurses and that sometimes measures were required that are not usually condoned in other settings, but because of the length of the relationship were appropriate with chronically ill patients. Since one of the primary concerns of the staff in this setting was to mobi-lize patients into occupational, physical, or vocational therapy, sometimes nurses had to be stern with patients. By saying things of this nature the researcher hoped to give the staff-members the per-mission to act as they ordinarily would, without feeling that they might be censured.

The researcher then clarified her own role on the unit by saying that although she was a nurse and would be wearing uniform and cap while doing the study, she would be busy with the recording and could not take part in patient care. However, should there be an emergency and her help be required, she would give it without hesitation. As events developed, she found that she could partici-pate minimally in patient care — picking up things that fell on the floor, opening windows, pushing a wheelchair, helping a nurse get a patient into bed — without distorting either her role or the interac-tion. The researcher then demonstrated the tape recorder, recorded a bit of the small group session, and played it back for the nurses. She explored with them their feelings about being tape recorded and followed around and explained that the data obtained were confidential and would not be shared with anyone in the hospital. The researcher encouraged the nurses to do their duties in normal fashion and to forget about her presence (an impossible task, of course). During data collection, the researcher did not talk with patients while she monitored the nurses and did not attempt to involve the nurses in technical discussions; neither did she attempt to validate with the nurses her subjective impression of the interaction.

The researcher spent two weeks on the unit, just being there and accompanying various staff-members, helping them move or turn patients, and generally establishing rapport through coffee breaks, light conversation, and lunches with staff. She also visited every patient on the ward and obtained signatures on permission forms (hospital policy). This two-week period enabled members of the staff to become accustomed to her presence and to identify her as an interested person, but one who would neither report on the staff nor be critical of their nursing abilities. The interval also allowed her to become acquainted with the physical facilities of the unit and to become known to the patients and medical staff, to know the routine, and to decide on the best times for data collection.

When time came to start the official data collection period, the researcher chose to accompany the head nurse for the first period, feeling that if the head nurse accepted her presence, the staff would be more likely to cooperate. This also helped to establish rapport with the head nurse and to remove any lingering administrative blocks. Before accompanying any of the staff-nurses, the researcher contacted each one of them to reinforce her explanations of what she was doing, clarify questions, reassure them of the confidentiality of the research, or explore their feelings about being recorded. By taking what may seem like an inordinate amount of time in making these preliminary arrangements with the nursing personnel, the researcher felt that she had obviated most of the problems that could interfere with the data collection or make the staff uncomfortable. It was apparent that staff-members accepted her well, since they invited her to coffee and called her by her first name. This acceptance did not seem to interfere with their normal routine, however, since the staff-people very shortly stopped telling her when they were going to another room or down the hall, and the researcher often had to run to keep up with a staff-member.

There is one additional problem with collecting data in this way. If the investigator is a nurse, it can be agonizing not to be able to help patients or to interact with them. Since the nurses on the ward knew that the researcher was a psychiatric nurse, there was some attempt to enlist her aid in dealing with patients with psychiatric or neurotic problems. The researcher tried to avoid being drawn into lengthy discussions of this nature and merely supported what the nurses were already doing with the patients. This approach seemed to be effective in that the nurses received some support for what they were doing, and the investigator avoided a role change that might have complicated data collection. At the same time, however, the investigator had to be very clear about what her function was and to accept the fact that it was painful to withhold advice that could possibly have been of some help to the nurses. There is also some evidence that the one nurse who was particularly insecure about her method of working with patients, and who often asked for help, probably did change her usual method of working with patients to include more of the psychological dimension of nursing, perhaps in an effort to impress the researcher. This was not, however, a consistent pattern either with her or with anyone else.

The initial curiosity of the nurses about what the reseacher was doing and why gave way rather quickly to an acceptance of her presence and what seemed to be a comfortable relationship for all concerned — with one exception. One of the nurses was so uncomfortable about being followed about and tape recorded that all of the researcher's efforts to reassure and placate her were futile. This nurse was dropped from the study and no more data were collected from her.

Category Construction

The tape recordings were transcribed almost as quickly as they were made, and simultaneously the transcripts were reviewed to try to develop categories. The "method" at this point consisted of discussion with a colleague and mulling over and rereading the data. The colleague, a fellow graduate student, was not a nurse and had little experience with hospitals, so that he was able to provide an objective eye. Researcher and colleague met several times a week, reread the data, and debated categories and variables.

The first stab at categorization came from a feeling that frequently the nurse's conversation was not focused on the patient and his experience and that when it was, it was mainly focused on the patient's physical well-being. At the same time the investigators seemed to see in the data instances of responses which the nurse made that cut off the patient or at least made it difficult for him to continue the conversation. Thus the first content analysis scheme used was called (because it made a good acronym) "Focus on Patient (FOP) Scale." The categories included:

Focus on patient condition
feeling
thinking
knowing
doing
other

No focus on patient condition
social
not social

These were the content categories. To pick up the process information, each unit was to be coded twice, using in addition the categories depicted in Figure 3-1.

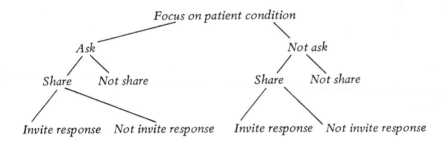

Fig. 3-1. Coding of the Focus on Patient (FOP) Scale.

The "share" dimension came from Orlando [66]; the others were relatively obvious kinds of categories, based primarily on grammatical distinctions.

Coding was very difficult with this system and reliability was low. But this first primitive attempt carried the seeds of categories later to become the NOS.

Reading over the body of data as it was being accumulated revealed two basic distinctions: (1) patient-centered nursing vs task-oriented nursing (a distinction then widely held in the nursing literature) and (2) focus on patient or focus on task (these were conceptual distinctions, not categories), but a patient-centered nurse focusing on the task is a logical inconsistency. Since the distinctions were taken from actual recorded material, we knew that that behavior happened. This deductive process led us to discard the use of "focus" as a concept and broaden it to the concept of "orientation." Thus a nurse could be "oriented" to the patient while "focusing" on the task. The next step was to define orientation *to what*.

Armchair thinking produced two general categories of orientation. The nurse could be oriented to a person (the patient, herself, or others) or to a non-person, hence the following categories were defined:

Object Orientation. The nurse is oriented to object(s). An object is regarded as anything that is not a person or not a single person. Examples: a newspaper, book, diet tray, wheelchair, bed, and so on; also such "objects" as a baseball team and things that may have some relation to a person but are not a body, e.g., blood pressure, TPR, urine specimen, treatments, prostheses.

Person Orientation. The nurse is oriented to a person other than herself as the actor or potential actor in the situation or the possessor of certain physical feelings, e.g., a tired person, possessor of the feeling of weariness; the patient as developer of bedsores; and emotional feelings, e.g., a sad person or possessor of the feeling of sadness.

Self Orientation. The orientation is to the nurse herself as the actor, potential actor, or "possessor" of physical or emotional feelings.

A second dimension was a system reference that included: "internal" — having to do with the immediate situation or context in time and place, and "external" — having to do with other times or places. This distinction came in part from Mills' work [63] and the transcripts which indicated that nurses often talked about the past with patients.

The last set of distinctions completed the system. These categories were the three "levels" or dimensions of nurse orientation to the patient or herself and included:

Feeling-Evaluating. The nurse is oriented to the patient on the patient's or her own (emotional) level; feeling in this system does not include physical feelings; also orientation to the patient as the possessor of the faculty of evaluation. Conditions such as need, desire, or want are scored here.

Knowing-Thinking. The nurse is oriented to the patient on the cognitive level; she is oriented to him (or to herself) as a knowing-thinking person or as a remembering, forgetting, suppressing, or not-knowing person.

Being-Doing. Orientation to the patient (or herself) as an actor or potential actor or the possessor of certain physical feelings.

The remnants of the FOP system can be seen here. In addition we had abstracted from psychosocial theory the cognition-cathexsis distinction [29, 69]. The inclusion of evaluation came from Bales [3] and part of his definition was used.

The entire NOS, as it was now called, is shown in Table 3-1.

Table 3-1. Nurse Orientation System (first version)

Object Orientation
    Internal-personal
    Internal-non-personal
    External-personal
    External-non-personal

Person Orientation
    Internal
        Feeling-evaluating
        Knowing-thinking
        Being-doing
    External
        Feeling-evaluating
        Knowing-thinking
        Being-doing

Self-Orientation
    Internal
        Feeling-evaluating
        Knowing-thinking
        Being-doing
    External
        Feeling-evaluating
        Knowing-thinking
        Being-doing

The object orientation categories were almost immediately telescoped into just one category, since we were not very interested in object orientation anyhow, and the distinctions seemed too trivial. An "other orientation" category with the same breakdowns as *person* and *self-orientation* was soon added to make the system logically exhaustive.

As it evolved, the NOS became neither a content nor a process system [6]. We experimented with several versions of process categories during the same period, but none of them seemed to contribute much information. Agreement between coders was very high with this system (90–93 percent), and the categories were sensitive to differences in interactions between patients whom nurses preferred and those whom they did not, older vs younger patients, and diagnostic subgroups [21]. But the internal-external dimension was not useful; external categories were rarely used and hence were eliminated, reducing the NOS to 10 categories in its final form (Table 3-2).

Table 3-2. Nurse Orientation System[a]

Category Number	Category
0	Object Orientation
	Patient Orientation:
1	Feeling
2	Knowing-thinking-evaluating
3	Being-doing
	Nurse Orientation:
4	Feeling
5	Knowing-thinking-evaluating
6	Being-doing
	Other Orientation:
7	Feeling
8	Knowing-thinking-evaluating
9	Being-doing

[a] Coding instruction available on request.

THEORETICAL BACKGROUND OF NOS

The NOS was developed specifically for nursing-practice research to quantify the dialogue between patient and nurse.

Orientation is a variable that has its roots in communication theory. The communication between nurse and patient most often is purposeful; they come together because of actual or anticipated needs related to the patient's health. The situation is circumscribed and the roles of each actor are predefined. The patient assumes or is placed in a dependent, if not a sick, role wherein his role behavior, including his verbal behavior, can be determined by another, the nurse. The labels attached — "nurse" and "patient" — clearly identify both roles and the relative power held by each. Weinstein and Deutschberger call the process of determining another's role behavior "altercasting" [90]. Altercasting is built in to the nursing situation because of the roles that the actors assume. The nurse is the helper and the patient the help-needer, which relationship allows the nurse the power and demands of the patient his cooperation.

Closely allied to altercasting, a sociological term, is the notion of perceptual set, a psychological phenomenon [10]. We tend to perceive and act on what we perceive on the basis of learned regularities or expectations — in our terms, "orientation." Orientation means the perceptual stance taken by one actor toward the other (or himself).

The major categories of NOS represent the focus of orientation, i.e., to what the speaker (actor) attends. Persons are attended to as feeling, thinking (cognitive), or being-doing persons, according to the minor subcategories. The major categories exhaust the empirical possibilities of that to which one can attend — objects or persons. The minor categories exhaust the possible dimensions of orientation.

Orientation is not a literal translation of the subjects of conversation but rather a reflection of the meaning to the person who is speaking. In coding, judgment is based on the meaning to the speaker rather than on grammatical form. A brief example from an interaction will illustrate.

The nurse begins: "Where you get the needles, is that sore?" (This unit would be coded in category 3; the nurse is oriented to the patient as a physical being who may be hurt.)

The patient replies: "Certainly." (He too is oriented to himself as someone who hurts.)

The nurse then says: "I imagine just having somebody new coming in all the time is hard" (which would be coded in category 1, i.e., the nurse is oriented to the patient but as a person who may be having feelings).

The patient says: "You never know who it's going to be" (which would be coded in category 2; the patient is oriented to himself as a person who is not-knowing).

The nurse concludes: "Is there anything else I can do for you?" (Grammatically this would probably be coded as orientation to the nurse, but the meaning to the nurse is: "Is there anything else you need?" which is orientation to the patient in category 3.)

The coding unit is the complete, uninterrupted utterance. As de Sola Pool has said: "The unit counted should be at least as long as the unit in whatever is assumed to be the relevant psychological process in the communicating organism and not so much longer so as to lose sensitivity [20]." It is assumed that whatever message is intended, it is probably conveyed by the whole utterance, rather than by single words, phrases, or clauses.

METHODOLOGICAL CONSIDERATIONS

The methodological considerations in an interaction study are the same as in any other research. Of particular interest in our study was establishing the reliability and validity of the NOS and examining the sources of data, work that was necessary to assure confidence in the findings of the clinical experiments using NOS as the measurement of the independent variable.

Reliability Study

Most investigators attempt some measure of consistency (agreement over time within one coder) and equivalence (agreement between two coders). In addition to these dimensions of reliability, we were interested in assessing the effect of coding method (coding data in context or out of context) and in the effect of coder training on consistency and equivalence. We wondered if in some cases reported "reliability" was really an effect of indoctrination of one coder by another through a long training period or perhaps a spurious effect of a mental set toward the data, developed over time by coding in context, rather than a true assessment of the reliability of the categories.

The aspects of reliability tested in this part of the study included: agreement between coders, agreement within one coder over time, effect of coding method on agreement, and effect of coder training on agreement.

One basic issue in reliability assessment is selection of coders. Often researchers depend on their graduate students who may have ulterior motives for producing high agreement on coding. Previous experience indicated that two nurses with similar graduate school preparation could attain very high intersubjective agreement even on the unrefined NOS categories. We wondered if this was a result of the likeness in backgrounds of the coders rather than of a real index of the ability of the categories to classify consistently. Therefore, in the first attempt at assessing reliability, a non-nurse coder whose education and personal background were very different from the investigator's was selected and trained. The hypothesis was somewhat supported in that reliability between the principal investigator and the non-nurse coder was never as high as it was between two nurses.

In reexamining the reasons for selecting a non-nurse coder, it became apparent that rather than treating the likeness of backgrounds between coders as an obstacle to be overcome, we should capitalize on it, i.e., the NOS has been specifically designed for nursing interactions and for nurses to use. At this time we were not much interested in its wider applications. This suggests that a nursing frame of reference in the coder should be sought not eliminated. In view of future planned uses of the system as a guide for nursing intervention, we were most interested in whether or not two nurses could agree on the categorization of units, not in whether or not a nurse and a non-nurse could agree.

The second coder chosen shared a somewhat similar background with the principal investigator, i.e., she was a nurse with a master's degree from the same university. However, her clinical specialty was not the same, nor was her experience in research or nursing.[2] She therefore represented probably the lower limit of "likeness" available within the institution. The adequacy of the NOS with respect to the consistency of coding from these two coders probably has been well tested.

SAMPLE

There were approximately 65 transcribed interactions from three experimental studies available [4, 26, 82]. We selected two samples of nine each so that every treatment group from every study would be represented by at least one interaction in each sample. The variability in the samples was maximized and presented the coders with the widest possible range of units.

The samples were selected proportionately. One-sixth of the interactions in all treatment groups were randomly selected by drawing the appropriate number of interaction code numbers from a hat. This proportion afforded a large enough number of units (total N = 818 units) for the statistical analysis, assured adequate representation from each group of interactions, and did not overwhelm the coders. The two samples were drawn independently. The second sample was drawn without replacement since for the statistical tests to be done, the two samples had to be independent of each other. Two interactions with only two units each were later eliminated since percentage of agreement was meaningless.

PROCEDURE

The first nine interactions drawn were turned over to a third person who numbered the units within the interaction in sequence, then typed every unit on a separate IBM card, together with a code number indicating the interaction from which it was taken and the point in the sequence where the unit fell. These units were then separated into nurse units and patient units and were shuffled within each group. We then had two groups of units, one group of nurse units and one group of patient units, arranged in random order. The same procedure was applied to the second sample, which was used after training. Thus there were four "samples," including: (1) the first nine interactions with units in sequence but ordered randomly with respect to the study from which they were drawn; (2) the same nine interactions, separated into individual nurse and patient units, with *units* in random order; (3) the second nine interactions; and (4) the second nine interactions separated into individual nurse and patient units in random order. The interactions with units coded in sequence were called "in-context" codings; the coding of units in random order was called "out-of-context" coding. The sequence of coding was: out-of-context nurse units, out-of-context patient units, in-context nurse units, and in-context patient units. The second coder repeated the sequence after a lapse of about three weeks.

The definition of "unit" — a complete utterance — makes agreement on unitization automatic, so that the percentages of agreement can be calculated by cross tabulating one coder on another. Percentages of agreement are therefore agreement *on the same units.*

The category numbers assigned by the coders were transferred to the backs of the IBM cards, and through the use of colored pens the coding from the out-of-context could be distinguished from the coding of the same unit in context. In this way the six codings of any one unit can be seen at a glance on the back of the card containing the appropriate unit. This method means that one can simply go through the cards to cross tabulate coders or codings or to count the number of agreements per interaction. The cards used had numbers already printed on the back in columns of 0 to 9, which coincidentally are the same numbers as the categories of the NOS.

CODER TRAINING

The second coder was furnished with a clean copy of the coding instructions. She was given no other information about the system. The use of the coding forms was explained briefly, and there was no systematic contact between coder and trainer during the first coding period. The coder coded all the data, in context and out of context, twice.

The trainer, meanwhile, cross tabulated the agreement between herself and the other coder in an effort to identify patterns of disagreement that could be worked on in the training period.

The second coder kept a running account of any ideas she had about the coding or of any questions about specific units or categories. This material became part of the coder training.

After all the first period's coding was done, the coders met for a series of training sessions. The first session was a general discussion of issues in coding, the questions the coder had noted, and the difficulties that ensued. This conversation was tape recorded so that suggestions about more precise wording of the coding instructions could be on record for future revisions or refinements of the definitions. The first session also gave the coders the opportunity to ventilate some of their feelings and perceptions about the data, coding, and NOS.

In the second session the trainer reviewed in some detail all of the categories, providing examples and particularly stressing those areas already identified through discussion or cross tabulation as difficult areas. The purpose of the session was to clarify the categories and point out distinctions between them that had not been made clear before. At the end of the second session the two coders together coded an interaction drawn from the same population as the sample nine and discussed any units or categories that seemed to give problems.

The coder was then provided with an interaction that she had not seen before and was told to code it. The trainer also coded it, and the two codings were cross tabulated to identify any consistent patterns of disagreement still present. The coders again discussed these patterns, and this procedure was repeated until both coders felt reasonably sure of themselves. The coder was then provided with the second sample of data, which she coded in the same way as the first sample. The second sample is called the "after training" sample and, although drawn from the same population as the first, is independent of it.

EFFECT OF METHOD OF CODING

We were interested in whether or not the method of coding (in-context or out-of-context) made a difference on the agreement within and between coders. In theory, if the system is sensitive and precise enough, the differences attributable to the method of coding should be minimal. In addition we felt that this exercise would give us some hypotheses that would be useful in later experiments, e.g., we were planning an experiment in which the nurse, in the course of the interaction, would immediately have to code the patient unit mentally in order to respond in the same category. Therefore consistent patterns of agreement on data coded out of context should lend some support to the idea that such coding is possible. Of course we had no data on how long a nurse coder would need to code each individual unit other than some informal data which indicated that an expert coder can code as fast as she can read and write — about 200 units/hour.

We were also concerned that some reliability figures reported in earlier versions of this study and other studies might be artificially inflated owing to the continual coding in context where one derives a general "feel" for the interaction and codes units not in terms of the categories as defined but in terms of some overall impression of the total interaction. Therefore we decided to partial out the effect of contextual coding. The effect of method of coding is presented in Table 3-3. To obtain this table, percentages of agreement between coders/interaction across all categories were computed for in-context and out-of-context codings, using the coder's *second* coding. Before and after training, codings were combined, giving an N of 16 interactions. There is a trend for agreement to be lower out-of-context on nurse units and in-context on patient units, but the difference is neither practically nor statistically significant (paired t tests, t = .83 for nurse units, t = .48 for patient units).

This suggests that the category definitions are precise enough to characterize the unit whether it is seen in context or by itself. In truth, of course, even out-of-context one experiences a feel for what is being talked about, but the tendency for a halo effect (judgment on the coding of one nurse unit affecting judgment on the coding of other nurse units) is minimized.

The effect of coding method on one coder's agreement with herself is presented in Table 3-4. Again both the before and after training samples are combined. Note that percentage agreement within one coder over time is higher than between two coders, which is to be expected.

Table 3-3. Effect of Method of Coding on Intersubjective Reliability

Nurse Units (% agree)		Patient Units (% agree)	
In context	*Out of context*	*In context*	*Out of context*
46	34	57	56
37	48	45	48
68	68	58	42
61	51	55	49
68	35	58	52
60	59	56	47
50	69	19	38
32	68	48	52
83	83	85	66
77	74	41	71
87	79	74	80
71	76	81	84
79	59	72	89
76	59	65	53
80	40	50	75
57	67	75	65
$\bar{x}$ 64.5	$\bar{x}$ 60.56	$\bar{x}$ 58.68	$\bar{x}$ 60.44
t = .83 NS		t = .478 NS	

The effect of coding method on one coder's agreement with herself is not significant for nurse units. However, in coding the patient units, the coder consistently agreed more with herself on the out-of-context data than on the same data coded in context. This pattern appeared equally before and after coder training. In theory, if this is a consistent pattern, it should have also affected the intersubjective agreement, unless the other coder were doing the opposite, i.e., agreeing less with herself on the patient out-of-context units. Unfortunately the other coder coded the data only once, so that we have no comparison.

Table 3-4. Effect of Method of Coding on Intrasubjective Reliability

Nurse Units (% agree)		Patient Units (% agree)	
In context	*Out of context*	*In context*	*Out of context*
57	59	49	71
68	89	42	79
51	62	72	76
87	75	25	62
87	71	65	52
68	48	60	76
43	53	58	70
67	65	77	81
79	72	61	71
72	75	79	83
83	71	83	91
81	73	73	76
79	90	96	86
76	82	65	88
80	80	75	75
80	82	77	78
$\bar{x}$ 72.37	$\bar{x}$ 71.69	$\bar{x}$ 66.06	$\bar{x}$ 75.94
t = .245 NS		t = 2.755	.05 > p > .02

EFFECT OF TRAINING

Significance tests were performed on the effect of coder training. As before, the percentage of agreement comparing the coder's with the investigator's second coding was used, and a mean percentage of agreement computed. A test for difference of means was performed with the results presented in Table 3-5.

Even before coder training, agreement between coders was about 50 percent. After training, there was about a 20 percent increase in agreement, which is considerable. The probability figures, although greater than what is usually accepted as significant (.05), are encouraging since they indicate such difference would have occurred by chance

Table 3-5. Effect of Training on Intersubjective Agreement

	% Agree		
	$\bar{x}$ *Before*	$\bar{x}$ *After*	*p under* H_o [a]
Nurse Units			
Out of context	55.50	67.12	.20 > p > .15
In context	51.25	76.25	
Patient Units			
Out of context	48.00	74.12	.15 > p > .10
In context	49.50	66.63	

[a]One tailed t test.

between 10 and 20 times out of 100. This may in part be due to the lowered possibility of difference, since we started with a before mean of about 50 percent. In previous reliability studies, agreement between coders was somewhat higher after training.

Coder training also had the effect of increasing the consistency of coding. As expected, agreement within one coder is always higher than agreement between coders. Therefore, even before coding, the agreement was about 65 percent (Table 3-6).

Again the probability of such differences occurring solely by chance ranges from 10 to 25 in 100. This is not discouraging, for we have some indications that the increases in agreement within and between coders increases only minimally over time alone. The effect of time alone — comparing agreement of the first coder with the second coder's first codings and the first coder with second coder's second coding — is presented in Table 3-7.

Both before and after training, the time lapse between the second coder codings did not change her pattern of agreement much with that of the first coder. These data merely substantiate the high percentage of agreement that the coder had with herself, especially after training.

This study is limited by having only one second coder. We have no data on her perceptions of the NOS, the coding procedure itself, or on her relationship with the investigator, all of which may have

Table 3-6. Effect of Training on Intrasubjective Agreement

	% Agree		
	$\bar{x}$ Before	$\bar{x}$ After	p under H_o [a]
Nurse Units			
Out of context	63.55	80.55	$.25 > p > .20$
In context	64.22	81.11	
Patient Units			
Out of context	70.87	81.00	$.25 > p > .20$ [b]
In context	56.00	76.12	$.15 > p > .10$

[a]One tailed t test.

[b]Data not combined since significant difference found; see Table 3-4.

Table 3-7. Intersubjective Agreement Over Time

Coder	Nurse Units (% agree)	Patient Units (% agree)
	In context	
1-2, first coding	$\bar{x} = 60.4$	53.5
1-2, second coding	$\bar{x} = 59.96$	55.7
	Out of context	
1-2, first coding	$\bar{x} = 53.3$	53.2
1-2, second coding	$\bar{x} = 59.2$	56.9

affected reliability, either by raising or lowering agreement figures. In later studies, agreement between coders (with a different coder) was somewhat higher, but the later coder had extensive experience with NOS and with the entire project.

The statistical treatment of reliability data deserves (and has warranted) deep consideration [92]. Computing reliability estimates can be done by percentage agreement on the same units (as was done here), by percentage agreement on frequency of category use [78, 79], by Pearson's r or other interval scale correlation technique, or by chi-square or other non-parametric test [2]. The straight cross-tabulation percentage agreement was the method chosen here because it seemed to be the simplest and most basically understood method. All of the other methods have built-in mathematical difficulties. Pearson's r, e.g., produces inflated correlations if there is a systematic pattern of disagreement between coders. Agreement on frequency of use over categories is an insensitive measure and produces spuriously high agreement when coders use categories at the same rate but put different units in them. But the percentage agreement method will only truly be useful when it is possible to obtain multiple codings on exactly the same units. This condition can be met if: (1) a stable source of data is used (transcripts); and (2) the definition of unit requires no judgment on the coder's part.

An arbitrary definition of unit has conceptual problems. There may indeed be more than one "orientation" in the course of a large NOS unit. Some data are lost by not considering smaller units. The use of transcripts has its own problems, and we were sufficiently concerned with the loss of data occasioned by transcribing that we conducted yet another study.

Tape Recordings and Transcripts

Errors or bias in findings in reported research are often attributed to inadequate sampling procedures, insufficient sample size, incorrect statistical manipulation, or lack of reliable categorization techniques. That the data collected may comprise a less-than-accurate representation of reality must also be considered. This is especially true of studies of interaction in nursing when the analysis system is being used to make operational the variations in nurse behavior. We considered the adequacy of tape recordings and transcriptions concurrently with an ongoing clinical experiment, testing the effects of varied nursing approaches (behaviors) on patient welfare [57].

The interaction data in the experimental study were analyzed in two ways. Percentages of the units that occurred in all of the NOS categories were computed for each coded interaction and were called "percentage profiles." In addition pairs of nurse-patient units were examined to determine *concordance*. Concordance was defined as the percentage of the total number of paired units in which both nurse and patient are coded in the same category.

The nurse-researcher tape recorded her own conversations with patients, with their knowledge and permission, on an inconspicuous miniature tape recorder. The tape recordings were later transcribed by a secretary who used equipment that had considerably higher fidelity than the original recording equipment. The investigator was asked to pick nine tapes for use in the tape-transcript study. Whether any one interaction was to be coded first from its tape or from its transcript was determined randomly.

The original intention was to compare the coding from the tape recording with the coding obtained from the transcript. Since we suspected from the beginning that the major difference between the tape recording and the transcript of the tape was a certain loss of data, the tape and transcript could not be matched unit for unit. Therefore an alternative procedure was devised. The coder read along from the transcripts while listening to the tape to make sure that the units coded on the transcript were the same ones that she heard on the tape. It was decided by convention that if a unit did not appear on the transcript it was not coded at all. Findings reported in the following paragraphs represent a comparison on only those units that are included both on the transcript and on the tape recordings.

It is hardly surprising that the first finding was that transcripts were not nearly so complete as tape recordings. Of the total number of transcript units, 155 or 9.6 percent were considered to be uncodable, whereas only 23 or 1.5 percent of the tape units were considered to be uncodable because they were incomplete ($N = 1,608$ units). It should also be noted that in addition to the loss represented by units regarded as uncodable, there were also units lost because there was no indication of their existence on the transcript at all.

There were other differences between tapes and transcripts. The following examples, all taken from the same interaction, illustrate how units can be codable but garbled.

Transcript	Tape
Nurse: "Hm, hm."	*Nurse*: "Hm, hm."
Patient: "That's how it feels . . . . The pain in the head is worse . . . ."	*Patient*: "That's how it feels. You try to straighten out and

N: "Hm, hm."
P: "I've never been on a drug. . . ."

N: "Hm, hm."
P: ". . . so if anybody asks, that's what it feels like."

P: "She's in psychiatric health herself, the teacher."
N: "Yes."
P: ". . . and the kids there . . ."

N: "Hm, hm."
P: ". . . and here I am, all bottled up. Sometimes I wonder if it's me or is it them?"

you go numb. The pain spreads. It's like not being able to straighten it, but the pain in the head is like . . ."
N: "Hm, hm."
P: "I've never been on a drunk."

N: "Hm, hm."
P: "But if anybody has, it's like everything's on an angle, like I'm pie-eyed . . . that's what it feels like."

P: "She's in psychiatric help herself, the teacher."
N: "Yes."
P: "An the kid's on Librium. Oh, my God."

N: "Hm, hm."
P: "And here I am all bottled up. It makes me wonder, is it me or is it them?"

There were many instances in the transcripts in which a conditional ("if I do this . . .") had been transcribed with a conjunction ("*and* I do this . . .") which may change the category of the unit from thinking to being-doing. Even a single word transcribed inaccurately can change the meaning of a unit. "Worth" has been transcribed as "worse," "lack" as "black," "but" as "and," "bad" as "mad" or "sad," and so forth.

Two of the nine interactions (218 units) were coded twice from the tape and twice from the transcript. There was a lapse of about two weeks between codings. The overall agreement on coding from tapes was 78.4 percent. The coder agreed with herself on 84.1 percent of the units coded from the transcript. It is not unreasonable to assume that a coder would obtain higher agreement scoring from a relatively more stable source of data, a transcript, than from a tape recording.

The percentage profiles computed from transcripts and tapes were compared. There was very little difference between the percentage profile of the combined nine interactions. The overall agreement between the sources of data is 71 percent on nurse units and 69 percent on patient units.

The effect of the source of data on concordance was measured. Concordance was higher when coding was done from tapes than from transcripts. The variation seems to be attributable mostly to the uncodable units. In determining concordance, if a nurse unit is coded with a category number but the accompanying patient unit is uncodable, that pair of units is not "concordant." The concordance measure was clearly affected more by the difference in data than were the percentage profiles.

The amount of the variation in coding that could be attributed to coder inconsistency and the amount that could be attributed to the source of data were analyzed. There were two tapes on which the coder had coded the data twice from the tape and twice from the transcript. Therefore for each unit there were four codings. *Coder error* was defined as instances in which the coding, either between the first and second tape coding or between the first and second transcript coding did not agree. Error attributable to the *source of data* was defined as instances in which, although there was agreement on the tape and agreement on the transcript, there was not agreement between the two sets of coding. *Mixed errors* included all errors in which it was impossible to tell if the variation could be attributed to either the source or the coder herself.

Of the errors involved, the largest percentages are those in which the source of data and the coder unreliability interact in some unspecified way. This finding suggests that the difference in the source of data compounds whatever unreliability there is already in the coder's interpretation of the categories.

Probably the most pertinent difference between the body of data contained on the tape recordings and that on the transcripts is the loss of data from tape to transcript. This is not solely a loss of content. Also lost are the "heard" components of speech, those linguistic qualities of pitch, speed, and pauses and the paralinguistic qualities such as drawl, clipping, loudness, softness, slurring, and articulation. This kind of data increases in importance as one tries to assess the emotional content of the interaction.

Despite the loss of data, transcripts are usually adequate in giving a comprehensive view of the interactions and the changes that occurred within each one.

The best way to reduce differences between tape recordings and transcripts of the tapes is to be sure that the recordings are acoustically clear. This may be possible with high fidelity equipment used in an interference-free (noise-free) setting. In clinical nursing studies it is rarely possible to obtain 100 percent verbatim recordings. Discarding those that are less than perfect would result in both a great loss of data (often most fruitful) and an exorbitantly high cost in researcher time and effort. The sacrifice in fidelity is recognized as a consequence of the need to keep the clinical situation as natural and as comparable to practice as possible.

Unit of Analysis

Interaction analysis schema suffer from the same problems of validity as any other measurement technique. The first problem involves the size or way of calculating the unit of analysis. Verbal interaction comes in units — seconds, minutes, words, phrases, clauses, sentences, paragraphs, topics, interactions, and so on. The major criterion for determining the size of the unit is the purpose of the analysis. If one is interested in the structure or formal aspects, or both, of the material ("text" is the term used by linguists), then phonetic or grammatical units are probably most appropriate. If the information or message conveyed is of major concern, as it has been for the NOS studies, determining the size of the unit becomes more difficult and there is less agreement among the experts. As de Sola Pool has said:

"Both experimental work on how people read and write and theoretical work in linguistics suggest that there may be units more closely geared to the actual processes of communication than the single word. In the previous sentence the phrase 'the single word' and not 'the' or 'single' or 'word' was in some sense a unit of meaning .... We leave this matter of 'basic units' vague. It is not one to which satisfactory answers yet exist [19]."

As a general rule, any sort of arbitrary or convention-determined unitization plan increases reliability. When coders do not have to decide how much of the data to encompass in one unit, they are freer to think about the category in which to put it. Therefore arbitrary units such as those relating to time or grammar or transcription, e.g., sentences, clauses, paragraphs, and utterances have a certain appeal. But whereas reliability of coding may go up, the meaningfulness of the data may go down by using arbitrary units that are determined by the transcriber. For example, in the NOS, the "utterance" — one uninterrupted passage of speech, no matter how long — is the unit of analysis. It is up to the transcriber or coder to determine whether or not a unit has been interrupted, and it becomes especially tricky when interjections like "hmmm," "uh huh," or "huh?" are frequently used. Unless the coder catches all or most of them, the coding will underestimate the number of units of speech and the percentage profiles may be thrown off considerably, especially in the frequency with which any large category is used.

Small units — words, clauses, or seconds — are appealing too because they produce very large numbers of units with which to work. On the other hand, it is questionable if single words or even the total number of words spoken in a given period are meaningful ways of regarding interaction data. Verbal messages may indeed be conveyed by a single word in a long utterance, but that assumption should be tested.

Conant [13] has used an interesting way of coding data. Her unit of analysis is an arbitrary time unit — 15 seconds — which essentially converts her categories into dichotomies, namely, did the category occur during the period or not? Data are then converted into rates/time period and compared across categories.

Category Range

The problem with validity of interaction categories is the same as any validity problem: do they measure what they are supposed to measure? With interaction categories the problem is compounded by the fact that interaction itself is such a complicated process, subject to so much variation and capable of being made operational in so many different ways that any one set of categories can only hope to tap a tiny portion of what is happening. The temptation in constructing categories is always to try for the global ones that will account for as much as possible. When these kinds of categories turn out to be unreliable and imprecise, the impulse then is to try for the very tiny categories usually employing grammatical distinctions because they are easier. Somewhere in the middle lies the better way.

The categories of NOS are such middle-range categories. The global categories of "patient" and "nurse" are counterbalanced by the specific categories of "feeling," "thinking," and "doing." Any coding difficulties, however, do not usually come from deciding on which of the large categories to use but rather from distinguishing among the subcategories. Once one has grasped the notion of what orientation is, then distinctions between "feeling" and "being-doing" are rather easy. Problems of coding errors creep in as one tries to distinguish content reflective of orientation to the person as a purely feeling being, i.e., attention to only the affective dimension, and of orientation toward evaluation of how or why one is feeling, as well as distinguishing orientation to the person as just being (having physical sensations) and orientation to him as thinking and evaluating those sensations. Coder training with much discussion of the theoretical fine points helps to reduce this source of error.

Confining categories to verbal data alone misses an enormous amount of meaning, but trying to include non-verbal data as well is about twice as complicated. Conant [13] included some non-verbal data cleverly in her give-and-take category scheme, and Christoffers [11] made a stab at the same technique. Bales [2] includes some non-verbal cues to categorization in his system, too, and scoring "live" one cannot help but use whatever cues are there to help determine the classification of units. All three of these schemes use the same terminology for both non-verbal and verbal categories, which is probably a sound idea. Conant has a "predisposing" category which includes head nods as well as certain kinds of statements. Christoffers uses the concept of "orientation" for both verbal and kinesic activity.

Kinds of Categories

Another validity problem in interaction studies pertains to the kinds of categories used and the way in which the data are analyzed.

There seem in general to be two kinds of category systems classified by how data are analyzed with them, to wit, those which essentially consist of single or dichotomous categories and those which consist of categories in relation to each other. Behymer's "administrative" and "social" categories, e.g., constitute a dichotomy, even though they have subclassifications, so that interactions can be compared according to the amounts of conversation in the two categories taken singly or contrasted [5]. On the other hand, Bales' categories are not taken singly but in various combinations: the two orientation, the two evaluation, and the two suggestion categories are combined for certain analyses.

The NOS also uses categories in combination; it is not so important how much, say, feeling orientation is present by itself but how much in combination with thinking and doing orientation. Data analysis procedures with combined categories can be extremely complicated. It is difficult to handle three categories at once in comparing groups of interactions, especially when the frequencies of category use are not independent of each other. For that reason probably, statistical treatment of interaction data is usually confined to the simplest sorts of tests that do not depend on independent samples or interval levels of measurement.

Validity of the NOS has had some empirical tests. Face and content validity were assumed when the categories were constructed, and tests for construct and concurrent validity have been made.

Validity Tests

Fairly early in the development of NOS an attempt was made to relate the concept of orientation to a concept called "altercasting" [90]. "Altercasting" is putting the other ("alter") into a particular role or identity. There are six dimensions to the concept:

1. Structural distance: how much authority ego is willing to delegate.
2. Evaluative distance: how much worth ego assigns.
3. Emotional distance: how much intimacy or personal involvement with ego is presumed.
4. Support: ego's indications that alter requires help or assistance.

5. Interdependence: how much ego and alter are tied by bonds of common fate, perspective, or interest.
6. Degree of freedom: the range of behavior allowed alter by ego.

Altercasting seemed to be related to orientation. To the extent that orientation means the perceptual set of one person toward another or himself, the "set" is altercasting. Weinstein has developed a rating scale to measure altercasting. The tool consists of seven-point rating scales for each dimension, plus a count of the personal pronouns used by each actor. Each interaction is evaluated once for each dimension.

Arrangements were made with Dr. Weinstein for one of his graduate assistants to score the interactions from McBride's first study [57] with the altercasting tool as a small test of the validity of the nursing approaches, and hence, of the NOS. Although usually altercasting is scored from tapes and only after a lengthy training period, in this case the tapes had been erased and the investigator had no training other than a study of the Weinstein article. Nevertheless reliability between coders averaged about 50 percent agreement, with some dimensions being as high as 90 percent agreement.

In McBride's study, interactions with patients in Group I were composed of relatively equal percentages of feeling, thinking, and doing orientation. Group II interactions were less feeling oriented and more thinking and doing, and Group III was almost wholly doing oriented.

There were no significant differences among the groups on the dimensions of structural distance, evaluation, support, or degree of freedom, which was encouraging. We would hope that the nurse did not vary her approach in these dimensions across the groups — that she would be equally sharing of authority, equally positively evaluating, equally supportive, equally indicating her perception of the patient's need for assistance, and equally freedom-allowing. The other two dimensions showed significant differences among the groups in the directions that would have been predicted had we predicted them: emotion, with Group I approach showing more intimacy than Group II and Group II more than Group III; and interdependence, with Group I showing more identity of nurse and

Table 3-8. Mean Altercasting Scores

	Group I	Group II	Group III	
Emotional	3.14	4.42	5.28	F = 10.47 d.f. = 2,19 .01 > p > .001
Interdependence	3.85	5.00	5.73	F = 6.79 d.f. = 2,19 .05 > p > .01

patient than Group II and Group II more than Group III (Table 3-8).

A count of personal pronouns was also illuminating. There was no difference across the groups in numbers of first- or second-person pronouns used, but there were consistent differences between nurses and patients. Nurses used about twice as many second-person pronouns (you, your) and about half as many first-person pronouns (I, me, my, mine) as patients did. This finding tends to validate the person orientation categories in NOS, as the NOS coding showed that the nurse was consistently oriented to the patient. The pronoun count may also suggest that part of the decision on categorization of units with NOS depends on the pronoun used, an element that is built into the coding instructions.

Construct validity has been tested by applying NOS to interactions with autistic children [85] and interactions with dying children and their mothers [75]. In the first study, NOS was sensitive to predicted changes in interaction patterns over time. In the second, interactions with mothers whose children were dying differed in predicted ways from interactions with mothers whose children were seriously ill but not dying.

INTERACTION ANALYSIS IN PREDICTIVE STUDIES

The most frequent use of interaction analysis has been in descriptive, i.e., non-experimental, studies. Interactions from various sources are compared, sometimes with differences hypothesized, sometimes not. Correlations are made between personality variables or social variables and interaction, or personality variables and interaction, or length of training and interaction, and so on. One whole sequence of studies relates to the relationship between various categories of nursing interaction and "effectiveness" [9, 36, 74, 86, 88].

At some point in discussing descriptive studies one must step back to evaluate their contributions. There are many interaction studies, all of which have devised different category schemes, used different sources of data, have different findings, and have never been replicated.

There is a point of diminishing returns in *ex post facto* analysis of interaction at which one realizes that one could go on forever inventing new ways to pick apart interaction data and never completely describe them. The proliferation of different categories for the same data is perhaps necessary to bring the research to the point at which its efforts can be reevaluated and perhaps realigned. It is not wasted effort to come up with years of interaction studies out of which one can draw one paragraph of very tentative conclusions. If the state of theory were more thoroughly developed, contributions to changing the practice situation would proceed faster. However, in the development of theory in a practice discipline, movement is from simply descriptive studies to prediction, but description is necessary to build the theory from which the predictions can be tested.

The greatest reward from interaction study seems to come in using interaction analysis to contribute more rigor to experimental tests of the effect of nursing on patient welfare. As Walter Johnson observed: "It seems probable that direct empirical studies of interaction will never make more than a limited contribution to a complete understanding of role variation [41]." He goes on to advocate "experimental tests of nurse tactics" but without apparently seeing how empirical interaction study can be useful in experimentation.

To our knowledge only two studies — ours and Conant's [13] — have used interaction analysis in experimental prediction.

The NOS was originally developed simply to describe interaction, but McBride saw in the categories a way to define nursing approaches for a study of patients in pain. The studies reported here are replications of McBride's early work.

Study Design

A clinical experiment with three treatment groups was designed. With minor variations the same study was repeated three times with three different nurses [15, 22, 57].

INDEPENDENT VARIABLE

The three nursing approaches were defined in terms of the relationship among NOS categories 1, 2, and 3. In the first approach (Group I) the patient was viewed as a feeling, thinking, and doing person, and the nurse tried to maintain approximately even distributions of her verbal behavior across all three dimensions. The approach in Group II minimized the feeling orientation, and the patient was seen as a thinking and doing person. Interaction in Group III was confined primarily to the doing dimension. In all three approaches the nurse focused on the patient's experience, including his emotional, cognitive, or physical needs. The difference among the approaches was in the scope of orientation that the nurse promoted and therefore the amount of attention that she paid to the various dimensions. In all three groups the nurse was free to give whatever physical care that she felt was indicated.

Briefly the theory guiding these definitions of nursing approach holds that the more of the patient's experience that is included in the nurse's interaction with him, the better he will be. Thus patients who are treated as "whole" persons fare better than patients who receive an approach that systematically lacks orientation to one or two dimensions of his experience. The more dimensions the nurse perceives or is oriented to, the more information she is likely to take in regarding the patient's needs, and therefore she is more likely to be able to provide appropriate ministrations.

The nursing approaches as they actually sounded have been described elsewhere [58, 59]. Here it is perhaps only necessary to emphasize that the NOS is deliberately constructed to allow extensive latitude for verbal interaction. The nurse is free to adapt the categories to her own usual verbal style and still maintain the relationship among them specified in the study design. Since "orientation" is neither exclusively interaction content nor process, it is possible to be oriented to the patient as, say, a feeling person in many different ways, discussing many different topics. The nurse is not as confined in her choices of things to say as she would be by a script, but she is still able to vary her verbal behavior consistently for a valid experiment.

DEPENDENT VARIABLE

In addition to varying in nursing approach, the three treatment groups varied in the theory of pain being employed. In Group I pain was viewed as a psychosomatic phenomenon — partly physical, partly emotional, and partly cognitive [45, 60]. It was assumed that patients had needs or at least experiences in all three dimensions, and the nursing approach was therefore geared to all three. In Group II it was assumed that pain was a physical entity but that patients could experience relief from pain if they were helped to analyze and reason out its causes and their reactions to it and the best treatment to relieve the pain [65]. In Group III it was assumed that pain was mostly physical, and the effort was to help the patient deal with the physical aspects of the experience.

Measures of the dependent variable — relief from pain — were pulse and respiration rate changes, verbal reports of patients, and non-verbal behavior.

HYPOTHESIS

Following from the interaction and pain theories, it was predicted that patients who received a nursing approach oriented to them as physical, cognitive, and emotion-feeling persons would experience more relief from pain than patients who were viewed either as only cognitive and physical or as only physical persons. In operational terms this means that patients in Group I would experience more relief than patients in Group II who would fare better than patients in Group III.

DATA COLLECTION

Patients who complained of pain to the staff nurse were randomly assigned to one of the three treatment groups with a block randomization scheme that produced equal numbers in all three groups. The research nurse then approached the patient, explained the study, asked the patient for his consent to be tape recorded and having received it, admitted the patient to the study. (Only one patient refused in the three studies.) The nurse administered the p.r.n. pain medication as ordered and spent about 15 minutes talking with the patient, using the verbal approach assigned. Any patient who complained of pain was eligible for the study except patients who (1) were addicts; (2) ineligible to receive the p.r.n. medication; (3) on placebos; (4) deaf or mute; (5) did not speak English; or (6) had undergone operative treatment less than 24 hours earlier.

The first and third studies were conducted on the general surgery units of a large urban medical center. The same units were used for both studies. The second was carried out in a middle-sized community hospital in an industrial city in the same general geographical area as the first.

At the beginning and at the end of the interaction and about one hour later, the patient's pulse and respiration rates were taken, and descriptions of his non-verbal behavior written according to a checklist. Patient's verbal statements were subsequently obtained from the tape recordings. Pulse and respiration rates were counted for one-half minute each and multiplied by two. The same wrist was used for each patient and the same body position. Items recorded for non-verbal behavior included facial expression, body position (posture), tears, crying, sobbing, perspiration, sighing, moaning, smiling, or sleeping, and any activity in which the patient was engaged.

The nurses also collected data from the patient's chart on medication dose and route, age, sex, religion, social class, and diagnosis. Ethnic background and site of pain were obtained by asking the patient.

The three descriptions of non-verbal behavior for each patient were transcribed onto cards, one card for each of the three time periods, and submitted to judges (two judges in Studies I and II, three in Study III) who did not know the patient's group assignment or the hypothesis. Judges were asked to compare card 1 (before interaction) with card 2 (end of interaction), 1 with 3 (an hour later), and 2 with 3, and rate the amount of change in behavior in each time period on a five-point scale from −2 (greatly increased discomfort) through 0 (no change) to +2 (greatly increased comfort). Non-nurse judges were used in the first two studies, nurses in the third.

The same judges rated the patients' statements about their conditions from transcriptions of the tape recordings. In Studies I and II the entire transcript was submitted to the judges; in Study III only the question "how are you feeling now?" asked at the three time periods, and the patient's response were submitted for judging. In all three studies the nurse returned to the patient after about an hour, asked again "how are you feeling now?" and recorded the answer. Again judges rated changes between time periods on a five-point scale.

There were a few small differences in procedure among the three studies. In Study II only one-half of the patients were tape recorded. In Study III the time between the end of the interaction and the third measurement was 45 minutes instead of one hour. Nurses in Studies I and II used different tape recorders than were used in Study III, and there was a consequent difference in the auditory fidelity of the recordings. Nurses in Studies I and II did not consistently ask the patient at the beginning and end of the interaction to rate how they were feeling at that moment, so that judges had to make their ratings from the entire transcript.

All three nurses wore uniform and cap and introduced themselves as nurses working temporarily on the floor, interested in the patient's experience with pain. Patients were assured of the anonymity of the tape recordings, and their permission to be recorded was itself recorded on tape. Thirty-six patients were included in Study I, 30 each in Studies II and III for a total N = 96.

Findings

Relief from pain was analyzed according to three time periods. From the beginning to the end of the interaction is called "initial relief" and is assumed to be a product of the interaction itself, since the medication had no time to "work." From the beginning to about one hour after the end of the interaction is called "long-range relief" and is a combination of the effect of nursing approach and medication. From the end of the interaction to one hour later is the "medication interval," and relief seen in this period is assumed to be a product of medication.

PULSE CHANGE

In the first study the changes in pulse rates tended to support the hypothesis. Patients in Group I had a mean pulse change of −6.0 beats/minute, Group II a mean change of 5.3, and Group III a mean change of −5.17 for the initial interval. The differences among the three groups are significant (one way analysis of variance: $F = 6.23$, 2,33 d.f., $.05 > p > .01$). Pulse changes in the "long-range relief period" did not quite approach statistical significance although they were in the predicted direction ($F = 3.16$). Pulse changes for the medication interval were not significant.

In Study II pulse rates did not change significantly from beginning to end of the interaction, or in the long-range and medication intervals. Differences among the three groups were not significant.

There were no significant differences in pulse-rate changes for any of the time periods in Study III although the trends are in the direction hypothesized.

When the three studies are combined, the trends become significant and results support the hypothesis.

Two-way analysis of variance was performed on pulse changes for the three studies combined. The main effect for groups (nursing approach) is significant for the initial interval and is not significant for the long-range period. The main effect for studies (nurse) is not significant (Tables 3-9 and 3-10). There is also a significant interaction effect for the initial period, indicating that pulse changes were influenced by the combination of study (nurse) and group acting together. The combined mean changes for the initial period were: Group I, −2.69; Group II, 2.06; and Group III, −2.75. For the long-range period they were: Group I, −3.69; Group II, 2.19; and Group III −3.09. Pulse changes in the medication interval were not significant either in individual studies or in all three studies combined.

Pulse-change data lend some support to the hypothesis. In addition nursing approach was more effective than medication alone. However, patients in Group II tended to have increases in pulse

Table 3-9. Analysis of Variance for Pulse Changes, Initial Relief Period (three studies combined)

Source of Variance	SS	d.f.	MS	F	p
Total	4041.96	89			
Subclass (cells)	918.76	8			
Study	45.42	2	22.71	.589	NS
Treatment group	370.75	2	185.37	4.81	.05 > p > .01
Interaction	502.59	4	125.65	3.26	.05 > p > .01
Within (error)	3123.20	81	38.56		

Table 3-10. Analysis of Variance for Pulse Changes, Long-Range Relief Period (three studies combined)

Source of Variance	SS	d.f.	MS	F	p
Total	6186.6	89			
Subclass (cells)	625.6	8			
Study	64.8	2	32.4	.474	NS
Treatment group	305.86	2	152.93	2.24	NS
Interaction	254.94	4	63.74	.93	NS
Within (error)	5561.0	81	68.65		

rates, whereas patients in Groups I and III tended to have decreases. This can be interpreted to mean that patients encouraged to analyze their experience (patients viewed as thinking persons) experienced arousal, seen in small pulse increases.

RESPIRATION CHANGES

Respiration rate changes were not significant for any time period in the first study. All three groups showed a mean decrease in the initial relief period, Groups I and II a decrease in the long-range relief period, and little mean change in any group for the medication interval. In both the second and third studies respiration changes were significant in the initial relief period but not in any other. However, when the three studies were combined and two-way analysis of variance performed, respiration changes were not significant for any time period. The trend was as predicted, with Group I having the greatest decrease, Group II next, and Group III having either a very small decrease or an increase in respirations/minute.

Judgments of non-verbal behavior, originally made on a five-point scale were converted into three categories — worse, better, or the same. Scores from .5 to 2.0 became "better"; from −.5 to +.5 "same"; below −.5 "worse." Findings in Study I support the hypothesis. During the initial period, 100 percent of the patients in Group I, 75 percent in Group II, and only 17 percent in Group III were judged to feel better. A similar pattern occurs in the long-range relief period, and there is no relationship between group assignment and relief for the medication interval.

Non-verbal behavior changes were not significant across the groups for any time period in Study II. In the initial period Groups I and II were nearly identical, with 20 percent of the patients in each group (two each) judged as feeling worse, and the other 80 percent judged as feeling the same or better. In the long-range period all three groups had identical frequencies — 9 of the patients in each group judged as feeling better; 1 in each group judged as having no change. The medication interval shows almost the same pattern. The lack of statistical significance is an effect of the lack of variation among groups. In the third study non-verbal behavior ratings were significant for all three time periods in the direction predicted.

When the three studies were combined, the findings supported the hypothesis: more patients in Group I than in Group II or Group III were judged to feel "better." Further, the changes are significant for nursing effect but not for medication alone (Table 3-11).

VERBAL STATEMENTS

Judgments of verbal statements of the patients were also telescoped into three categories. In Study I there was no significant

Table 3-11. Non-Verbal Behavior (three studies combined)

Group	Initial Relief			Long-range Relief			Medication Interval		
	Worse	Same	Better	Worse	Same	Better	Worse	Same	Better
I	2	4	26	0	2	30	3	7	22
II	4	13	15	1	11	20	4	14	14
III	1	23	8	5	9	18	3	12	17
		N = 96			N = 96			N = 96	
	X^2 = 25.63 d.f. = 4 $p < .001$			X^2 = 16.74 d.f. = 4 $p < .01$			NS		

relationship between group assignment and relief in the initial relief period, but both in the long-range and medication intervals the distribution is significant. A general lack of variation in the initial relief period — with one exception no patient felt worse — explains the absence of statistical significance.

Verbal statements of improvement showed no significant difference in any of the intervals in the second study. Again most of the patients in all three groups indicated that they felt the same or better, with little or no difference among the three nursing approaches.

The same was true of the third study, with only 1 patient in the sample indicating that he felt worse in any time period.

Verbal statements were close to significance in the direction predicted for the initial interval when the three studies were combined and reached significance for the long-range relief period and the medication interval (Table 3-12).

ANTECEDENT VARIABLES

There were no significant differences in the distribution of antecedent patient variables within any of the studies; neither were

Table 3-12. Verbal Statements (three studies combined)

Group	Initial Relief			Long-range Relief			Medication Interval		
	Worse	*Same*	*Better*	*Worse*	*Same*	*Better*	*Worse*	*Same*	*Better*
I	0	5	22	0	2	25	1	3	23
II	2	8	17	1	10	16	4	10	13
III	0	12	15	4	11	12	5	7	15
	$N = 81$[a]			$N = 81$			$N = 81$		
	$X^2 = 8.40$			$X^2 = 16.57$			$X^2 = 9.59$		
	$d.f. = 4$			$d.f. = 4$			$d.f. = 4$		
	$.10 > p > .05$			$.01 > p > .001$			$p < .05$		

[a] Only one-half of patients in Study II were tape recorded.

length of interaction, number of units, or amount of medication given different across groups within any study. Religion, social class, site of pain, and diagnosis were somewhat differently distributed across studies. Patients in the second and third studies tended to list a Protestant preference, whereas more patients in the first study were Catholic. More patients in the third study fell in the lower social classes (IV and V). There were more patients in the second and third studies with incisional pain (about three-fourths of all groups) than in the first study, and more patients in the last study had orthopedic, genitourinary, or gynecological diagnoses than in the first two. However, none of these differences is statistically related to either interaction or outcome variables.

Reliability and Validity

In all three studies the nurse-researcher herself took all the physiological measurements and wrote her own descriptions of non-verbal behavior. Since she knew the group assignment and the hypothesis of the study, there is possibility of bias and unreliability. No systematic checks were made either on the accuracy of pulse and respiration counts or on the recording of non-verbal behavior. The judges knew neither the patient's group assignment nor the hypothesis; still it is possible that the nurses unconsciously biased their written descriptions or their counts of pulse and respiration rates in the direction intended. The patient's verbal report of how he felt has, on the face of it, validity. However, in these studies the patient was reporting to the same nurse who had tried to help him and he may have been loathe to report feeling as badly as he did. That the verbal reports showed little difference among the groups tend to support this idea, although there is enough difference in the direction predicted to indicate that verbal report is sensitive to the effects of nursing approach.

The measures of the dependent variable were chosen not only on the basis of previous research but because they are easily accessible in nursing practice. This selection may result in imprecise or insensitive indices, but the variables that nurses use in practice to measure their effect are equally, if not more, imprecise. The decreased methodological rigor is accepted as a consequence of increased clinical relevance. However, respiration rate change appears to be little affected by nursing approach [28].

The tape-recorded interactions were all coded with NOS to check on the validity of the experiment itself.[3] Each nurse conducted the three approaches a little differently. The nurse in Study III seemed to conceive of the Group I approach as a "feeling" one, and her interactions are consistently more feeling oriented than those in either of the other two studies. The nurse in Study I came closest to the stated definitions of nursing approach, and the findings from that study more often support the hypothesis. The nurse in Study II seemed to have the most difficulty in sustaining the Group I (feeling-thinking-doing) approach; and she had more interaction in the feeling category in Group II than did either of the other nurses. Thus there is less variation in nursing approach in the second study than in the other two, and perhaps not coincidentally, less variation in results on the dependent variable.

The theories behind the approaches did not specify exact rules for orientation to the patient as a feeling, thinking, and doing person — only guidelines. When the nurse actually encounters the patient, however, she must take into account what the patient presents, while at the same time trying to adhere to the study design. This is precisely the dilemma in these kinds of studies: maintaining the clinical relevance by allowing a nurse some freedom to tailor her approach to the patient and at the same time defining her approach with enough specificity so that it can be repeated. The time may never come when it is possible to define "nursing" as tightly as it is possible now to define some independent variables in other disciplines. Until more is known about what in nursing affects what in patient welfare, we must live with some muddiness in definition and a good deal of tentativeness in results. The advantage of using an interaction analysis scheme to make operational the independent variable is that it is then possible to check on the conduct of the study and build a better understanding of the nature of the nursing "treatment."

DISCUSSION

We have reported in this chapter the development of one facet of research into nursing practice. Previous to the development of NOS, most content analysis schemes were borrowed from the social sciences and applied to descriptive studies in nursing.

The series of studies using NOS demonstrate that a content analysis scheme designed on the basis of nursing as well as on socio-psychological theory can be used in both descriptive and predictive studies.

In developing the NOS an attempt has been made to strike a balance between clinical relevance and the need for the nurse to perform in a style suited to her and to her patient and for precision and accuracy in measuring that nursing care. The NOS has made replication — a powerful tool for developing research-based theory — a possibility. It has been successfully used by different nurses with different nursing styles. In fact it has been sensitive to those differences.

Defining the independent variable by using interaction analysis categories furnishes guidelines to other investigators that afford some specificity while at the same time allowing latitude for individualized care. The validity of the experiment can be better assessed when more precise data on the independent, as well as on the dependent, variables are collected.

The power of this approach is clear. If one has more complete data on the independent variable, then theory development about its effects can proceed on a much broader plane than if only the dependent variable is considered. For example, had we not used interaction analysis after McBride's original study, we would have known only that the hypothesis was supported. After the first replication we might have been a bit surer of that. But after the second replication we would have left thinking the study did not replicate with another nurse. Instead interaction analysis helped determine *why* the results were not the same and encouraged us to forge ahead, incorporating a new dimension to the theory.

An interaction analysis scheme to define nursing approach is a compromise between the other two designs most often seen in tests of the effect of nursing: a script, which the nurse just follows without variation, and a loosely defined experimental nursing process, which is then contrasted to regular care given by hospital nurses. The first design, although rigorous methodologically, has low generality and perhaps questionable clinical relevance. Nurses resent being programmed to the extent of not being allowed to individualize their care, so that even if the results from a script study supported the hypotheses, it is unlikely that the results would be translated into changes in patient care. Even in behavior modification studies the nursing approach, although programmed, is individualized for each patient within a given theoretical orientation to social reinforcement, whereas the script design allows for no such variation.

Historically the early clinical experiments in patient care used the second method — a nurse with special training (usually a graduate student) approached patients using an interaction defined by theory. The results of her nursing were compared with the results obtained by staff nurses with no special preparation. While this design may be a valid test of a very general hypothesis, as more knowledge accumulates about the internal structure of the nursing process it becomes possible to design tests of rather smaller differences in approach. Also we have learned through painful experience that the general hypothesis testing approach is methodologically questionable and politically odious. The specially trained nurse with no clinical responsibilities has literally hours to spend with patients, and comparing her treatment to that of the busy staff nurse is unsound.

It should be remembered that much work remains in developing measures of nursing care, and NOS taps but one dimension, that of orientation. Nurse-patient interaction is a complex phenomenon which includes far more than verbal exchange. We need to learn more of how the non-verbal fit with the verbal components of communication, as well as how the technical aspects of care influence the communication. Hopefully researchers will develop such tools so that sound practice and theory will be developed to guide the nurse in giving optimum care to all patients.

NOTES

1. Over the years of this study we have used several different recorders. In general the larger the recorder, the higher the fidelity. An Ampex 601 recorder (Redwood City, Calif. 94063) at 7½ips with a very high fidelity microphone (Altec Lipstek, Anaheim Calif. 92083) produced recordings of unbelievable fidelity. It was even possible to count respirations from the tape alone, with the microphone about four feet from the patient's head. However, the Ampex is very large and not portable. The Uher 4000S recorder (Martel Corp, New York, NY 10001) has also been used with some success. It is portable but weighs about 20 pounds. The faster the recording speed, the higher the fidelity but the shorter the tape time, so that while it is possible to obtain four hours of tape time on one side of tape recording at 15/16ips, the fidelity is low. The Fi-Cord 101 miniature tape recorder (Lanier Products, Atlanta, Ga. 30304) and the Dictet miniature (Dictaphone, Bridgeport, Conn. 06602) have the advantage of size. They are small enough to fit into a uniform pocket. The Fi-Cord uses small reels that are compatible with other playback equipment; the Dictet requires special transcribers. Both are adequate in a noise-free environment, with speakers within a few feet of the microphone. The best recorder for our purposes is the Sony TC100 cassette recorder (Sun Valley, Calif. 91352). It is small enough to be unobtrusive and portable, it is easy to operate, and its fidelity is excellent. Its disadvantage is that it requires a cassette transcriber.

2. Mrs. Ann Hempy, Research Assistant, served as the second coder. The investigator gratefully acknowledges her assistance not only in coding, but in conceptualizing the issue of reliability.

3. Reliability of categorization has been reported elsewhere [23]. Coder

agreement assessed in the third study remained high: 80 percent on units, 95.5 percent on categories. Coders also guessed which nursing approach was being used and were correct more than 95 percent of the time. The possibility for "halo effect" — knowing group assignment affecting coding of individual units — must be mentioned as a limitation.

REFERENCES

1. Anderson, B. J., Dumas, R., and Johnson, J. Two experimental tests of a patient-centered admissions process. *Nursing Research* (New York) 14:151, 1965.
2. Bales, R. F. *Interaction Process Analysis*. Cambridge: Addison-Wesley, 1950.
3. *Ibid.*, p. 192.
4. Barron, M. A. The Effect Varied Nursing Approaches Have On Patients' Complaints of Pain. Master's report, Yale University School of Nursing, 1964.
5. Behymer, A. Interaction patterns and attitudes of affiliate student nurses in a psychiatric hospital. *Nursing Outlook* (New York) 1:205–207, 1953.
6. Berelson, B. Content analysis. In G. Lindzay (Ed.), *Handbook of Social Psychology*. Cambridge: Addison-Wesley, 1954.
7. Birdwhistell, R. *Kinesics and Context*. Philadelphia: University of Pennsylvania Press, 1970.
8. Bursten, B., and Diers, D. Pseudo patient-centered orientation. *Nursing Forum* (Hillsdale, N. J.) 3(2):38–50, 1964.
9. Cameron, J. An Exploratory Study of the Verbal Response of the Nurse in Twenty Nurse-Patient Interactions. Master's report, Yale University School of Nursing, 1961.
10. Cantril, H. Perception and interpersonal relations. *American Journal of Psychiatry* 114:119, 1957.
11. Christoffers, C. Patients' Orientation and Nurses' Perceptions. Master's report, Yale University School of Nursing, 1967 (see Section V).
12. Conant, L. Use of Bales' interaction process analysis to study nurse-patient interaction. *Nursing Research* (New York) 14:304–309, 1965.
13. Conant, L. An Exploratory Study of Nurse-Patient Give and Take. Terminal progress report to USPHS grant NU 00181, 1967.
14. Daubenmire, M. J. A Study of the Communicative Interaction Process. USPHS grant NU 00401, Division of Nursing, Department of Health, Education, and Welfare, May, 1971–April, 1974.
15. Davis, B. L. A Replication of the Effects of Three Nursing Approaches on Pain: A Clinical Experiment. Master's report, Yale University School of Nursing, 1971.
16. Davitz, L. J. Inferences of physical pain and psychological distress. *Nursing Research* (New York) 19:388–401, 1970.
17. Davitz, L. J., and Pendleton, S. H. Nurses' inferences of suffering. *Nurs-*

ing Research (New York) 18:100–107, March-April, 1969.

18. de Sola Pool, I. (Ed.) *Trends in Content Analysis.* Urbana: University of Illinois Press, 1959.

19. de Sola Pool, I. Trends in content analysis today: A summary. In S. Soporta (Ed.), *Psycholinguistics – A Book of Readings.* New York: Holt, Rinehart and Winston, 1961, pp. 300–301.

20. *Ibid.,* p. 310.

21. Diers, D. K. The Nurse Orientation System: A Method for Analyzing Nurse-Patient Interactions. Master's report, Yale University School of Nursing, 1964.

22. Diers, D. K. Studies in Nurse-Patient Interaction. USPHS grant NU 00179, Bureau of Health Manpower Education, 1965–1971.

23. Diers, D. K., and Schmidt, R. L. Transcriptions and tape recordings in interaction analysis. *Nursing Research* (New York) 17:235–241, 1968.

24. Dollard, J., and Auld, F. *Scoring Human Motives.* New Haven: Yale University Press, 1959.

25. Downey, D. Public health nurses' attitudes toward a patient with a psychiatric diagnosis. *Nursing Research* (New York) 18:244–250, 1969.

26. Dumas, R. G. Clinical Experiments in Nursing Practice. Terminal progress report to USPHS grant 00060, 1966.

27. Dumas, R. G., and Leonard, R. C. The effect of nursing on the incidence of postoperative vomiting. *Nursing Research* (New York) 12:12–15, 1962.

28. Elms, R. R., and Leonard, R. C. Effects of nursing approaches during admission. *Nursing Research* (New York) 15:39–48, 1966.

29. Freud, S. Formulations regarding the two principles in mental functioning. In S. Freud (Ed.), *Collected Papers, vol. IV.* New York: Basic Books, 1959, p. 14.

30. Gill, M., Newman, R., and Redlich, F. *The Initial Interview in Psychiatric Practice.* New York: International Universities Press, 1954.

31. Gottschalk, L. A., and Gleser, G. C. *The Measurement of Psychological States Through the Content Analysis of Verbal Behavior.* Berkeley: University of California Press, 1969.

32. Graffam, S. Nurse response to the patient in distress: Development of an instrument. *Nursing Research* (New York) 19:331–336, 1970.

33. Greenleaf, N. P. Content Analysis of Verbal Interaction Between Psychiatric Nurses and Patients. Master's report, Boston University School of Nursing, 1967.

34. Greer, S. Use of the Nurse Orientation System to Evaluate Problem Solving Abilities of Student Nurses. Master's report, University of Rochester, 1969.

35. Griffin, G. J., Kinsinger, R. E., and Pittman, A. J. Clinical nursing instruction and closed circuit TV. *Nursing Research* (New York) 13:196–204, 1964.

36. Hinshaw, A. S. Identification and Analysis of the Nurse's Focus. Master's report, Yale University School of Nursing, 1963.

37. Hulicka, I. M., and Hulicka, K. To design experimental research. *American Journal of Nursing* (New York) 62:100–103, 1962.

38. Jensen, J. The Development of a Nurse-Psychiatric Patient Interaction Inventory. Master's report, University of Utah, 1966.
39. Johnson, B. S. Relationships between verbal patterns of nursing students and therapeutic effectiveness. *Nursing Research* (New York) 13:339–342, 1964.
40. Johnson, W. *Content and Dynamics of Home Visits of Public Health Nurses, vol. II.* New York: American Nurses Foundation, 1969.
41. *Ibid.*, pp. 126–127.
42. Johnson, W., and Hardin, C. *Content and Dynamics of Home Visits of Public Health Nurses.* New York: American Nurses Foundation, 1964.
43. Kerrigan, Sr. M. R. Analysis of conversations between selected students and their assigned patients. *Nursing Research* (New York) 6:43–45, 1957.
44. King. J. M. A nurse's communication patterns and a patient's use of denial. *Nursing Research* (New York) 16:137–140, 1967.
45. Kolb, L. Symbolic significance of the complaint of pain. In L. Kolb (Ed.), *Clinical Neurosurgery.* Baltimore: Williams and Wilkins, 1962, p. 249.
46. Leak, A., and Runyon, N. Process recordings — are they accurate? In W. Hargreaves (Ed.), Patterns of Psychiatric Nursing. Progress report to USPHS grant NU 00201, 1968.
47. Leary, T. *Interpersonal Diagnosis of Personality: A Functional Theory and Methodology for Personality Evaluation.* New York: Ronald Press, 1957.
48. Leary, T., and Coffey, H. Interpersonal diagnosis: Some problems of methodology and validation. *Journal of Abnormal and Social Psychology* (Washington) 50:110–124, 1955.
49. Lennard, H. I., and Bernstein, A. *Anatomy of Psychotherapy.* New York: Columbia University Press, 1960.
50. Leonard, R. C., Tryon, P., and Elms, R. R. The Effect of Tape Recording on Short Dyadic Interactions. Unpublished paper, 1968. (The data come from Clinical Experiments in Nursing and The Effect of Varied Nursing Approaches During Admission to a General Hospital. The former study was supported by USPHS grant NU 00060 and the latter by the American Nurses Foundation.)
51. Levine, E. Experimental design in nursing research. *Nursing Research* (New York) 9:203–212, 1960.
52. Lonergan, M. M. Measurement of Person-centeredness as Demonstrated by Basic Baccalaureate and Diploma Student Nurses During their Psychiatric Nursing Experience. Master's report, University of Washington, 1964.
53. Lorenz, M. Expressive behavior and language patterns. *Psychiatry* (Washington) 18:353–366, 1955.
54. Lum, J. L. Interaction patterns of nursing personnel. *Nursing Research* (New York) 19:324, 1970.
55. Mahaffey, P. R., Jr. The effects of hospitalization on children admitted for tonsillectomy and adenoidectomy. *Nursing Research* (New York) 14:12–19, 1965.
56. Matarazzo, J. D., et al. Studies of interview speech behavior. In L. Krasner, and L. P. Ullman (Eds.), *Research in Behavior Modification.* New York: Holt, Rinehart and Winston, 1965, pp. 179–210.

57. McBride, M. A. B. Nursing approach, pain and relief: An exploratory experiment. *Nursing Research* (New York) 16:337–341, 1967.
58. McBride, M. A. B. The additive to the analgesia. *American Journal of Nursing* (New York) 69:974–976, 1969.
59. McBride, M. A. B., Diers, D., and Schmidt, R. Nurse-researcher: The crucial hyphen. *American Journal of Nursing* (New York) 70:1252–1260, 1970.
60. Meiding, C. Differential characteristics of pain. *ANA Monograph No. 10, 1962.* New York: American Nurses Association.
61. Methven, D., and Schlotfeldt, R. The social interaction inventory. *Nursing Research* (New York) 11:83–88, 1962.
62. Meyers, M. E. The effect of types of communication on patients' reactions to stress. *Nursing Research* (New York) 13:126–131, 1964. Reprinted in J. K. Skipper, and R. C. Leonard (Eds.), *Social Interaction and Patient Care.* Philadelphia: Lippincott, 1965, pp. 92–101.
63. Mills, T. M. *Group Transformation: The Analysis of a Learning Group.* Englewood Cliffs: Prentice Hall, 1964.
64. Molde, D., and Weins, A. Interview interaction behavior of nurses with task versus person orientation. *Nursing Research* (New York) 17:45–51, 1968.
65. Moss, F., and Meyer, B. The effects of nursing interaction upon pain relief in patients. *Nursing Research* (New York) 15:303–306, 1966.
66. Orlando, I. J. *The Dynamic Nurse-Patient Relationship.* New York: Putnam, 1961.
67. Osser, H. A. Distinctive Features Analysis of Vocal Communication of Emotion. Ph.D. dissertation, Cornell University, 1964.
68. Park, M. M. The Relationship Between Scores on a Nurse-Psychiatric Patient Interaction Inventory and Nurse Performance. Master's report, University of Utah, 1967.
69. Parsons, T., and Shils, E. *Working Papers in the Theory of Action.* Glencoe: Free Press, 1953.
70. Pride, L. F. An adrenal stress index as a criterion measure for nursing. *Nursing Research* (New York) 17:292–303, 1968.
71. Putt, A. One experiment in nursing adults with peptic ulcers. *Nursing Research* (New York) 19:484–494, 1970.
72. Quint, J. C., et al. Delineation of qualitative aspects of nursing care (including discussion papers). *Nursing Research* (New York) 11:204–213, 1962.
73. Rademacher, M. L. A Study of Person-centeredness as Demonstrated in the Verbal Responses to Psychiatric Patients by Basic Baccalaureate and Diploma Nursing Students During the Psychiatric Nursing Program of Studies. Master's report, University of Washington, 1963.
74. Rhymes, J. P. A Description of Nurse-Patient Interaction in Effective and Ineffective Nursing Activity. Master's report, Yale University School of Nursing, 1962.
75. Ross, S. The Dying Child: Direct Observation of Nursing Interactions. Master's report, University of Utah, 1972.
76. Saslow, G., and Matarazzo, J. A Technique for Studying Changes in Interview Behavior. In E. A. Rubenstein, and M. B. Parloff (Eds.), *Research in*

Psychotherapy. Washington, D.C.: American Psychological Association, 1959, pp. 125–159.

77. Scheflen, A. E. The significance of posture in communication systems. *Psychiatry* (Washington) 27:316–331, 1964.

78. Schutz, W. C. Reliability, ambiguity and content analysis. *Psychological Review* (Washington) 59:119–129, 1952.

79. Scott, W. A. Reliability of content analysis. *Public Opinion Quarterly* 55:321–325, 1955.

80. Semradek, J. Methods of Analyzing Interactions in Public Health Nursing Home Visits. Master's report, Yale University School of Nursing, 1962.

81. Sethee, U. K. Verbal responses of nurses to patients in emotion laden situations in public health nursing. *Nursing Research* (New York) 16:365–368, 1967.

82. Severin, N. The Effect of Different Nursing Approaches on Patient Distress in the Emergency Admission. Master's report, Yale University School of Nursing, 1965.

83. Sharp. E. S. Development of a Tool to Measure Patient Welfare. Progress report to USPHS grant GN-8922, 1962.

84. Spring, F. E., and Turk, H. A therapeutic behavior scale. *Nursing Research* (New York) 11:214–218, 1962.

85. Spurgeon, R. K. Development and Test of a Measurement for Evaluating the Effects of an Experimental Nursing Process on the Behavioral Manifestations of Autistic Childhood Psychosis. Master's report, Yale University School of Nursing, 1965.

86. Taylor, S. A Measure of Nurse-Patient Verbal Interaction. Master's report, Yale University School of Nursing, 1962.

87. United States Public Health Service, Nursing Resources Division. How to Study Nursing Activities in a Patient Unit (Publication No. 370). Washington, D.C.: United States Government Printing Office, 1954.

88. Varney, H. An Exploratory Study of the Deliberative Process. Master's report, Yale University School of Nursing, 1963.

89. Weins, A. N., et al. Interview interaction behavior of supervisors, head nurses and staff nurses. *Nursing Research* (New York) 14:322–329, 1965.

90. Weinstein, E., and Deutschberger, P. Some dimensions of altercasting. *Sociometry* (Albany) 26:454–466, 1963.

91. Wilcox, J. Closed circuit television: A tool for nursing research. *Nursing Research* (New York) 13:211–216, 1964.

92. Wooldridge, P. J. Scorer Reliability: The Study of a Measurement Problem. Ph.D. dissertation, Yale University, 1965.

Models for Data Analysis
II

AS research in nursing becomes more complex, the need for developing models and computer programs to handle and analyze complex data increases. Part II of this textbook presents the contributions of four authors who examine the dilemma of complexity from different points of view.

In Chapter 4, Daniel Howland makes some general comparisons between engineering and science. He presents the specific steps of model building, making references to operations and systems analysis research approaches. He then uses systems analysis research models to examine nursing- and patient-care problems. He intends this approach as a means of ultimately developing theoretical bases for nursing and health care.

Chapter 5 is by Janelle C. Krueger, who outlines guides for computer analysis of data. The data that she uses to illustrate computer programming are etiological variables of decubitus ulcer patients. This chapter is also illustrated with various computer printouts, and their applicability to nursing research is described.

Alton L. Taylor, in Chapter 6, has a different approach to computer analysis, emphasizing models of multiple linear regression analyses. Interestingly Dr. Taylor also uses data on decubitus ulcer variables to illustrate his approaches.

The concluding chapter is by John P. Young, a noted investigator in operations research. He discusses operations-research approaches in terms of examining health care and patient problems. Specific formulas are used as examples for attacking complex problems systematically.

Models in Nursing Research
Daniel Howland

4

AMERICANS are much more comfortable with engineering than with science. The impatient manager may remark that he doesn't need all that "theoretical stuff," he needs something practical. Nothing, however, is more practical than theory, the product of science. Our entire technological society is based on it. Engineers use it to design the systems that transport us to and from our jobs, send men to the moon, and design the mechanical devices used in health-care delivery systems [6]. If we can do all of these things — the impatient planner demands — why can we not solve the problems of the ghetto and health-care delivery systems. The answer is that we lack the theory needed to understand their behavior. Before we can be prescriptive, we must be descriptive.

What is the difference between science and engineering? Quade states it well: ". . . Science finds things out while engineering uses the results of science to do things cheaply and well [17]." The science on which space flight is based is founded on sidereal observations made by Copernicus who hypothesized that the planets revolved around the sun. Newton related observation and thought in a mathematical language. Nothing comparable to Newton's work has happened in health-care delivery systems. Furthermore nothing is likely to happen until we can provide the empirical data needed for theory development and test.

Because of the complexity of health systems, it is doubtful if the theories needed will result from the work performed in the classic mode of the physical sciences, namely, eliminating or holding constant all but two variables at a time. Furthermore it is doubtful if either the substantive information or method required will be developed in any single discipline. As Ashby has pointed out, complexity is needed to deal with complexity [2]. Interdisciplinary research is required if we are to understand behavioral phenomena as complex as health-care delivery systems.

Despite both the societal role that science plays and the practical importance of its philosophy and methods, the nature and utility of theory and models is not well understood. Theories are general statements of relationships between observable phenomena. Von Bertalanffy defines theory as "a conceptual system which permits explanation of the empirical fact [23]." Models are statements of relationships for a particular set of empirical facts, collected by observing the behavior of a particular system. Theories are general; models are specific. Given a theory of nursing, we should then be able to map a specific nursing unit into a model and make predictions about how it would behave under specified conditions.

The scientist observes a phenomenon and measures selected aspects of it. He then develops functional relationships between the variables measured. Once the relationships have been developed and tested, the engineer uses them to "do things cheaply and well." This distinction is drawn between science and engineering because, as Quade points out: "Operations research, and to an even greater degree systems analysis, seems to be more nearly engineering than science [17]."

The operations research models used to provide information for executive decision making are analogous to the physical models used to design mechanical systems. The major difference between engineering and science, however, is not the technical one between inventing and using relationships. A fundamental difference is one of attitude of philosophy. Where the engineer is likely to adopt an a priori, normative attitude about what *should* be done, the scientist is concerned with discovering *how* things behave, in inventing relationships between variables and in testing them empirically. This distinction in no way disparages the engineer. It is simply that there *is* a difference and that one should be aware of it. In the investigation of systems, e.g., the same person may be required to operate in both modes — but *not* simultaneously.

Development of Systems

The scientist's insistence on observation and measurement raises problems in the case of unbuilt systems. Very few systems are new in the sense that what we have today is not the product of evolutionary development. Thus we are concerned not with the "new" systems but with the next step in the evolutionary development of old ones. What is "new" about a new system is usually the result of technological or organizational change in equipment and the way things are done, not in the tasks themselves. We start, therefore, by modeling the system as it is. Until we can do this, we are not in a very good position to explore possible alternatives.

We assume that the tasks which the systems perform are relatively constant and that what changes is the way tasks are performed. This of course is the assumption that the engineer makes when he uses his models to generate information for the design of new structures and machines. It seems particularly appropriate in health systems because man, the center of it all, has changed little in thousands of years.

The second major difference between the engineer and the scientist is in their reliance on mathematics. Philosophically the engineer is likely to be a formalist, whereas the scientist, who is concerned with understanding complex systems, may be more an empiricist. As Newton so brilliantly demonstrated, modern science combines these views [3]. The scientist views mathematics as a language to be used when it is appropriate. As Dantzig pointed out, mathematicians are like tailors who make suits. When someone enters their shop, and a suit fits, there is "general rejoicing [9]." Cramer noted that "mathematics tells us nothing about the real world [8]." The language of mathematics should be used when it is appropriate, but phenomena must not be cut solely to find a mathematical model that fits.

Formulating The Research Question

Having discussed the differences between engineering and research approaches, I shall now review some of the problems of research on health-care delivery systems.

The first problem is to formulate a research question. Since models are devices for generating information to answer questions, a clear statement of the problem and the questions it raises must precede research. This is necessary to select a model to generate the information needed. As Wilson points out, many scientists ". . . owe their greatness not to their skill in solving problems but to their wisdom in choosing them [24] "; and Quade in discussing systems analysis indicates that it ". . . is associated with the class of problems where the difficulty lies in deciding what ought to be done — not simply how to do it — and honors go to people who have the ability or good fortune simply to find out what the problem is [17] ."

Once a problem has been identified and the information required to solve it specified, it is possible to define the characteristics of a model that can be used to provide the information. Having identified the type of model required, one can decide if engineering is possible, i.e., whether or not a model can be selected from the available inventory or if research is needed to develop a new one. If a model is available that will provide the required information, engineering is possible.

Building System Models

Given the need to build a model, the first requirement is to select a world view, of which there are essentially three. First there is the incrementalist, non-model approach of "muddling through," in which the focus is on the process, not the goal [15, 18]. Second there is the optimizing approach, which evolved historically from the economic concept of rational man optimizing a utility function. Third there is the adaptive view that holds that resources are allocated to maintain a dynamic equilibrium [1, 2, 3, 13].

If we view the system manager's job as one of adapting to change by allocating resources to insure goal achievement, we can focus on the problems of providing the sequential information needed for selecting and using resources in response to information about system behavior. To manage a system the following general questions must be answered:

1. What are system goals; They must be operationally defined so that they can be operationally defined and measured.
2. What information and resources are required to achieve them?
3. What information is required to insure that the required resource allocations take place?

System Goals

Since models are abstractions of reality and provide limited information, it is imperative that the model builder develop an operational definition of the goals of the system to be modeled in order to specify the information required for resource allocations. Because goals are often obscure, covert, and conflicting, the systems researcher must be familiar with the behavior of the system that he wishes to model in order to define goals operationally.

Real-world problems with which we are concerned involve the direct and indirect allocation of resources to patients. Basically what we want to know is: What resources are required to maintain patients in desired states, and how are these resources provided? For the acutely ill patient, the objective may be to establish and maintain physiopsychological homeostasis [4, 14]. In the chronically or terminally ill patient, this goal may not be achievable, and the goal may be simply to relieve pain. If we define health-system goals in terms of patient states [13], we can ask a number of questions about the resources and the information required to achieve these states.

Resource Allocation and Model Availability

If we assume that the system is "state determined," i.e., that resources are not allocated at random but in response to patient or organization needs, we must be able to define this "need," recognize it when it arises, and provide an information system that will insure that resources are allocated quickly and accurately to meet it [2].

Patient and organizational needs are assumed not to conflict. This, however, may not be the case. The needs of the terminally ill patient, e.g., may be markedly different from those of the young nurse. The patient may in fact supply emotional support for the nurse, not the other way round.

Models are available to describe behavior at various levels of a health system, ranging from the bedside to the community. The "bedside" models describe patient-nurse or patient-physician interactions. Verhonick, e.g., has studied the problem of decubitus ulcers [22], and the physiological responses to drugs are found in a text on anesthesiology [10].

A second group of models may be used by health-system managers to represent the demands of groups of patients. The operations research models, e.g., may be used to describe the behavior of health subsystems such as radiology, and central supply. Inventory, queuing, and programming models are useful to study these subsystems. In addition there are epidemiological models that can predict the incidence of various disease types in the population.

The problems of designing managerial health-care delivery systems, however, cannot be solved at any one level. Resources are available for the nurse or physician at the bedside because resource-allocation decisions were made at higher system levels in different time frames. For this reason it is imperative that patient needs be used as the basis for resource-allocation decisions at all levels. If this is to be done, system models must tie the levels together in terms of information and resource flows. Community-level decisions affect patients. Patient requirements, therefore, must be explicitly considered in these decisions. Since such models do not now exist, procedures for developing them will be discussed.

Developing A Health-System Model

Having described the general characteristics of models and pointed out how they are used, the next step is to describe a method for their development.

Modeling starts with a "world view" or philosophical orientation to the behavior of the real world. One might say, e.g., that the real world acts "as if" it is optimizing or searching through possible alternatives to select the "optimum" configuration to some criterion. Or we may say that it adapts, coping with inputs from the environment by utilizing its resources to survive. Most system modeling has been based on the economic optimizing philosophy. Hitch and McKean outline the procedure in terms of stating system objectives, selecting alternative ways of reaching the objectives, assigning cost to the alternatives, developing models to ". . . trace the relations between inputs and outputs, resources, and objectives, for each of the systems to be compared, so that we can predict the relevant consequences of choosing any system," and choosing a criterion to guide in system selection [12]. The least-cost system may be selected that meets effectiveness requirements or alternatively, the most effective system may be selected, given a budget [12].

These methodologies, first introduced into the Department of Defense in 1961, were implemented in all departments of government by presidential directive in 1965. This requirement has given rise to numerous problems, which have been discussed at length in legislative-branch committees and by Lindblom [15], Etzioni [11], Simon and March [19] and others. It is beyond the scope of this chapter to discuss these problems in detail. In general, however, the methods have not supplied the kind of information needed by systems managers, and alternatives have been sought, particularly in health systems [26].

ALTERNATIVE FRAMES OF REFERENCE

An alternative is to select another frame of reference and to view organizational behavior as adaptive. If this is done, cybernetic models may be selected to study their adaptive behavior. This world view is based on Cannon's concepts of homeostasis applied to organizations [4, 5]. Rather than optimization, this view holds that organisms or organizations adapt to disturbances from their environment by using their resources to maintain survival variables within limits. Organizations may be modeled after living organisms because of similarities in their behavioral characteristics. System behavior, as Cannon pointed out, is essentially similar to the behavior of living organisms. The machines of man-machine systems are viewed as extensions of man's sensorimotor system [7]. If we adopt the organismic view of systems, we are primarily interested in modeling the procedures by which they use their information and resources to adapt to environmental disturbances.

Examples of systems that exhibit adaptive behavior are ubiquitous, particularly in the medical setting. The anesthesiologist administering sodium thiopental for intubation is an example. As he administers the drug in 2-mgm doses, he observes the reaction of the patient. If the drug is tolerated, administration of the drug continues until the patient's eyelash reflex is lost, indicating arrival at the desired level of anesthesia [10]. The anesthesiologist can then intubate and proceed with the administration of a gaseous agent. No two patients respond to this process in the same way, and the anesthesiologist must regulate patient states on the basis of information feedback.

Feedback of information between physician and neurosurgical patient is another example of adaptive behavior. The surgeon, by asking the patient to perform simple tasks, draws inferences about damage to the sensorimotor system which he cannot observe directly. As a final example, the relationship between information and anxiety has been demonstrated in a number of settings. To obtain the information he needs, however, the patient frequently discusses problems with those who have no competence for providing information rather than with the physician or nurse who has. This phenomenon may reflect the patient's perception of his role in the system.

Having selected a philosophy to guide our work, the next question involves how to proceed. Traditionally there have been two paths: the formal, deductive route with its roots in Greek philosophy; and the empirical, inductive route stemming from the philosophy of Bacon, and other English empiricists [3]. Because of the dangers inherent in model development without empirical feedback to insure that axioms and postulates are valid, the hypotheticodeductive methods that combine observation and measurement with mathematical schemes for combining them should be used [20].

Having selected a problem and identified the information required to solve it, the next step is to develop a model to provide the information. The required information usually takes the form of functional relationships between system components and the resources that can be used to modify system behavior. Mapping the real world into a model is a process of abstracting from the real world into the model world. By abstracting the real world into a qualitative model, a "list of variables," it is possible to take the first step toward the development of relationships between sets of variables in functional form [2]. In a general way the variables that are controlled are the dependent variables; resources that can be used to control them are the independent variables. This formulation of a qualitative model may take the form of a set of differential equations [1, 23]. Unfortunately, however, the sets of equations needed to describe the behavior of complex systems may be mathematically intractable. If this is the case, computer approximation may be used.

The next step is to develop a quantitative method from the qualitative model. This is done by a combination of the inductive and deductive methods of science and mathematics. It makes little difference where one starts as long as both aspects are considered. It is best to start with data that describe real-world behavior, in order to avoid the dangers of a priori normativism. These data can be used to build a qualitative model that can be tested by experiment and accepted or rejected on the basis of predictive capability.

Once this relationship has been developed and validated, the research is finished. Using the models to make predictions in any specific instance is engineering, and using the information generated by the model to make an impact on the real world is management.

Cybernetic Modeling

Originally, our methodology was a mixture of engineering and science [13]. It soon became apparent, however, that we did not understand the hospital system well enough for engineering, and our emphasis shifted to research. Since 1961 we have been developing and testing procedures for relating the behaviors of components to that of the overall system. Our views have changed significantly during this period, and it may be of interest to see why. Our problem, which has not changed, we view as one of relating hospital resources and levels of patient care. In our original model, shown in Figure 4-1, we spelled out what we thought were the relationships and resources. It developed, however, that there was no operational definition of patient care to serve as the dependent variable in our

$$\text{PATIENT CARE} = A_1 X_1 + A_2 X_2 + A_3 X_3 + A_4 X_4$$

Fig. 4-1. Original disciplinary formulation of problem. (Suggested by W. A. Gomberg, *A Trade-union Analysis of Time Study*. New York: Prentice-Hall, 1955.)

model. Since no definition was available and we were unable to obtain one from anyone in the health systems, it was necessary to change our operational rationale from the kind of model represented by this regression equation to the adaptive system—cybernetic model that has guided our subsequent work.

Having elected to develop a cybernetic model to represent the adaptive characteristics of health systems, we found that the first problem was one of partitioning the system into interacting levels to reduce the number of variables and to avoid the dangers of sub-optimization. The partitioning scheme which is being used is shown in Figure 4-2. At the bottom, or individual level, we represent the nurse, patient, and physician behaving as an integrated team. At the second, or operational level, we find the management functions of the health system, the work of the administrator. At the top level, strategic long-range decisions are made by lay groups and health-system professional planners. Each level deals with resources, information, and goals. The modeling objective is to relate these levels and show how information is transmitted from patient through hospital system to community where it is used to make resource-allocation decisions.

STRATEGIC LEVELS

Having partitioned the system in this way, the next problem is one of deciding where to begin modeling. Many researchers

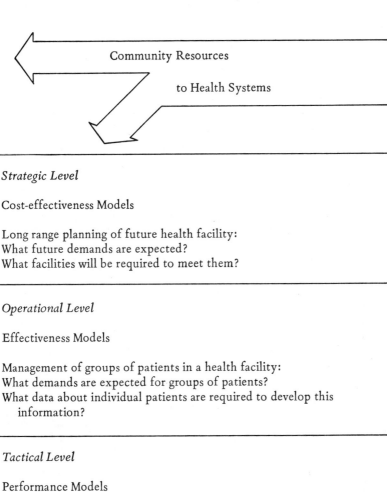

Community Resources

to Health Systems

Strategic Level

Cost-effectiveness Models

Long range planning of future health facility:
What future demands are expected?
What facilities will be required to meet them?

Operational Level

Effectiveness Models

Management of groups of patients in a health facility:
What demands are expected for groups of patients?
What data about individual patients are required to develop this
    information?

Tactical Level

Performance Models

Management of the individual patient:
How does the use of a specific resource affect a given patient?

Fig. 4-2. Functional levels of health system.

recommend that modeling start at the top level. This is the way it
was done in the cost-effectiveness studies in the U.S. military. If
this route is chosen, the information obtained from the tactical
units is usually in the form of assumed probability distribution of
events. Since strategy depends on tactics, we have elected to start
at the lowest, or individual patient level. Unless the model really

represents nurse-patient-physician behavior, model conclusions may be in error and strategic plans may fail. Another reason for starting at the bottom is that the distributions are a function of the behavior of the individual units. The shape of the operational relationships can be changed only by making changes in individual-level behavior.

Having elected to start at the patient (direct care level), the next problem is one of developing a conceptualization of how the system behaves at this level.

Conceptualizing the system in this way, the next decision is one of what data are collected and how to analyze it. Registered nurse observers were selected and trained to record interactions between patients and all members of the health team. These recordings were then coded in such a way that interactions between patient and the system at any moment in time could be analyzed [16].

The analysis comprised three general steps. In the first step the data were plotted as sets of continuous variables in time. Plotting can be done manually or by computer, using either an X-Y plotter or a cathode-ray tube. These graphic time plots make it possible to identify events that lead to changes in system behavior. Events such as diverging systolic and diastolic blood pressure will be followed by the allocation of system resources in an attempt to bring these back into the desired relationship. The graphic plot or the cathode-ray tube make it possible for the experimenter to search through the data and locate those critical incidents that led to the unscheduled allocation of resources.

Having identified a number of events, the search program can be used to examine the data in specific time increments preceding and following the event to find out what was going on prior to their occurrence and how they were handled.

The third program develops a "play and outcome" table [1] to relate disturbance from the environment, resource allocations, and the consequences for patients. It is developed over time and across patients. It is a tabular function showing how disturbances on the system were dealt with and what the consequences were. Disturbances may be known and regulatory action may be routine; or they may not be known, and the regulator may have to respond to changes in patient states by "hunt and stick" methods to cope with disturbances [2].

Row headings show what resources were utilized to cope with disturbances and cell values show the consequences of a disturbance and regulatory action. The functions that we were developing, therefore, may be used like trigonometric or logarithmic functions. They offer information for coping when closed-form, analytical solutions are impossible.

In conclusion we have described a method for relating patient states to the allocation of health-system resources. Our methodology is based on observation and measurement of systems behavior and analysis of the measurements to discover what disturbances impinge on the patient and how they are coped with. The result of the analysis is the table, showing the coping mechanisms used and the consequences. Having developed valid descriptive relationships, it may be feasible to arrive at normative decision rules. This method avoids the dangers of moving too quickly to an a priori normative position which may ignore some of the realities of life. Although the method is time consuming and expensive, so too are the consequences of decisions based on poor information. For this reason extensions of this research will be focused on procedures for data collection and reduction for computer analysis as we move up through the system levels. Computer programs for conducting part of the analysis are available, but manual methods can always be used if the amount of data is not extensive. The methods described herein are not specific to the analysis of health systems; in fact they have been used to improve understanding of undersea warfare systems and pilot and co-pilot relationships in an aircraft.

REFERENCES

1. Ashby, W. R. *Design for a Brain* (2nd ed.). New York: Wiley and Sons, 1960.
2. Ashby, W. R. *An Introduction to Cybernetics.* New York: Wiley and Sons, 1957.
3. Bronowski, J. Operations research as an example of the contemporary evolution of science. Review of P. M. Morse and G. E. Kimball, *Methods of Operations Research. Scientific American* 185:75–77, 1951.
4. Cannon, W. *The Wisdom of the Body.* New York: W. W. Norton, 1932.
5. Cannon, W. The body physiologic and the body politic. *Science* 93:1-10, 1941.

6. Conant, J. *On Understanding Science*. New York: Mentor, 1957.
7. Craik, K. J. W. *The Nature of Explanation*. Cambridge, England, University Press, 1952.
8. Cramer, H. *Mathematical Methods of Statistics*. Princeton: Princeton University Press, 1946.
9. Dantzig, T. *Number, The Language of Science*. New York: Macmillan, 1930.
10. Dripps, R. D., Eckenhoff, T. E., and Vandam, L. D. *Introduction to Anesthesia*. Philadelphia: Saunders, 1957.
11. Etzioni, A. On the Process of Making Decisions. *Science* 152:746–747, 1966.
12. Hitch, C. J., and McKean, R. N. *The Economics of Defense in the Nuclear Age*. Cambridge: Harvard University Press, 1960.
13. Howland, D. (Ed.). *The Development of a Methodology for Evaluation of Patient Care*. Columbu᷄ ̄he Ohio State University, Systems Research Group, 1961.
14. Howland, D., and McDowell, W. E. The measurement of patient care: A conceptual framework. *Nursing Research* 13:4–7, 1964.
15. Lindblom, C. E. *The Intelligence of Democracy*. New York: The Free Press, 1965.
15a. Lindblom, C. E. The science of muddling through. *Public Administration Review* 19, 79–88, 1959.
16. Pierce, L., Brunner, N., and Larabee, J. *Procedures for the Reduction of Data*. Columbus: The Adaptive Systems Research Group, Ohio State University, 1968.
17. Quade, E. S. (Ed.). *Analysis for Military Decisions*. Chicago: Rand McNally, 1965.
18. Schick, A. Systems politics and systems budgeting. *Public Review* 29: 137, 1969.
19. Simon, H. F., and March, J. G. *Organization*. New York: Wiley and Sons, 1958.
20. Stevens, S. Mathematics, measurement and psychophysics. In S. Stevens (Ed.), *Handbook of Experimental Psychology*. New York: Wiley and Sons, 1951.
21. Stimson, D. H., and Stimson, R. H. *Operations Research in Hospitals: Diagnosis and Prognosis*. Chicago: Hospital Research and Educational Trust, 1972.
22. Resio, D. T., and Verhonick, P. J. On the measurement and analysis of clinical data in nursing. *Nursing Research* 22:388–393, 1973.
23. von Bertalanffy, L. General system theory. In L. von Bertalanffy, and A. I. Rapoport (Eds.), *General Systems, Yearbook of the Society for General Systems Research*. Washington, D. C.: Society for General Systems Research, 1956.
24. Wilson, E. B. *Introduction to Scientific Research*. New York: McGraw-Hill, 1952.

Computerized Data for Nursing Research
Janelle C. Krueger

5

THE purpose of this chapter is to present some of the types of nursing and health data that are amenable to computer analysis, together with examples of printouts of some specific programs that have been utilized for health-related data. Introductory statements about questionnaire design and coding will precede descriptions and examples of data analysis.

A trite but true statement is that any data that can be categorized, classified, or aggregated are fair game for computerization. The assignment of symbols (numbers) to nominal, ordinal, interval, or ratio scale data is a simple process that opens the door to rapid, accurate manipulation by the computer. The computer's manipulations can range from the simple act of counting and printing out frequency distributions to complex statistical computations such as multivariate analysis.

Computer centers are becoming as common and as important to colleges and universities as libraries. They are equipped and staffed to make services available to all who wish to use the computer. Staff-members encourage use of facilities since the more hours/day that the computer operates, the more economical is its operation. Generally, limited computer time is made available to faculty and students for educational and research purposes. Staff-members are available to assist the novice and the expert through consultation in programming and finding and correcting errors made by the programmer (debugging).

A "program" is a logical step-by-step outline or set of instructions that the computer must follow to solve a problem. A "programmer" considers the problem, designs a flow chart to indicate how the program is to flow from start to finish, and translates the flow chart into statements in a language such as Fortran.

One need not be an expert programmer or computer specialist to use the computer. Most computer installations have libraries containing "canned" programs such as the Biomedical Computer Programs [2] and the Non-parametric Statistical System (NPAR) [10]. These procedures make actual "programming" unnecessary for the researcher.

Although skill in writing computer programs is not imperative, an understanding of the potentialities and limitations of the data on hand is necessary. The computer can only follow directions and cannot correct for the researcher's errors of judgment as to the kind of statistical procedure which represents the most powerful and appropriate tool for analyzing data. Programming the computer to do a t-test on data that do not meet the underlying assumptions of random sampling, normal population, and the interval scale level of measurement will result in a t-score value, even though inappropriate.

In summary the researcher who wishes to utilize the computer needs to know how to transfer his information to data processing cards and to be able to explain to the programmer how he wishes his data to be processed. With this information the programmer will either set up the data deck structure to retrieve and run the canned program desired or show the researcher how to do so. One successful "do it yourself" experience goes a long way toward building confidence in self and the computer.

Some practical suggestions for having information translated into numbers that can then be punched onto data cards are presented in the following sections.

QUESTIONNAIRE DESIGN

The analysis of data — one of the chief functions of the computer in research — should be in the investigator's thoughts from the inception of the research design. Once the question or hypothesis is formulated and the information needed to answer the research question is decided on, the collecting instrument comes under consideration. In addition to drafting "good" questions, the researcher needs to consider the logical sequence of the items, spacing for easy recording by the respondent or interviewer, and the convenience of the coder and keypunch operator. The researcher may and often does do his own coding and keypunching.

Coding is the term used to describe the process of translating the questionnaire responses to symbols, usually numbers, which are then punched onto a machine data card containing 80 columns. One or more cards are used for each respondent; the cards of all respondents compose the data deck, which is manipulated by the computer according to the researcher's instructions or program.

A data card punched with (1) the digits from 0 through 9, (2) the letters of the alphabet, and (3) other characters used in communicating with the computer is shown in Figure 5-1.

Each *digit* has a "single punch" which corresponds to its row number. Each *letter* of the alphabet is assigned two punches or rows on the card. Other special characters are used for basic arithmetic operations, including: addition (+), subtraction (−), multiplication (*), division (/), and exponentiation (**). Left and right parentheses, comma, period, and the equal sign complete the series of symbols that the computer translates to its language in order to make computations.

PRECODING AND CODING

Ideally the answer to every item on the collection instrument is precoded, i.e., a number is assigned to every item in advance. The assigned number coincides with the columns on the data card to which the data are transferred. Reserving a space to the left or to the right of the item for coding purposes makes keypunching from the questionnaire a relatively simple task. The keypuncher only needs to run his eye down the left or the right side of the page and pick up the numbers, which are then keypunched in the appropriate columns on a data card. Coding instructions are prepared prior to the

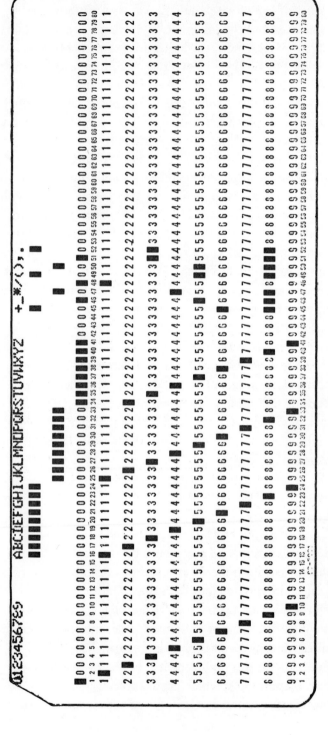

Fig. 5-1. Data card with digits, alphabet, and special characters.

distribution of the questionnaire and are revised to coincide with any changes resulting from a pilot study.

In large-scale surveys in which more than one person collects data from informants, the interviewers should be instructed by the researcher in the use of the instrument to insure consistency. Interviewers should be familiar with the coding system so that the responses received are recorded in the appropriate spaces on the instrument and in the form designated by the researcher. A sample of a few biographical items from a questionnaire are shown in Figure 5-2. Note the space at the top left-hand side which has a column to its left marked C1, C2, C3. The C1 stands for column 1 on the data card, C2 and C3 for columns 2 and 3. Likewise, the C4, C5, C6, and C14 to the left of the biographical responses also correspond to columns on the data card.

The coding instructions for translating the answers to items in Figure 5-2 to numbers which then are punched onto a data card are shown in Figure 5-3.

Generally the researcher will profit from writing the instructions for coding before the questionnaire is in its final form. The decision concerning the need for one or more columns on the data card is based on the number of categories required for an item. The expected size of the sample, e.g., will determine how many columns are needed for the identification number for respondents. One column (single punched) will handle from one to nine respondents and two columns are sufficient for as many as 99 respondents (01 to 99). In the example in Figure 5-3, three columns were provided because there were more than 99 respondents to be assigned identification numbers.

If the questionnaire has open-ended questions in which the total number of categories is uncertain, the researcher may wish to allow extra data columns to handle each possible response; or he may choose arbitrarily to limit the number of categories to a total of nine (one column) and instruct the coder as to the kinds of responses that will fit into preassigned categories. Often one sees a question with several categories to which one may respond followed by an open-ended category titled "other, please specify." If the latter is to be coded, the researcher needs to take this into account in writing instructions for the coding.

```
C1
C2
C3_____
```

I. BIOGRAPHICAL INFORMATION

Directions: Please answer the following questions by supplying the appropriate words, circling or checking the responses which pertain to your particular situation. (Please do not write in the space in the left margin.)

_____C4. Name of Employing Organization_____

_____C5. Unit in which you work_____

_____C6. Age: (Please circle) 18-21; 22-30; 31-45; 46-59; 60+

_____C14. Please check your present job classification:

       _____ Nurse Aide, Home Health Aide, Orderly or Attendant

       _____ Licensed Practical Nurse

       _____ Staff Nurse

       _____ Team Leader

       _____ Head Nurse

       _____ Clinical Specialist

Fig. 5-2. Excerpts from biographical section of questionnaire.

CODING INSTRUCTIONS

I. *Biographical Information Section*

Nursing Service Project

Column	Item or variable	Description of code
1, 2, 3	Identification number of respondents	001-029-Aide 030-080-L.P.N. 081-160-R.N.
4	Name of Employing Organization	1 = Stonyfield Hospital 2 = County Hospital 3 = Mt. View Extended Care 4 = Cragstone Rehab. Center
5	Area of work	1 = Pediatrics 2 = Maternity 3 = Newborn Nursery 4 = ICU, CCU 5 = Geriatrics 6 = Recovery Room 7 = Medical, including Psychiatric 8 = Surgical, including Orthopedics
6	Age	1 = 18–21 2 = 22–30 3 = 31–45 4 = 46–59 5 = 60+
7	Blank	
14	Job Classification	1 = Nurse Aide, Home Health Aide, Orderly or Attendant 2 = Licensed Practical Nurse 3 = Staff Nurse 4 = Team Leader 5 = Head Nurse 6 = Clinical Specialist

Fig. 5-3. Coding instructions for biographical section of questionnaire shown in Fig. 5-2.

The coding instructions are invaluable in communicating with the programmer. The instructions serve as a map which enables him to identify in which location on the data cards he should tell the computer to look for information. He cannot take a data deck and "run it" without the translation provided by coding instructions.

As is shown in Figure 5-2, using the column number from the coding instructions to identify each piece of information to be placed on the data card simplifies coding and keypunching. Placing a blank to the left of each item in which to record the coded response for each column permits greater speed and accuracy in keypunching. As can be seen, the uniform alignment of coding in the previously described procedure facilitates keypunching data directly from the collecting instrument.

The answers to the biographical questions shown in Figure 5-2, using the coding instructions in Figure 5-3, are keypunched on the data card shown in Figure 5-4.

The researcher may prefer to use a questionnaire or instrument that follows conventional outline protocol with each item numbered or lettered in chronological sequence. In the latter case accuracy in keypunching may require the intermediate step of placing the coded responses on master coding forms or tabulation sheets containing clearly marked columns of 80 spaces which correspond to the 80 spaces on the data cards. When the coder completes and rechecks the master sheets for all of the data collected, the data from the sheets are keypunched onto cards. If the researcher has a small amount of data, or as is more likely, little financial support, he is likely to be his own coder and keypunch operator. Accordingly the simplification of collecting and coding procedures is of great practical concern.

FREQUENCY DISTRIBUTIONS OF DATA

Assuming that data collection has been completed and that all of the information has been punched on data cards, the next step is to form a picture of the distribution of the data by categories. Breakdowns or frequency distributions that show the number of respondents in each category of the important demographic or intervening

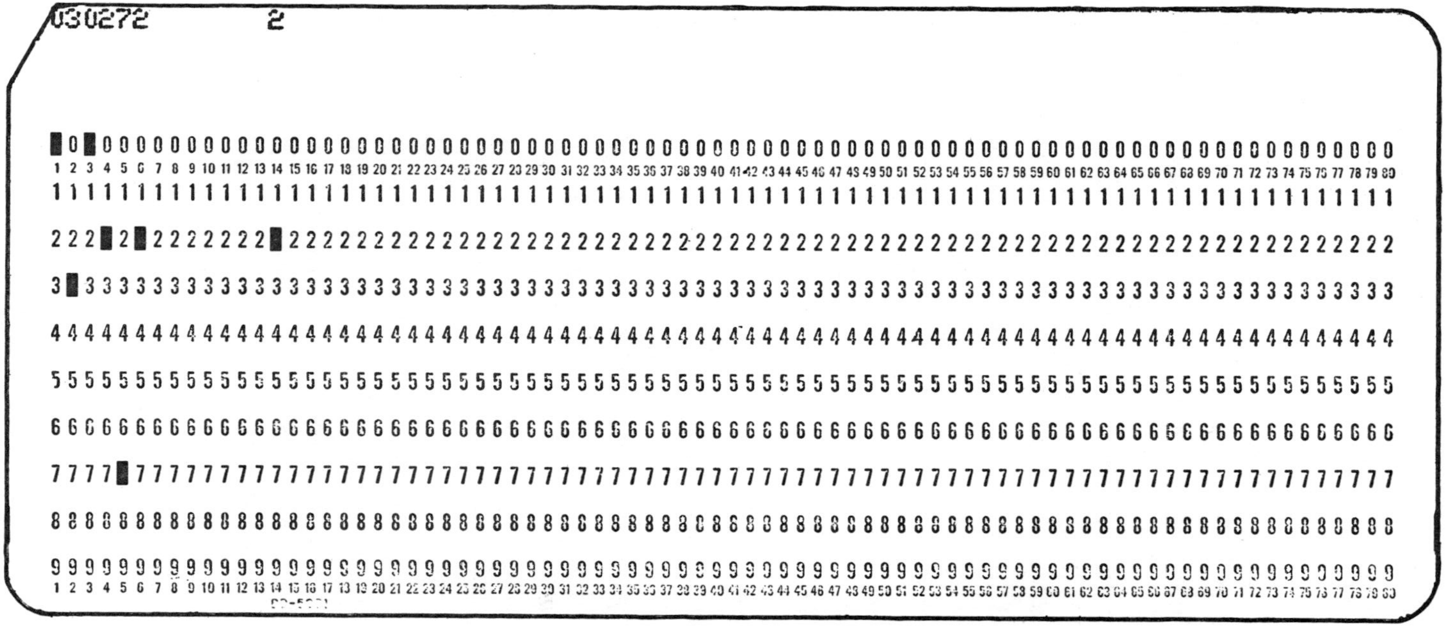

Fig. 5-4. Data card punched with biographical information shown in Fig. 5-2.

157

variables and the items in the questionnaire give the researcher preliminary ideas about the data which he wishes to compare or study further.

Frequency distributions can be accomplished by a counter-sorter, a standard piece of equipment at a computer facility. This machine counts and sorts the cards in a data deck column by column — a tedious operation if one must record the count manually. On the other hand, sorting, counting, and printing out the frequency of occurrence of responses are simple processes for the computer. Two examples of computer printouts of frequency distributions are included here. The first is a bare-bones tabulation, whereas the second includes titles, cumulative frequency and percentage, mean, variance, standard deviation, and median. Both of them report the responses of a group of respondents (licensed practical nurses) to one item on a questionnaire. The instructions to the respondent and one item chosen for tabulation are shown in Figure 5-5.

A simple-to-run library program entitled Alphanumeric Frequency Count (AFC) [2] was used to give the researcher an estimate of the spread of responses to each question in a research instrument. The printout of the responses of 27 licensed practical nurses to variable number 62 — "Talk with patients who are critical or demanding and try to find reason for their behavior" — is in Table 5-1.

The great advantage of the AFC program is its simplicity. Only a few cards are needed to communicate to the computer that the user wishes the program designated BMD04D taken from the computer's storage file and run, using data (cards or tape) supplied by the user.

Simplicity of programming is of little value if inordinate amounts of time must be spent in labeling and making sense of the printout. The lack of labels on printed output is a serious drawback if there are several pages of frequency distributions identified only with the variable numbers. Unless the researcher is able to link in his memory the variable number with its content, he may find himself writing above each frequency count words which remind him that variable 62 is concerned with "talking with demanding patients."

The AFC shown in Table 5-1 is an example of a "non-labeled" canned program. This type of program has limited usefulness if much hand labeling is required, i.e., the saving of time effected by using the computer is soon consumed by doctoring the printout.

INSTRUCTIONS: For each item, we would like you to circle the response which comes closest to your expectation for yourself. Given your nursing education and experience. To what extent do you feel that you have an obligation to do or not to do the item? There are no right or wrong answers. We are interested in your view.

There are six possible responses:

ABSOLUTELY MUST — If you think the item describes a type of behavior that, given your education and experience, you feel you absolutely must do, after the item circle AM (absolutely must).

PREFERABLY SHOULD — If the item is one that you feel you preferably should do, circle PS (preferably should).

MAY OR MAY NOT — If the item is one that you feel that a nurse with your education and experience may or may not do, circle MMN (may or may not).

PREFERABLY SHOULD NOT — If the item describes a type of behavior that you feel you preferably should not do, circle PSN (preferably should not).

ABSOLUTELY MUST NOT —If the item represents behavior that you feel one with your education and experience absolutely must not perform, circle AMN (absolutely must not).

NOT APPLICABLE — If the item does not apply to you, circle NA (not applicable).

EXAMPLE: If you feel that you absolutely must talk with patients who are critical or demanding and try to find reasons for their behavior, draw a circle around AM.

62 Talk with patients   AM PS MMN PSN AMN NA
    who are critical
    or demanding and
    try to find reason
    for their behavior.

Fig. 5-5. Sample instructions for questionnaire.

Table 5-1. Frequency Count[a]

Number of Observations	27
Variable Number	62[b]

Symbol	*Frequency*
1[c]	10
2	8
3	5
4	2
5	0
6	2

[a] Printout using BMD04D, Alphanumeric Frequency Count, BMD Biomedical Computer Programs, p. 66.

[b] Variable number 62. Talk with patients who are critical or demanding and try to find reason for their behavior.

[c] 1 = Absolutely must; 2 = Preferably should; 3 = May or may not; 4 = Preferably should not; 5 = Absolutely must not; 6 = Not applicable.

Often the researcher has a need for more thorough analysis than that provided by the AFC; FREQY [4] is a frequency count program that labels variables and responses and computes and prints out not only frequencies but also percentage of total, cumulative frequency, cumulative percentage, mean, variance, standard deviation, and median. A FREQY printout of the responses of Licensed Practical Nurses to Item 62 is shown in Table 5-2.

Note the contrast between the kind of information supplied in Tables 5-1 and 5-2 concerning the same responses to a question. Additional time must be spent in making label cards to achieve the elegance of printout shown in Table 5-2. The choice is with the researcher.

The reader may question whether or not the categories in Table 5-2 which range from "Absolutely Must" through "Not Applicable" represent interval data. These are adapted from a study in which the categories were treated as equal intervals [16]. This is included as a reminder that only the researcher can make this judgment. The

Table 5-2. Printout of Frequency Distribution. 62. Talk With Demanding Patients To Find Cause For Their Behavior.

	Category Code	Frequency	Percent of Total	Cumulative Frequency	Cumulative Percent
Absolutely must	1	10	37.04	10	37.04
Preferably should	2	8	29.63	18	66.67
May or may not	3	5	18.52	23	85.19
Preferably should not	4	2	7.41	25	92.59
Not applicable	6	2	7.41	27	100.00
Total number of cases equals		27			

Mean = 2.259   Variance = 2.046   Standard Deviation = 1.430   Median = 1.938   Variable Number = 62 computer treated the categories as if they were indeed equal distances from one another and computed the mean, variance, and standard deviation, as well as legitimate median value.

CLUSTER ANALYSIS

Assume that the researcher has obtained a frequency distribution of the data collected from several groups of nurses with different job categorizations. He now has a general idea of each group's standing with respect to each item but would like to know what similarities and differences there are among the *items* and among the *groups* with respect to the behavioral items. In other words, are there groupings of behavior that nursing personnel perform and are there groupings of personnel around these behaviors?

Cluster analysis is a method that provides answers to these questions. This type of analysis derives domains of behaviors by placing into clusters those items that show high correlations between themselves (similarity) and low correlations with other items in other clusters (differences).

In 1939 Robert C. Tryon published a monograph on cluster analysis in which all of the computations were done by hand [12]. The task of finding the correlations and intercorrelations among a number of variables using a desk calculator was unbelievably time consuming. When computers became available to Tryon in the 1950s, he and other investigators began the task of translating his quantitative methods into a computer program called the BC-TRY System of Cluster Analysis. Tryon and Bailey present a theoretical and applied description of cluster analysis for the reader who wishes more detail [13].

To obtain the output presented in this section the BC-TRY Cluster Analysis Computer Program [14] was employed in a utilization study conducted among hospital and health-department nursing personnel [9]. The instrument developed for data collection contained 88 behaviors taken from nursing literature, which might be expected of registered nurses educated in baccalaureate and associate degree programs as well as licensed practical nurses and other auxiliary nursing personnel. Implicit in the choice of activities included in the questionnaire was the idea that differing types of personnel are required for the care of patients whose illnesses vary from mild to acute.

In contrast to the "ideal" response requested in the example in Figure 5-5, respondents were asked to indicate their "real" behavior by indicating the frequency with which each specific behavior was performed. Instructions for choices were:

Often - If an item is one which you perform often or on a regular basis, circle "often."
Sometimes - If the item is one which you sometimes perform, circle "sometimes."
Never - If you never perform the behavior stated in the item, circle "never." (Figure 5-6).

Responses to the questions were coded and the identifying information plus the responses to each question were punched on data cards. Two cards were required for each respondent since the number of responses exceeded the 80 column limit on one card. The interface or control cards needed to check out the BC-TRY System from the library file were then put with the data deck and run on the computer.

According to Bailey: "The data amenable to cluster analysis are those of multivariate experiments in which a number of different objects (subjects, respondents, etc.) are each assessed (observed, measured, counted, etc.) on a number of different variables [3]." Generally the variables are limited to ordinal or dichotomous characteristics of the objects.

Representativeness of variables and respondents is necessary if generalizations beyond the sample are to be pertinent. In cluster analysis a sound rule of thumb is to have at least twice as many objects (subjects) in the sample as there are variables in the study [3]. To meet this rule, the analysis reported here should have had either fewer variables or more respondents. (There were 88 variables and 140 objects or respondents.)

In the variable analysis (V-analysis) successive subsets of homogeneous (similar) variables are selected. The BC-TRY System selects a pivot variable, which is the most general single variable, and then

ITEM	RESPONSE		
16_____ Assist in formation of written nursing care plans for patients in my area	Often	Sometimes	Never
17_____ Make notation on chart of patient's condition and care given	Often	Sometimes	Never
Observe and report symptoms or changes in patient's condition			
18_____ To team leader	Often	Sometimes	Never
19_____ To head nurse	Often	Sometimes	Never
20_____ To supervisor	Often	Sometimes	Never
21_____ To physician	Often	Sometimes	Never
Give medications	Often	Sometimes	Never
23_____ Oral	Often	Sometimes	Never
24_____ Hypodermic	Often	Sometimes	Never
25_____ Intramuscular	Often	Sometimes	Never
26_____ Intravenous	Often	Sometimes	Never
27_____ Know expected results and bad side-effects of medications which patients assigned to me are taking	Often	Sometimes	Never
28_____ Explain procedures or treatments to patient or family	Often	Sometimes	Never
29_____ Keep relatives informed about patient's condition	Often	Sometimes	Never

Fig. 5-6. Example of items contained in nursing utilization study questionnaire.

selects variables to complete the subset which are mutually colinear with one another and the pivot variable. Homogeneity (similarity) is insured by setting a lower limit for the variables which define the cluster. A printout of the correlation matrix of the first cluster selected from the data is shown in Table 5-3.

In the matrix in Table 5-3, Variable 24, which is "Give medications — hypodermic," is the pivot variable in Dimension 1. "Dimension" can be equated with the terms "cluster" or "domain." Definers of the Dimension are Variables 25, 24, and 26 — give oral, intramuscular, and intravenous medications — plus Variables 60 and 52 which relate to assigning staff-members to carry out necessary care and being a team leader, respectively. As can be seen in Table 5-3, the mean correlation between the key cluster variables is .8378. The correlations were very high — between .7048 and .9870. The face validity of the items was accepted at the intuitive level and labeled "team nursing."

In cluster analysis, clusters are relatively independent of one another. (In addition to correlation matrices, the BC-TRY System plots out the various clusters in a program called SPAN-spherical analysis to give the researcher a graphical picture of the Euclidean distance between clusters of items.)

Cluster analysis is described as a special case of factor analysis in which all of the variables are "pure" [5]. That is, a variable as a unit is assigned to a cluster, whereas in factor analysis different parts of the variance of a variable may be placed in different factors. In other words variables that have been placed in clusters are extracted from the population of variables and are not available for selection for subsequent clusters.

The V-analysis aspect of cluster analysis gives answers to the question concerning the *groupings* of *behavior* that nursing personnel perform. The 88 original behavioral variables were reduced to nine clusters containing 36 items considered to be representative of the total items. The items in each cluster have high correlations with one another, indicating that the behaviors have a common underlying dimension. The nine dimensions or clusters selected by the computer are listed in Table 5-4. The correlation matrices are not given. Instead the nursing behavior variables composing each dimension are included to give the reader a qualitative summary of the V-analysis results.

Table 5-3. Correlation Matrix for Key Cluster Variables (as Reflected) of Dimension 1 — Nursing Utilization Study

	24	25	23	60	52	26
24	.9861	.9870	.9380	.8281	.8141	.8519
25	.9870	.9798	.9334	.8261	.7938	.8415
23	.9380	.9334	.9127	.7982	.7623	.8033
60	.8281	.8261	.7982	.8078	.8219	.7048
52	.8141	.7938	.7623	.8219	.7835	.7485
26	.8519	.8415	.8033	.7048	.7485	.7868

Mean Correlation Between The Key Cluster Variables (as reflected) of Dimension 1 = .8378

Variable 24 = give hypodermic medications (pivot variable — one with highest variance). Variable 25 = give IM medications (definer variable). Variable 23 = give oral medications (definer variable). Variable 60 = be a team leader (definer variable). Variable 52 = assign staff to carry out necessary care based on patient's need and staff's ability (definer variable). Variable 26 = give IV medications (definer variable).

Table 5-4. Nursing Behavior Variables Defining Dimensions of Patient Care

Dimension	Nursing Behavior Variables
1. Team leader	Give medications: oral, hypodermic, IM, IV; assign staff to carry out necessary care; be team leader
2. Vital signs	Observe and record vital signs: temperature, pulse, quality and rhythm of pulse, respiration rate, quality of respirations, tone, temperature and color of skin, blood pressure
3. Organizational activity	Be active in nursing organization; belong to nursing organization; represent agency or nursing on local, state, or national committees
4. Post-surgery planning and care	Give direct patient care to: recovery room patients after minor and major surgery; plan nursing care for: recovery room patients after minor and major surgery
5. Plan care	Plan nursing care for patients (mildly ill and convalescent, chronically ill, acutely ill and mentally confused)
6. Evaluate care	Evaluate quality of care given to your patients as evidenced by: skin condition, mental attitude, degree of self-help in bathing, eating, elimination, patient mobility; does his activity match doctor's orders?
7. Sociopsychological care	Give emotional support to patient, family, help create therapeutic environment through development of productive interpersonal relationships with patient; encourage patient to make decisions about his desire to maintain identity as a social being (wear own clothes, set own hours of sleep, consider food habits)
8. Bedside care (complex)	Give direct patient care to: acutely ill and critically ill patients
9. Bedside care	Give direct care to: mildly ill, convalescent, and chronically ill patients

Following the V-analysis, the computer executed the object or O-analysis program of cluster analysis to obtain an answer to the question concerning the *groupings* of *personnel*. O-analysis operates on the same principle as V-analysis except that the *respondents* rather than the *variables* are placed into clusters based on their similarity to one another with respect to the behavioral clusters, i.e., respondents are placed into typologies on the basis of similar scores on the dimensions obtained through V-analysis. The composition or membership of the O-types is printed out according to the identification code for respondents supplied by the researcher. The O-type mean on each of the nine dimensions is shown in Table 5-5.

Since the O-types describe a group of individuals who have similar scores on multiple variables, the predictions which can be made for any member of a given O-type are better than if based on only one variable or one dimension. The O-type mean score is based on a standard score of 50 and a standard deviation of 10. A score greater than one deviation from the mean permits O-types to be categorized as high or low on each dimension.

In Table 5-5 a mean score that is one standard deviation or more below the mean of 50 indicates that the O-type members frequently perform the behaviors comprising a given dimension, i.e., members of O-Type 1 (OTP001) with a mean score of 39.1359 on Dimension 1 (FSC001) reported that they frequently performed the behaviors listed under Dimension 1 in Table 5-4. A score of 40 or less is considered to be high, and a score of 60 or more is labeled low. The reversal of the terms high and low is an artifact of coding. Had behavior that was reported as "frequently occurring" been coded 3 rather than 1, the means would have been directly rather than inversely related to the high and low designations.

In the interest of space the composition, education, and reported utilization of the 13 typologies of nurses are summarized in Table 5-6. The answer to the question concerning the groupings of personnel according to their reported behaviors is apparent.

The typologies are hierarchically arranged with dimensions of behavior performed only by registered nurses in the first three groups and behaviors reported most frequently by licensed practical nurses and aides in the last three typologies. The composition of the intermediate typologies is a mix of registered nurses and practical nurses.

Table 5-5. O-Type Means for Nine Dimensions of Nursing Behavior

O-Type Means		Dimensions								
		1 FSC001	2 FSC002	3 FSC003	4 FSC004	5 FSC005	6 FSC006	7 FSC007	8 FSC008	9 FSC009[a]
1	OTP001	39.1359	46.2622	35.3993	32.6043	39.4040	42.4700	36.4166	45.6596	48.8387
2	OTP002	39.5423	48.9788	52.7921	42.0490	41.9652	45.1396	43.8141	43.7032	51.9847
3	OTP003	39.9783	53.2493	52.4748	44.0045	48.1796	53.0819	59.7987	42.1838	60.7744
4	OTP004	41.6153	54.1953	50.3770	60.0104	49.4909	46.0272	45.4888	43.2402	63.2745
5	OTP005	44.5471	43.5871	36.2001	36.1796	43.1951	45.3118	46.5602	42.1838	40.8746
6	OTP006	53.7230	43.4014	34.7207	52.1714	43.6438	42.4700	44.7103	45.5642	40.8745
7	OTP007	47.0614	45.1774	45.6763	42.8053	48.4650	50.4806	54.8733	49.0400	40.8745
8	OTP008	43.0691	45.6538	60.0309	60.5117	48.0359	51.0321	49.8268	50.8733	43.3730
9	OTP009	41.3863	61.9283	58.4420	48.6560	46.5200	45.6573	50.8122	57.6317	59.6841
10	OTP010	46.7678	60.6587	45.9638	59.7634	47.8297	58.0581	48.9098	61.1426	54.4393
11	OTP011	61.1630	42.8286	43.4596	48.3743	66.1924	44.5999	50.2756	44.2966	42.1135
12	OTP012	62.2861	44.7998	56.8098	48.7494	45.0623	51.6205	55.8676	49.0718	42.1054
13	OTP013	61.3557	43.6871	58.3464	59.1071	66.9682	47.6047	53.3013	55.1881	45.8640[b]

[a] FSC001, Team leader dimension; FSC002, Vital signs; FSC003, Organizational activity; FSC004, Post-surgery planning and care; FSC005, Plan care; FSC006, Evaluate care; FSC007, Sociopsychological care; FSC008, Bedside care (complex); and FSC009, Bedside care (simple).

[b] Mean = 50; standard deviation = 10.

Table 5-6. Education and Utilization of 13 Nursing O-Types

| O-Type | | Utilization | |
Composition	Education	High	Low
1. Registered nurses	Diploma (3), baccalaureate (2)	1. Team leader 3. Organizational activity 4. Post-surgery planning and care 5. Planning care 7. Sociopsychological care	
2. Registered nurses	Diploma (17)	1. Team leader	
3. Registered nurses	Diploma (7)	1. Team leader	7. Sociopsychological care 9. Simple care
4. Registered nurses	Diploma (5), baccalaureate (3)		4. Post-surgery planning and care 9. Simple care
5. Registered nurses and practical nurses	Diploma (1), baccalaureate (2), practical (1)	3. Organizational activity 4. Post-surgery planning and care	

6. Registered nurses and practical nurses	Diploma (2), practical (3)	
7. Registered nurses and practical nurses	Diploma (2), baccalaureate (1), practical (2)	3. Organizational activity
8. Registered nurses	Diploma (3), baccalaureate (1)	3. Organizational activity 4. Post-surgery planning and care
9. Registered nurses	Diploma (6), baccalaureate (3)	2. Vital signs 8. Complex care
10. Registered nurses	Diploma (3), baccalaureate (8)	2. Vital signs 4. Post-surgery planning and care 8. Complex care
11. Registered nurses	Practical (8)	1. Team leader 5. Planning care
12. Practical nurses and aides	Practical (9), aides (6)	1. Team leader
13. Practical nurses and aides	Practical (6), aides (4)	1. Team leader 5. Planning care

ANALYSIS OF VARIANCE

Analysis of variance or ANOVA is a statistical test that is frequently used with nursing data. The test, in which a single interval scale can be related to one or more nominal scales, has the same assumptions of normality, independent random samples, and equal population standard deviations as does the difference of means test. Both protocols also test the null hypothesis that the population means are equal [1].

Analysis of variance is particularly useful in analyzing data collected in experimental nursing studies. Putt, e.g., used analysis of variance in an experiment in nursing adults with peptic ulcers [11]. Her study utilized a post-test-only experimental design. Patients were randomly assigned to groups to test the effectiveness of two nursing approaches, psychological support and instruction by the nurse, against the control of the usual hospital nursing care to patients hospitalized with confirmed peptic ulcers. One of the hypotheses that she tested was: In decreasing the mean length of hospitalization of the ulcer patients in the study: (1) treatment III, instruction, is significantly more effective than treatment II, psychological support; (2) treatment II, psychological support, is significantly more effective than treatment I, control; and (3) treatment II, instruction, is significantly more effective than treatment I, control.

The adjusted mean hours of hospitalization (interval scale level) for the three main effects of treatment group, sex, and type of ulcer (nominal scale levels of measurement), shown in Table 5-7, were keypunched on data cards.

Other information punched on the cards included data describing length of time that discomfort was reported by patients, antacid consumption by patients, Institute for Personality and Ability Testing (IPAT) Anxiety Scale mean scores, mean scores for four concepts measured by semantic differential scales, and mean scores on a structured interview scale. The deck was then computer analyzed using a library program for Harvey's least squares analysis of variance for unequal subclass members [8]. The program produced F ratios for the main effects of treatment groups, sex, and types of ulcer in addition to first-order interactions of group by sex, group by ulcer, and ulcer by sex. The interaction procedure makes possible the segregation of the source of variance, i.e., the interaction variation is

Table 5-7. Hours of Hospitalization: Adjusted Means

Factor	Group I	II	III	Total
Sex:				
male	194.05	96.53	266.40	185.66
female	446.32	178.62	198.93	274.62
Type of ulcer:				
duodenal	271.08	109.53	114.74	165.12
gastric	369.28	165.62	350.59	295.16
Total	320.18	137.57	232.66	230.14
Standard deviation				117.62

attributed to neither variable alone but to the joint effect of the two acting together [7]. The printout of the analysis of variance for only the length of hospitalization is shown in Table 5-8.

The interpretation of Table 5-8 is that the variables "groups" and "type of ulcer" showed a statistically significant difference at the .001 level in length of hospitalization. The interaction analyses indicated that the greatest difference (.001 level) in hospital stay was related to the joint effects of group and sex differences. In Table 5-7 the mean scores show that the males in the study were not hospitalized as long as were females.

STEPWISE REGRESSION ANALYSIS

Stepwise regression analysis is a statistical tool of great potential value to nurse-researchers. This test provides point-biserial correlations between multiple independent variables and a dependent variable. The multiple correlations show to what extent the dependent variable can be predicted by the independent variables.

Stepwise Regression Program BMD02R is a library program available to users of the BMD Biomedical Computer Programs [2]. This

Table 5-8. Least Squares Analysis of Variance for Job 1 (L. Hosp)

Job	Rhm	Source	D.F.	Sum of Squares	Mean Squares	F
1	4	Total	35	484190.305556		
1	4	T red.	9	346256.385343	38472.931705	7.252[a]
1	4	Error	26	137933.920213	5305.150777	
1	4	1 (Group)	2	135650.964814	67825.482407	12.785[a]
1	4	2 (Sex)	1	31871.184392	31871.184392	6.008[b]
1	4	3 (Ulcer)	1	74615.263494	74615.263494	14.065[a]
1	4	4 (Group and sex)	2	90030.555416	45015.277708	8.485[c]
1	4	5 (Group and ulcer)	2	16701.298282	8350.649141	1.574
1	4	6 (Sex and ulcer)	1	13965.981497	13965.981497	2.633

[a] Significant at .001 level.
[b] Significant at .05 level.
[c] Significant at .01 level.

program was utilized by Williams in the analysis of data from a comparative study of patients who develop decubitus ulcers with those who do not [15, 16]. The questions asked were: Are there factors other than pressure associated with decubitus formation? If there are such factors, what are they?

The formation of decubitus ulcers was the dependent variable. Patients were categorized using a dichotomous rating system that included the independent or intervening variables of age, sex, ethnicity, level of consciousness, self-movement, dryness of skin, body weight, edema, sensation, general circulation, genitourinary infection, urinary and stool incontinence, routine skin care, padding, corticosteroids, vitamins, other infection, calories/day, and temperature. These data were placed on data cards for computer analysis.

The computer is invaluable in multiple correlation analysis because of the numerous computations required. In stepwise regression the first independent variable selected is that which has the greatest predictive value relative to the dependent variable, in this case the formation of decubitus ulcers. In Table 5-9 the multiple correlations (R) and multiple correlation squares (RSQ) are shown for 20 variables. A multiple R is subject to the same kind of interpretation with respect to size and importance as is a Pearson product-moment coefficient (r). Guilford gives a rough estimate of the strength of relationship of a correlation of .70 to .90 as a high correlation and marked relationship [7]. The coefficient of multiple determination, as Guilford calls RSQ (R^2), denotes the proportion of variance in the dependent variable that is associated with the independent variable.

In step 1 in Table 5-9, .5221 or 52.21 percent of the variance in decubitus formation is accounted for by body weight. (This was a negative correlation, i.e., thin or very thin persons are more susceptible to decubitus formation than are persons judged to be normal, plump, or obese.) The steps are cumulative. Step 1, body weight, and step 2, other infection, together contribute .6322 or 63.22 percent of the variance. The predictive contribution of other infection is 11.01 percent, 63.22 − 52.21.

The computer continues serially to select from the remaining variables the independent or intervening variable which contributes the greatest predictive power until all variables have been entered

		Multiple	
Step	*Variable*	*R*	*RSQ*
1	Body weight	.7226	.5221
2	Other infection	.7951	.6322
3	Padding devices used	.8278	.6852
4	Sex	.8509	.7241
5	Incontinent feces	.8659	.7497
6	Edema	.8806	.7754
7	Temperature	.8957	.8023
8	Sensation	.9086	.8255
9	Calories/day	.9244	.8545
10	Vitamins	.9356	.8753
11	Corticosteroids	.9415	.8865
12	Level of consciousness	.9476	.8980
13	Age	.9570	.9159
14	Moves self	.9704	.9417
15	General circulation	.9725	.9458
16	Routine skin care	.9782	.9570
17	Dry skin	.9839	.9681
18	Genitourinary infection	.9897	.9795
19	Incontinent urine	.9908	.9817
20	Ethnicity	.9913	.9826

into the regression. Cumulatively the 20 variables in Table 5-9 contribute 98.26 percent to decubitus ulcer formation for the particular group of patients studied. Once again, without the rapid manipulation of the computer, analyses such as stepwise regression would be prohibitive in time and cost.

OTHER STATISTICAL TESTS

Computer programs are available for most statistical tests. A boon to social-science researchers who use qualitative data is the

NPAR Non-parametric Statistics Package compiled by the Computer Institute for Social Science Research at Michigan State University [10]. Included in this package are chi-square, K-sample tests, measures of randomness, Mann-Whitney and Wilcoxon tests, two-way and three-way analyses of variance, rank correlation coefficients, randomization tests, and Coombs non-metric scaling.

Each computer center has its own library of programs available to users. Exchange agreements among universities permit the researcher to utilize programs to fit almost any statistical problem amenable to computer analysis.

TIME-SHARED REMOTE CONSOLES

The programs discussed in this chapter were all run by "batch processing," using a digital computer. The data deck and control cards were either taken or sent to a computer center, placed in Intake together with other user's decks and retrieved from the center's Output after an interval sometimes referred to as turn-around time — the time required to process the batches of programs on hand at a given time. Sometimes programs were taken to the center after 10 P.M. when the number of users was minimal and the turnaround time was only a few minutes.

The time-shared remote console is a recent development that promises to simplify the process of running programs through the connection of a large computer by cables, telephone wires, or microwave links to multiple terminals located in departments around campus, laboratories, libraries, hospitals, or the researcher's home. All of the terminals are served simultaneously by the central computer and consist of a keyboard for communicating with the computer as well as a television-like screen. Other options are an audio speaker, a card reader, and a printer. These pieces of equipment permit immediate interaction between the researcher and the computer and allow programming problems to be corrected without the delays encountered in "batch" processing when each error must be traced and corrected, and the entire program run through the computer again with the lag of turnaround time.

A familiar prototype of remote control terminals is MEDLARS

(Medical Literature Analysis and Retrieval System), a federally supported endeavor which indexes about 200,000 papers in medicine and biology each year.

PROBLEMS AND POSSIBLE SOLUTIONS

The problems encountered by the researcher in learning to use the computer for the analysis of data seem small when one considers the increase in efficiency and in scope of research that is possible once the ability is mastered. The only insurmountable problem appears to be lack of access to a computer center with its library and technical assistance in statistics, programming, keypunching, and debugging of programs.

Given the computer center, the nurse-researcher needs to visit the center and become acquainted with the physical layout, the consultants, the services that are available without charge, and the cost of services that must be bought. Sources of funds for the latter may be (1) computer time available to the university and allocated to departments on request; (2) research funds within the department which may be requisitioned for purchase of computer services; (3) small or large individual or group research grants which may include categories for data analysis; or (4) use of time-shared consoles in agencies in which research is being conducted.

One of the problems encountered by some social scientists is related to communicating their desires for statistical or programming assistance to consultants. Familiarity with one's data, the kinds of statistical tests that are appropriate, and coding instructions which clearly show where the data are located on the data card will decrease the communication gap.

Although proficiency in programming is not essential, the researcher who has some knowledge of one of the computer languages probably will be less hesitant about beginning to use the computer for research purposes. Short courses in Fortran, Basic, Cobol, or whatever the language of the accessible computer frequently are offered by computer centers and departments such as systems engineering or university hospitals where the computer is a part of the daily life.

REFERENCES

1. Blalock, H. *Social Statistics.* New York: McGraw-Hill, 1960.
2. *BMD Biomedical Computer Programs.* Berkeley and Los Angeles: University of California Press, 1968.
3. *Cluster Analysis and the BC-TRY System.* Boulder: Tryon-Bailey Associates, 1970.
4. *FREQY, FREQYLS, FREQYVL, or FREQYST.* Test Analysis and Development Corporation, James K. Hoffmeister, 855 Inca Parkway, Boulder, Colorado 80302.
5. Fruchter, B. *Introduction to Factor Analysis.* Princeton: Van Nostrand, 1954.
6. Gross, N, Mason, W. S., and McEachern, A. N. *Explorations in Role Analysis: Studies of the School Superintendency Role.* New York: Wiley & Sons, 1958.
7. Guilford, J. P. *Fundamental Statistics in Psychology and Education.* New York: McGraw-Hill, 1956.
8. Harvey, W. R. *Least Squares Analysis of Data with Unequal Subclass Numbers.* USDA, ARS 20-9, Washington, GPO, 1960.
9. Krueger, J. C. The education and utilization of nurses: A paradox. *Nursing Outlook* 19:676–679, 1971.
10. *Non-parametric Statistical System.* Computer Institute for Social Science Research. East Lansing: Michigan State University, 1970.
11. Putt, A. M. An experiment in nursing adults with peptic ulcers. *Nursing Research* 19:484–494, 1970.
12. Tryon, R. C. Cluster analysis, a monograph. Ann Arbor: Edwards Brothers, 1939.
13. Tryon, R. C., and Bailey, D. E. *Cluster Analysis.* New York: McGraw-Hill, 1970.
14. Tryon, R. C., and Bailey, D. E. *User's Manual of the BC-TRY System.* Boulder, Colorado: Tryon-Bailey Associates, 1965.
15. Williams, A. M. A study of factors contributing to skin breakdown. *Nursing Research* 21:238–243, 1972.
16. Williams, A. M. A Comparison of Patients Who Do Develop Decubitus Ulcers With Those Who Do Not. Master's thesis, University of Arizona College of Nursing, 1971.

Applied Multiple Regression Approach to Research in Nursing
Alton L. Taylor

6

RESEARCH problems in nursing practice and preparation are multidimensional. Studies that deal with patient care to improve nursing practice need to consider important patient variables and appropriate therapy traits within a multidimensional behavioral scheme. So often the ability to control complex multidimensional factors of the nursing environment have been ignored owing, in part, to lack of sophisticated experimental designs and inadequate computer resources for processing large amounts of research data.

Not only have innovations in clinical research and practice in nursing been wanting, but also institutional self-study projects of academic programs in nursing have been treated in restricted fashions. The assessment of academic programs in nursing is very obviously multidimensional. It is both impossible to separate and foolish to ignore the interacting effects of student-nurse behaviors within the educational training environment. The multidimensional nature of student nurses includes the influence of the personalities of peers and professors, classrooms, dormitory life, clinical environments, interests in a career, factors associated with motivation, and so on.

The applied multiple regression approach allows an investigator greater flexibility in conceptualizing complex research problems [3].

Some very complex models of multiple linear regression analysis can be used for predictions, testing for interaction, accounting for non-linear and curvilinear vectors, cross-validating research, covariance designs, multiple correlation routines, multiple discriminant analysis, factor analysis, and canonical correlations [2].

Research on multivariate problems has been successfully conducted with the notable assistance of computer technology in medical research and the behavioral sciences.

COMPUTER TECHNOLOGY AND RESEARCH IN NURSING

Developments in computer technology have brought about computational capabilities for handling larger amounts and kinds of data than were previously considered to be useful. Improvements in research methodology and research design in nursing are also taking place in an unprecedented manner. With capabilities to control more data and improve research designs, it is necessary to strengthen means of collecting, organizing, and analyzing data and to refine techniques for stating and testing research hypotheses. A common problem in nursing research is that an investigator conceptualizes complex behavioral problems but fails to construct a research problem that reflects these complexities. This is attributable in part to restricted knowledge of statistical designs or lack of skills with the computer. One approach that allows an investigator to develop statistical models which reflect his original conceptualization of a complex and multivariate research problem and emphasizes the formulation of research questions for computer processing is the *multiple linear regression approach* described by Bottenberg and Ward [1].

Among the advantages for using the multiple regression approach: (1) the predictor variables in the linear regression models do not assume normal distributions, which allows an investigator to use dichotomous variables in a binary-coded form (1 or 0); (2) a large number of variables can be used to reflect complex behaviors under study; and (3) the investigator is allowed the opportunity to arrange systematically large numbers of research hypotheses without fear of restrictions normally imposed by other statistical designs and the usual existing or packaged computer programs [1].

The basic unit used in the multiple linear regression approach is the *vector*. A vector is defined as an ordered set of numbers. By using vector notations a large amount of data can be arranged and controlled without much difficulty. For example, percentile rank scores on the *National League for Nursing (NLN) Examination— Comprehensive Pharmacology* for five nursing students can be represented as a vector (Table 6-1).

Table 6-1. NLN—Comprehensive Pharmacology Scores Expressed as a Vector

Nursing Student	Score
A	65
B	70
C	61
D	92
E	84

The collection of NLN—Comprehensive Pharmacology scores is called a vector because each score or element in the set is a number (percentile rank), and the scores or elements are distributed in the order that nursing-student A had a score of 65, nursing-student B had a score of 70, and so on.

Vectors may also be used to describe a baccalaureate nursing student (Table 6-2). This description of the nursing student reports that she graduated from high school with a percentile rank of 92, obtained scores on the verbal section of the Scholastic Aptitude Test (SAT) of 514 and on the mathematics section of 520, for a total SAT score of 1034, and entered a baccalaureate nursing school after receiving the R.N. diploma. In describing the student as a column vector Y:

$$Y = \begin{bmatrix} 92 \\ 514 \\ 520 \\ 1034 \\ 1 \\ 0 \end{bmatrix}$$

A description of the nursing student as a row vector would be: $Y = [92, 514, 520, 1034, 1, 0]$.

A representation of using row and column vectors to describe several nursing students on the previous recordings is shown in Table 6-3. This is a graphic example of six column vectors including: percentile rank in graduating high school class, SAT verbal scores, SAT mathematics scores, SAT total scores, student type A (1 if R.N., 0 otherwise), and student type B (1 if generic, 0 otherwise).

The general way to note vectors is with subscripted capital letters. The elements or numbers in a vector are usually noted by subscripted lower-case letters. The capital letter designations are assigned at the discretion of the investigator. Vector notations describing the characteristics of the nursing students are shown in Table 6-4. Vector

Table 6-2. Selected Characteristics of Nursing Student Entering Baccalaureate Program

Characteristic	Score
Percentile rank in graduating high-school class	92
Scholastic Aptitude Test, Verbal	514
Scholastic Aptitude Test, Math	520
Scholastic Aptitude Test, Total	1034
Student type A (1 if RN, 0 otherwise)	1
Student type B (1 if generic, 0 otherwise)	0

Table 6-3. Several Vectors Describing Five Nursing Students

Percentile Rank in Graduating High-School Class	SAT, verbal	SAT, math	SAT, total	Student Type A	Student Type B
92	514	520	1034	1	0
91	520	510	1030	1	0
99	600	590	1190	0	1
92	580	560	1140	0	1
87	500	510	1010	1	0

Table 6-4. Nursing Students Expressed as Six Vectors

$$A = \begin{bmatrix} 92 \\ 91 \\ 99 \\ 92 \\ 87 \end{bmatrix} \quad B = \begin{bmatrix} 514 \\ 520 \\ 600 \\ 580 \\ 500 \end{bmatrix} \quad C = \begin{bmatrix} 520 \\ 510 \\ 590 \\ 560 \\ 510 \end{bmatrix} \quad D = \begin{bmatrix} 1034 \\ 1030 \\ 1190 \\ 1140 \\ 1010 \end{bmatrix} \quad E = \begin{bmatrix} 1 \\ 1 \\ 0 \\ 0 \\ 1 \end{bmatrix} \quad F = \begin{bmatrix} 0 \\ 0 \\ 1 \\ 1 \\ 0 \end{bmatrix}$$

notation is a convenient technique to define continuous variables (test scores, ratings, and so on) and categorical or mutually exclusive variables (sex, race, and so on). Once the vectors are constructed, they may have the same simple properties of ordinary numbers, i.e., they may be added, subtracted, multiplied, or divided.

RESEARCH DESIGNS FOR COMPUTER OPERATIONS FOR RESEARCH IN NURSING

Often research in nursing requires precise definitions of groups that are mutually exclusive so that observations or measurements may be recorded to but one group, e.g., R.N. student groups vs generic student groups, nursing-student dropouts vs nursing-student graduates, and active vs inactive R.N.s. The basic problem usually is to determine whether or not members of one group are the same as members of a comparative group on selected criteria or predictor variables. When a research problem is concerned with testing differences between groups or predicting certain variables for certain groups, problems can easily be formulated using vector notations of categorical variables in structuring the specific questions to be answered by the developed research models for computer operations.

Applied Multiple Linear Regression

Suppose a problem arises in a baccalaureate school of nursing involving categorical membership in three groups of nurses, including: students with R.N.s from hospital programs, students with associate degrees from community colleges, and students in the basic baccalaureate nursing program.

The question concerning the dean of the school of nursing might be whether or not the students in these three groups are of comparable levels of ability to perform successfully in the Bachelor of Science in Nursing degree program. If we accept the student's cumulative grade-point average (cum GPA) at time of graduation as an index of successful academic performance, we can restate the question more precisely: Do cumulative grade-point averages at time of graduation differ between students with an R.N. diploma, an Associate of Arts (A.A.) degree, or generic students? This question may be answered "yes" or "no" at some significant level, which indicates the preciseness of the investigator's thinking.

The logical implications for the research question is that "on the average" nursing students from one group will achieve higher grades in nursing school than at least one other group. Using the applied multiple linear regression approach, estimates of academic achievement can be computed from knowledge of group assignments, all other things being equal.

Suppose that we randomly select from a graduating class three students who entered the school of nursing with R.N. diplomas, two from community colleges with A.A. degrees, and four students who entered nursing school the first year without an R.N. diploma or A.A. degree. The vector notation for cum GPAs of the nursing students can be represented by vector Y, of dimension N, where N is the number of cum GPA scores:

$$Y = \begin{bmatrix} y_1 \\ y_2 \\ \cdot \\ \cdot \\ \cdot \\ y_n \end{bmatrix}$$

where

y_1 = cum GPA for nursing student 1
y_2 = cum GPA for nursing student 2

.   .   .   .

.   .   .   .

.   .   .   .

y_n = cum GPA for nursing student n

Next vector notations for group membership can be defined:

X_1 = vector in which the element is a 1 if the corresponding cum GPA element in Y comes from a nursing student with an R.N. diploma, and 0 if the cum GPA comes from a nursing student without an R.N. degree

X_2 = vector in which the element is a 1 if the corresponding cum GPA element in Y comes from a nursing student with an A.A. degree, and 0 if the cum GPA in Y comes from a nursing student without an A.A. degree

X_3 = vector in which the element is a 1 if the corresponding cum GPA element in Y comes from a generic nursing student, and 0 if the cum GPA in Y comes from a nursing student with an R.N. diploma or A.A. degree

In order to predict vector Y from X_1, X_2, and X_3, a linear combination of a set of vectors may be obtained by multiplying each vector X by a constant a_i and summing the products to obtain S, a predicted cum GPA: $S = a_1 X_1 + a_2 X_2 + a_3 X_3$, where a_1, a_2, and a_3 are undetermined at this point.

$$S = \begin{bmatrix} s_1 \\ s_2 \\ s_3 \\ s_4 \\ s_5 \\ s_6 \\ s_7 \\ s_8 \\ s_9 \end{bmatrix} = a_1 \begin{bmatrix} 1 \\ 1 \\ 1 \\ 0 \\ 0 \\ 0 \\ 0 \\ 0 \\ 0 \end{bmatrix} + a_2 \begin{bmatrix} 0 \\ 0 \\ 0 \\ 1 \\ 1 \\ 0 \\ 0 \\ 0 \\ 0 \end{bmatrix} + a_3 \begin{bmatrix} 0 \\ 0 \\ 0 \\ 0 \\ 0 \\ 1 \\ 1 \\ 1 \\ 1 \end{bmatrix} = \begin{bmatrix} a_1 \\ a_1 \\ a_1 \\ a_2 \\ a_2 \\ a_3 \\ a_3 \\ a_3 \\ a_3 \end{bmatrix}$$

Since the cum GPAs of the nursing students in the three groups are not identical, there will be differences between the observed and the predicted cum GPAs of the nursing students. If we call the variance between the observed and predicted scores residual vector E, then discrepancies may be expressed as: $E = Y - S = Y - [a_1 X_1 + a_2 X_2 + a_3 X_3]$. Then, $Y = S + E = [a_1 X_1 + a_2 X_2 + a_3 X_3] + E$.

$$\begin{array}{ccccc} Y & X_1 & X_2 & X_3 \\ \begin{bmatrix} 2.2 \\ 2.1 \\ 2.0 \\ 2.3 \\ 2.5 \\ 2.7 \\ 3.2 \\ 3.2 \\ 2.9 \end{bmatrix} = a_1 & \begin{bmatrix} 1 \\ 1 \\ 1 \\ 0 \\ 0 \\ 0 \\ 0 \\ 0 \\ 0 \end{bmatrix} + a_2 & \begin{bmatrix} 0 \\ 0 \\ 0 \\ 1 \\ 1 \\ 0 \\ 0 \\ 0 \\ 0 \end{bmatrix} + a_3 & \begin{bmatrix} 0 \\ 0 \\ 0 \\ 0 \\ 0 \\ 1 \\ 1 \\ 1 \\ 1 \end{bmatrix} + E \end{array}$$

Since the nursing students in X_1 did not have equal cum GPAs at the time of graduation from nursing school, there is no a_1 that will contribute to making a linear combination true. The same is also true for the nursing students in X_2 and X_3. If groups X_1, X_2, and X_3 were a true linear combination of criterion Y, a perfect prediction could be made using knowledge of group membership.

Since a perfect linear combination does not exist, we can construct a new vector (E_1) that, when combined with X_1, X_2, and X_3, will make the criterion vector Y a linear combination of the four vectors, namely: $Y = a_1 X_1 + a_2 X_2 + a_3 X_3 + E_1$.

In order to satisfy the equality conditions in this formula, E_1 would be the difference between the observed cum GPA of each nursing student and the weight associated with each student's group. In the weight to be assigned to each group which minimizes the squared values of vector E_1, the criterion mean for the particular group is best:

$$
\begin{array}{ccccc}
Y_1 & X_1 & X_2 & X_3 & E_1 \\
\begin{bmatrix} 2.2 \\ 2.1 \\ 2.0 \\ 2.3 \\ 2.5 \\ 2.7 \\ 3.2 \\ 3.2 \\ 2.9 \end{bmatrix}
= 2.1
\begin{bmatrix} 1 \\ 1 \\ 1 \\ 0 \\ 0 \\ 0 \\ 0 \\ 0 \\ 0 \end{bmatrix}
+ 2.4
\begin{bmatrix} 0 \\ 0 \\ 0 \\ 1 \\ 1 \\ 0 \\ 0 \\ 0 \\ 0 \end{bmatrix}
+ 3.0
\begin{bmatrix} 0 \\ 0 \\ 0 \\ 0 \\ 0 \\ 1 \\ 1 \\ 1 \\ 1 \end{bmatrix}
+
\begin{bmatrix} .1 \\ 0 \\ -.1 \\ -.1 \\ .1 \\ -.3 \\ .2 \\ .2 \\ -.1 \end{bmatrix}
\end{array}
$$

The "least-squares weights" give the minimal sum of the squared values of the E_1 vector. The sum of the squared values of the elements in E_1 is called the "error sum of squares" (ESS). The linear combination of nursing groups that will give the most accurate prediction of Y is $Y = a'_1 X_1 + a'_2 X_2 + a'_3 X_3$ where a'_1, a'_2, and a'_3 are least-squares weights.

The ESS values will be denoted hereafter as the letter q with appropriate subscripts, i.e., q_1, q_2, q_3.

The q_1 for the example shown can be described by: $q_1 = (.1)^2 + (0)^2 + (-.1)^2 + (-.1)^2 + (-.3)^2 + (.2)^2 + (.2)^2 + (-.1)^2 = .22$.

In order to test the hypothesis that there is no significant difference among the three nursing groups, we assume that our sample represents, on the average, the cum GPA performance of the population, other things being equal.

If there are no differences in cum GPAs of the three groups of nursing students, then $a_1 = a_2 = a_3 = a_c$, *where* a_c = weight to be used for all three nursing group vectors, a constant.

If we designate a vector T in which the actual cum GPA scores in vector Y are to be estimated, then T would be expressed as a linear combination of the three group vectors X_1, X_2, and X_3, i.e., $T = a_c X_1 + a_c X_2 + a_c X_3 = a_c(X_1 + X_2 + X_3)$.

Since each nursing student is in only one group, then

$$X_1 + X_2 + X_3 = \begin{bmatrix} 1 \\ 1 \\ 1 \\ 1 \\ 1 \\ 1 \\ 1 \\ 1 \\ 1 \end{bmatrix}$$

If we define this vector as U, the unit vector in which each element is a 1, with a dimension of nine elements, then vector T becomes $T = a_c U = a_c(1)$.

If no differences exist between the three nursing groups, all of the elements of T will be equal to Y. The elements of Y will differ from T whatever the value of a_c, $T \neq Y$. The differences between T and Y can be defined as vector D, in which $D = Y - T = Y - a_c U$, and $Y = T + D = a_c U + D$.

In a similar fashion to minimize the sum of squares of vector E_1, the logical choice for a value of a_c is one which will minimize the sum of squares for the element of vector D. The least-squares procedure will be used to find the value of a_c that minimizes q_2, the error sum of squares associated with vector D.

The values of the elements in the residual vector D and the error sum of squares q_2 are computed in the same manner as before, namely: $D = Y - a_c U$.

$$D = \begin{bmatrix} 2.2 \\ 2.1 \\ 2.0 \\ 2.3 \\ 2.5 \\ 2.7 \\ 3.2 \\ 3.2 \\ 2.9 \end{bmatrix} - 2.6 \begin{bmatrix} 1 \\ 1 \\ 1 \\ 1 \\ 1 \\ 1 \\ 1 \\ 1 \\ 1 \end{bmatrix} = \begin{bmatrix} -.4 \\ -.5 \\ -.6 \\ -.3 \\ -.1 \\ .1 \\ .6 \\ .6 \\ .3 \end{bmatrix}$$

The mean for Y, 2.566, rounded to nearest tenth is 2.6. Computation of q_2 total error sum of squares is:

$$q_2 = (-.4)^2 + (-.5)^2 + (-.6)^2 + (-.3)^2$$
$$+ (-.1)^2 + (.1)^2 + (.6)^2$$
$$+ (.6)^2 + (.3)^2$$
$$q_2 = 1.69$$

Now we are able to answer the hypothesis that no differences in cum GPAs exist among the three groups of nursing students. The error sum of squares q_1 denotes between-group variance, and q_2 denotes the total variance of all of the nursing students in the sample.

The F statistic is a method to test for the difference among means of two or more groups. The computation of the F value from the error sum of squares is:

$$F = \frac{(q_2 - q_1)/df_1}{q_1/df_2}$$

The F statistic is Snedecor's F ratio commonly used with analysis of variance techniques, in which:

q_1 = minimized error sum of squares obtained from an attempt to express the observed values in vector Y as a linear combination of an unrestricted set of predictors

q_2 = minimized error sum of squares obtained from an attempt to express observed values in vector Y as a linear combination of a restricted set of predictors that express an hypothesis

df_1 = a number related to (and sometimes equal to) the difference between the number of unknown parameters to be estimated in the unrestricted linear combination and the number of unknown parameters in the restricted linear combination. In this example the number of unknown parameters to be estimated in the unrestricted linear combination was three (X_1, X_2, and X_3), and the number of unknown parameters in the restricted linear combination was one (U, the unit vector); $df_1 = 3 - 1 = 2$

df_2 = a number related to (and sometimes equal to) the difference between the number of elements in the vectors, i.e., sample points, and the number of unknown parameters to be estimated in the unrestricted linear combination. In this example the number of elements in the vectors was nine (sample points), and the number of unknown parameters to be estimated in the unrestricted linear combination was three $(X_1, X_2,$ and $X_3)$; $df_2 = 9 - 3 = 6$

Therefore:

$$f = \frac{(1.69 - 0.22)\ /2}{0.22\ /6}$$

$$= \frac{1.47\ /2}{0.22\ /6} = \frac{.74}{.037} = 20$$

$F = 20$

An F ratio of 20 with $df_1 = 2$ and $df_2 = 6$ is significant beyond the .01 level. This indicates that there is a significant difference among the three groups of nursing students in relation to academic performance at time of graduation (Table 6-5).

The mean for Group 1 is $(2.2 + 2.1 + 2.0)\ /3 = 2.1$
The mean for Group 2 is $(2.3 + 2.5)\ /2 = 2.4$
The mean for Group 3 is $(2.7 + 3.2 + 3.2 + 2.9)\ /4 = 3.0$
The total mean is $(2.2 + 2.1 + 2.0 + 2.3 + 2.5 + 2.7 + 3.2 + 3.2$
$+ 2.9)\ /9 = 2.6$

To check for significant differences between the three means, the F statistic provides a measure to indicate how frequently the observed differences are likely to occur:

$$F = \frac{\text{Observed variance of group means}/df_1}{\text{Expected chance variance of group means}/df_2}$$

Table 6-5. Example Expressed in Traditional Analysis of Variance Design

Group	Mean
1 = 2.2	G1 = 2.1
2.1	
2.0	
2 = 2.3	G2 = 2.4
2.5	
3 = 2.7	G3 = 3.0
3.2	
3.2	
2.9	
	Total Mean = 2.6

To calculate the observed variance of group means, the total mean is subtracted from each group mean and the mean difference is weighed by the number of observations in each group and summed (Table 6-6).

The total variations squared (SS_a) = 1.47. The sum of squares (SS_a) divided by the number of subjects $(N = 9)$ from which the sum of squares was derived is the among-group variance or observed-group variance:

$$SS_a/N = \text{among-group variance} =$$
$$SD_a^2 = 1.47/9 = .16$$
$$SD_a^2 = .16 \text{ observed variance of group means}$$

The *expected chance variance of the group means* is calculated by subtracting each subject's group mean from his score.

The sum of the squared deviations $(X-\overline{X})^2$ = .22 and is called the sum of squares within groups (SS_w) (Table 6-7). The within-group variance is derived by $SS_w/N = .22/9 = 0.24 = SD_w^2$.

Table 6-6. Sum of Squares Among Groups

Group	Subject	$(\overline{X}_G - \overline{X}_T)$	$(\overline{X}_G - \overline{X}_T)$	$(\overline{X}_G - \overline{X}_T)^2$
1	1	2.1–2.6	−.5	.25
	2	2.1–2.6	−.5	.25
	3	2.1–2.6	−.5	.25
2	1	2.4–2.6	−.2	.04
	2	2.4–2.6	−.2	.04
3	1	3.0–2.6	.4	.16
	2	3.0–2.6	.4	.16
	3	3.0–2.6	.4	.16
	4	3.0–2.6	.4	.16
				1.47

Table 6-7. Sum of Squares Within Groups

Group	Subject	$(X - \overline{X})$		$(X - \overline{X})$	$(X - \overline{X})^2$
1	2.2	(2.2–2.1)	=	.1	.01
	2.1	(2.1–2.1)	=	.0	.00
	2.0	(2.0–2.1)	=	−.1	.01
2	2.3	(2.3–2.4)	=	−.1	.01
	2.5	(2.5–2.4)	=	.1	.01
3	2.7	(2.7–3.0)	=	−.3	.09
	3.2	(3.2–3.0)	=	.2	.04
	3.2	(3.2–3.0)	=	.2	.04
	2.9	(2.9–3.0)	=	−.1	.01
					.22

The degree of freedom of the observed variance of group means (df_1) is 3–1 or 2. The degrees of freedom for the expected chance variance of the groups (df_2) is $(3 - 1) + (2 - 1) + (4 - 1)$ or 6. The total degrees of freedom $= df_1 + df_2 = 2 + 6 = 8$, or the total observations minus 1 $(N - 1 = 9 - 1 = 8)$.

Given the SD_a^2, SD_w^2, df_1 and df_2, the F ratio is calculated as follows:

$$F = \frac{(SD_a^2)/df_1}{SD_w^2/df_2} = \frac{.16/2}{.024/6} = \frac{.08}{.004}$$

$F = 20$

The degrees of freedom are used to determine whether or not an F of 20 can be attributed to chance. By checking an F Table with 2 and 6 degrees of freedom, we find that an F of 20 or larger would be expected less than one time in 100 owing to chance alone [4]. We can conclude then that the group means of 2.1, 2.4, and 3.0 are significantly different. It appears that the generic students (Group 3) achieved significantly better results than the nursing students with an R.N. diploma (Group 1). Additional checks would have to be conducted to determine whether or not Group 3 achieved significantly higher results than Group 1.

The traditional analysis of variance table is shown in Table 6-8. The procedures involved in checking for significant mean differences between the applied multiple linear regression approach and the traditional analysis of variance approach can be revealed very easily. The squared deviations of the scores from the total mean $(\overline{X}_t)$ is

Table 6-8. Traditional Analysis of Variance Table

Source	SS	d.f.	MS	F
Between (among)	1.47	2	.74	20.00
Within	.22	6	.037	
Total	1.69	8		

defined as the total variance $(SD_t{}^2)$. In Table 6-8 the total variance was computed to be 1.69, using the regression approach. In Tables 6-6 and 7 using the traditional analysis of variance approach, the sum of squares among group means was 1.47, and the sum of squares within groups was .22, or a total variance of 1.69. Additional checks show that the F-ratios will be the same, computed by the two procedures.

The simple example of determining whether or not knowledge of groups can account for greater significant mean differences than would be expected by chance alone by the regression approach and the traditional analysis of variance approach shows how the computational results are the same. The applied multiple regression approach, however, provides greater flexibility in conceptualizing complex research problems for research in nursing.

REGRESSION MODELS USING CONTINUOUS PREDICTORS

To this point the regression models discussed were concerned with formulating and analyzing problems that tested differences between groups or categorical vectors. This approach revealed that knowledge of group membership can be used to improve the accuracy with which observed criterion scores are estimated. Oftentimes an investigator raises questions or hypotheses which take into account the influence of several continuous variables, i.e., which have more than two values such as "1" and "0" and which may be expressed as integral numbers or decimals.

Nursing schools are usually concerned about their admission policies. Predicting cumulative grade-point averages (cum GPA) after the first academic year is a frequent practice to test how successfully admission requirements have served to select entering students. To predict cum GPA at the end of the first year for a group of nursing students using selected admissions data as continuous predictors, the multiple linear regression approach allows an investigator to develop an efficient predictor system. By this approach each criterion variable is considered in relation to the set of predictor variables to establish different levels of values observed for each predictor.

Suppose a nursing school has questioned its admission requirements and desires to know how the requirements influence the
first year cum GPA of first year students. The full, or unrestricted
model, would be as follows:

$$Y = a_o U + a_1 X_1 + a_2 X_2 + \ldots + a_n X_n + E_1,$$

where

Y = cum GPA at the end of the first year in nursing school

a_o = the regression constant, Y intercept, when multiplied by U

U = Unit vector

$a_1 \ldots n$ = partial regression weights calculated so as to minimize
the sum of the squared elements in E_1

$X_1 \ldots n$ = vectors in which the elements are the scores or data
from admission records corresponding to the first year
cum GPA for each student

E_1 = a vector the elements of which are the difference
between the observed cum GPA and the predicted
cum GPA $(Y - \overline{Y})$

Using the formula, one can find the line of best fit so that the
sum of the squared deviations of the predictor variables are minimal.
This means that the symmetry of the distance between the cum GPA
scores and the predictor variable scores allows a straight line to be
the case which fits the midpoint of all the score distributions. This
reasoning is based on the equation for a straight line $Y = a + bx$,
where b is the slope of a straight line between pairs of scores which
have minimal differences of *total variance,* and a is the Y-intercept
(Figure 6-1).

Continuing with the example, let us suppose that 10 nursing students were randomly selected to be included for the analysis and

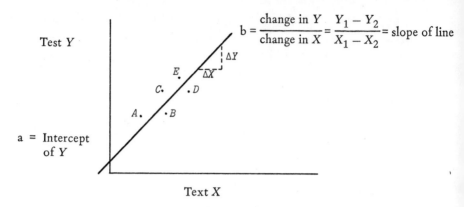

Fig. 6-1. Line of best fit between scores recorded on tests by five students.

had the records shown in Table 6-9. The research question raised would be: "Can knowledge of the percentile rank in graduating high school class help account for successful completion of the nursing program?"

The regression equation would be: $Y = a_0 U + a_1 X_1 + E_1$;

where

Y = observed cum GPA at time of graduation from nursing school

X_1 = a vector in which the elements are the percentile rank scores in graduating high school class which correspond to the cum GPAs of the criterion measure

U = the unit vector

a_0 = the regression constant, when multiplied by U

a_1 = partial regression weight computed to minimize the sum of the elements in E_1

E_1 = a vector the elements of which are the difference between the observed cum GPA and the predicted GPA

198 Models for Data Analysis

Table 6-9. Random Inclusion of 10 Nursing Students for Analysis

Students	Cum GPA at Graduation from Nursing School	Percentile Rank in Graduating High-School Class
A	1.8	54
B	2.1	63
C	2.2	78
D	2.4	83
E	2.6	96
F	2.2	56
G	2.6	60
H	2.9	77
I	3.2	83
J	3.4	90

The vector representation of these data is as follows:

$$
\begin{matrix} Y & & U & & X_1 \end{matrix}
$$

$$
\begin{bmatrix} 1.8 \\ 2.1 \\ 2.2 \\ 2.4 \\ 2.6 \\ 2.2 \\ 2.6 \\ 2.9 \\ 3.2 \\ 3.4 \end{bmatrix} = a_o \begin{bmatrix} 1 \\ 1 \\ 1 \\ 1 \\ 1 \\ 1 \\ 1 \\ 1 \\ 1 \\ 1 \end{bmatrix} + a_1 \begin{bmatrix} 54 \\ 63 \\ 78 \\ 83 \\ 96 \\ 56 \\ 60 \\ 77 \\ 83 \\ 90 \end{bmatrix} + E_1
$$

Computing for the values of a and b, which correspond to a_o and a, respectively, by the traditional routine:

$$
b = \frac{\Sigma XY - [(\Sigma X)\,(\Sigma Y)/N]}{\Sigma X^2 - \dfrac{(\Sigma X)^2}{N}}
$$

$$a = \overline{Y} - b\overline{X}$$

$$b = .02$$

$$a = 1.06$$

Given the values of a and b, the predicted cum GPA can be derived for each student from the regression model, as:

$$Y = a_o U + a_1 X_1 + E_1,$$

where

$$a_o = a = 1.06$$

$$a_1 = b = .02$$

$$Y = 1.06U + .02X_1 + E_1$$

Using the regression equation, the values of E_1 can be derived. The vector representation of these data would appear as:

Y		U		X_1		E_1
$\begin{bmatrix} 1.8 \\ 2.1 \\ 2.2 \\ 2.4 \\ 2.6 \\ 2.2 \\ 2.6 \\ 2.9 \\ 3.2 \\ 3.4 \end{bmatrix}$	$= 1.07$	$\begin{bmatrix} 1 \\ 1 \\ 1 \\ 1 \\ 1 \\ 1 \\ 1 \\ 1 \\ 1 \\ 1 \end{bmatrix}$	$+ .02$	$\begin{bmatrix} 54 \\ 63 \\ 78 \\ 83 \\ 96 \\ 56 \\ 60 \\ 77 \\ 83 \\ 90 \end{bmatrix}$	$+$	$\begin{bmatrix} -.35 \\ -.23 \\ -.43 \\ -.33 \\ -.39 \\ .01 \\ .33 \\ .29 \\ .47 \\ .53 \end{bmatrix}$

The sum of the values squared in E_1 is 1.32. The sum of $(E_1)^2$ is the within variance (SS_w) in an analysis of variance design. This variance can be attributed to the error sum of squares with knowledge of group membership of percentile rank in graduating high-school class.

When a restricted regression model is set up without knowledge of group membership of percentile rank in graduating high-school class, a new error sum of squares can be derived and used for SS_t.

If group membership in vector X_1 is not known, then $a_1 = 0$. Therefore the regression equation would be: $Y = a_o U + a_1 X_1 + E_2$, when $a_1 = 0$. Then $Y = a_o U + E_2$.

The weight assigned to a_o is that value which minimizes the sum of the difference between the observed cum GPA and the predicted cum GPA (E_2). This value is the grand mean of Y or 2.54.

The vector representation of these data in a restricted model and the sum of the squared elements in E_2 are:

Y	U	E_2	$(E_2)^2$
1.8	1	−.74	.55
2.1	1	−.44	.19
2.2	1	−.34	.12
2.4	1	−.14	.02
2.6	1	.06	.00
2.2	1	−.34	.12
2.6	1	.06	.00
2.9	1	.36	.13
3.2	1	.66	.44
3.4	1	.86	.74

with $U = 2.54$.

The sum of $(E_2)^2$ is 2.31.

The F ratio can be computed to determine if knowledge of group membership in X_1 is significant to consider for predicting cum GPA at time of graduation from nursing school:

$$F = \frac{(q_2 - q_1)/df_1}{q_1/df_2}$$

where

$$q_2 = \Sigma(E_{2_i})^2 = 2.31$$

$$q_1 = \Sigma(E_{ij})^2 = 1.32$$

$$df_1 = 2 - 1 = 1$$

$$df_2 = N - 2 = 10 - 2 = 8$$

$$F = \frac{(2.31 - 1.32)/1}{1.32/8} = \frac{.99}{.165} = 6.00$$

With one and eight degrees of freedom, an F of 6.00 would be expected to occur by chance alone less than five times in 100. In other words knowledge of group memberships of percentile rank scores in graduating high-school class is significant when predicting cum GPA at time of graduation from nursing school.

Obviously predicting cum GPA at time of graduating from nursing school would be improved by including other predictor variables in addition to percentile rank in graduating high-school class. The applied multiple linear regression approach allows an investigator to develop a prediction system. The prediction system considers individual predictors with the criterion vector in relation to other predictor vectors which improve the efficiency or reliability of the regression equation.

Suppose a nursing school is concerned about improving its admission procedures to increase the probability that entering students will successfully complete the academic program. The elements in the criterion vector, Y, include cum GPAs at time of graduation from the nursing school of a selected class or classes. Continuous predictor variables selected to be considered in the prediction system include: (1) percentile rank in graduating high-school class, (2) SAT verbal scores, (3) SAT mathematics scores, (4) SAT total scores, and (5) size of graduating high-school class.

The unrestricted or full model expresses Y in a linear combination as:

$$Y = a_0 U + a_1 X_1 + a_2 X_2 + a_3 X_3 + a_4 X_4 + a_5 X_5 + E,$$

where

Y = a vector containing cum GPAs for each nursing graduate

X_1 = a vector in which the elements are the recording of percentile rank in graduating high-school class corresponding to the criterion cum GPA score

X_2 = a vector in which the elements are the score on the SAT verbal test corresponding to the score of the criterion cum GPA

X_3 = a vector in which the elements are the score on the SAT mathematics test corresponding to the score of the criterion cum GPA

X_4 = a vector in which the elements are the score on the SAT total test corresponding to the score of the criterion cum GPA

X_5 = a vector in which the elements are the recording of size of high-school class corresponding with the score on the criterion cum GPA

E = residual vector resulting from use of the full model to estimate observed values of vector Y.

Values for vector E are obtained from the least-squares estimates of the unknown parameters in the regression equation. The values of E are used as the basis for obtaining the value of q_1, i.e., $q_1 = (E_1)^2 + (E_2)^2 + \ldots (E_n)^2$.

The investigator suspects that vector X_4 (SAT total) does not make a significant contribution to the prediction system. This hypothesis can be expressed as $X_4 = 0$ in the regression model. The restricted model to test for this restriction would be $Y = a_0 U + a_1 X_1 + a_2 X_2 + a_3 X_3 + a_5 X_5 + G$, where:

G = residual vector resulting from the use of the restricted model to predict the values in vector Y

The sum of the values obtained in G may be expressed as q_2. Now the hypothesis to test for the significant influence of vector X_4 in the prediction system can be determined by

$$F = \frac{(q_2 - q_1)/df_1}{q_1/df_2}$$

where

$$q_1 = (E_1)^2 + (E_2)^2 + \ldots (E_n)^2$$

$$q_2 = (G_1)^2 + (G_2)^2 + \ldots (G_n)^2$$

df_1 = The difference between the number of unknown parameters in the full or unrestricted linear combination and the number of unknown parameters in the restricted linear combination used to predict values in vector Y. In this problem the number of unknown parameters in the full model was 5, and the number of unknown parameters in the restricted model was 4

df_2 = $N - 2$, the difference between the dimension of the vectors and the number of unknown parameters in the unrestricted model

A versatile and robust feature of the regression analysis approach can be used at this point to examine the significance of individual predictor variables with the criterion. A systematic stepwise addition of the predictor variables in the regression equation will reveal the variance accounted for by any array of predictor variables in the regression model. The variance accounted for in Y by the predictor variables can be shown by changes in the multiple correlation coefficient squared, R^2. Testing preliminary hypotheses concerned with significant relationships between the predictor variables and the criterion allows an investigator to identify variables to be considered for more sophisticated research experiments.

The examples to depict the use of the applied multiple linear regression approach to develop prediction models or systems were briefly presented at an elementary level. The approach allows for checks on interaction effects if the investigator suspects that the predictor variables are functionally related. The prediction system may also consist of combinations of categorical and continuous vectors. The flexibility to test the complete conceptualizations of a research problem by linear combinations of categorical and continuous variables is one of the basic strengths of the applied multiple linear regression approach.

REGRESSION MODELS IN CLINICAL RESEARCH IN NURSING

Clinical research in nursing may be enhanced by using the applied multiple linear regression approach. So often in clinical nursing research the investigator is simply overwhelmed by the lack of control over a large number of variables which are functionally related in changes of patients' behaviors with nursing care. The strength of using the applied multiple linear regression approach with computer resources enables an investigator of clinical-nursing practice to control many and varied influences of the research project.

Suppose an investigator were interested in studying the influence of selected variables on patients with *decubitus ulcers*. The investigator seeks significant relationships between the development of decubitus ulcers by hospitalized patients and certain patient variables that are associated with the ulcers. Some patient variables that can be controlled by binary codes (1 and 0) may include a "diagnostic category,"

where

X_{11} = a vector in which the elements are 1 if arteriosclerotic heart disease, 0 otherwise

X_{12} = a vector in which the elements are 1 if coronary-myocardial infarction, 0 otherwise

X_{13} = a vector in which the elements are 1 if hypertension, 0 otherwise

$$X_{1_n}$$

Other categorical vectors may be set up to control diagnostic categories of neurology-neurosurgery, orthopedic-trauma, nutritional and metabolic disease, general surgery, and general medicine.

Categorical vectors can also be defined to control data concerning patient's diet, appetite, intake-output, mental state, type of position change, and the like. Even medical regimen can be controlled by categorical vector notation as:

X_{21} = a vector in which the elements are 1 if vitamin therapy, 0 otherwise

X_{22} = a vector in which the elements are 1 if hormone therapy, 0 otherwise

X_{23} = a vector in which the elements are 1 if antibiotic therapy, 0 otherwise

$$X_{2_n}$$

The decubitus ulcer can be described by categorical and continuous vectors. A few examples would be:

Location of lesion:

X_{31} = a vector in which the elements are 1 if sacrococcygeal, 0 otherwise

X_{32} = a vector in which the elements are 1 if trochanter, 0 otherwise

X_{33} = a vector in which the elements are 1 if ischial tuberosities, 0 otherwise

.

.

.

X_{3_n}

Drainage of lesion:

X_{41} = a vector in which the elements are 1 if serous, 0 otherwise

X_{42} = a vector in which the elements are 1 if serosanguinous, 0 otherwise

X_{43} = a vector in which the elements are 1 if purulent, 0 otherwise

.

.

.

X_{4_n}

Lesion size:

Y = a vector in which the elements are the lesion size in square
centimeters

A full regression model representing the linear combination of
the predictor variables with lesion size would be:

$$Y = a_o U + a_1 X_{1_i} + \ldots + a_1 X_{1_n} + a_2 X_{2_i} + \ldots + a_2 X_{2_n} + a_3 X_{3_i} +$$

$$\ldots + a_3 X_{3_n} + a_4 X_{4_i} + \ldots + a_4 X_{4_n} + E,$$

where

E = residual vector resulting from use of the full or unrestricted
model to predict vector Y

Restricted models can be set up to test hypotheses of significant
relationships of any of the predictor variables with the vector Y.
Examination for significant changes in the R^2 of each of the unrestricted models with the full model among the unrestricted models
can account for the variance of the criterion under study. Factor
analysis routines can also be conducted to identify groups of variables that associate among themselves as a similar variable.

The uses of the applied multiple linear regression approach in
clinical nursing research has been introductory in nature. The potential of an applied multiple regression approach with computer
resources is unlimited at the present time for research in nursing.

SUMMARY

The shortcomings of traditional research approaches in nursing
by methods of classic parametric and non-parametric statistical
designs can be improved by using an applied multiple linear regression approach. Advantages of using a regression analysis approach
are basically that: (1) the investigator can formulate research problems and test hypotheses in a comprehensive fashion for computer

analysis, (2) underlying normality of the variables is not assumed, and (3) the use of binary codes (1 and 0) enables an investigator to control variables with greater ease than traditional analysis of variance designs.

Similarities between regression analysis and analysis of variance designs were noted. Other applications of the regression approach include factor analysis, cross-validation routines, covariance designs, canonical correlation techniques, and several others.

In short, the multiple regression analysis approach adds preciseness and flexibility to multivariate research studies and is better suited to computer analysis than classic statistical designs. The requirement that investigators delineate precisely research hypotheses before collecting and analyzing data continues to take priority in conducting robust research and using an applied multiple linear regression approach.

REFERENCES

1. Bottenberg, R. A., and Ward, J. H., Jr. *Applied Multiple Linear Regression.* Technical Documentary Report PRL-TDR-63-6. Lackland Air Force Base, Texas, March, 1963.
2. Kelly, F. J., et al. *Research Design in the Behavioral Sciences: Multiple Regression Approach.* Carbondale: Southern Illinois University Press, 1969.
3. Walberg, H. J. Generalized regression models in educational research. *American Educational Research Journal* 8:71–91, 1971.
4. Winer, B. J. *Statistical Principles in Experimental Design.* New York: McGraw-Hill, 1962, pp. 642–647.

Operations Research
John P. Young

7

F ROM an administrative point of view, a health-services facility
may be conceived of as a complex system confronted with a
highly variable flow of patients presenting uneven sets of demands
for care that must be satisfied through the effective mobilization
and allocation of available resources. This kind of conceptualization
is valid whether one is dealing with a vast regional delivery network,
a large medical center, or an individual nursing unit. As the primary
decision-maker within such a system, the health-facility administrator encounters a variety of problems that have defied complete, or
in some instances even satisfactory, solutions. Indeed one can easily
argue that in spite of frequent claims to the contrary, basic organizational structures and procedures have not changed significantly in
response to the many sociological and technological changes of the
twentieth century. This is indirectly evidenced by the ever-rising
costs of care, the chronic shortages of appropriately trained personnel, and the perennial inadequacy of physical plant.

Problems related to the allocation of resources, especially while
maintaining at least an adequate level of quality of care, have
plagued health-services administrators for decades. Some have been
dealt with satisfactorily by capable persons, many of whom have
been physicians or nurses with little or no formal training in management techniques. But, with health-delivery organizations becoming

increasingly complex, the modern administrator needs more than experience and intuitive judgment on which to base decisions; he must have available a sound quantitative basis for the evaluation of the risks and outcomes involved in choosing from among many possible alternative courses of action.

Recently there has been increased emphasis on the application of "operations research" techniques to cope with a variety of problems in the health-services delivery process — problems involving both the organization for and the provision of care. For that matter a considerable amount of operations research has already been conducted during the past decade on problems of facilities utilization, delivery of nursing care, manpower allocation, and therapeutic strategies [42]. Simultaneously there has been the growth of an almost overwhelming interest in the development of management-information systems, reflecting the increased capabilities made available through the introduction of computer technology.

It is perhaps inevitable that the rapidly expanding use of operations research approaches and methodologies has been accompanied by occasional, but unfortunately rather extravagant, claims as to their capacity for solving health-oriented problems, derived largely from past successes in military and industrial areas. This has resulted in frequent confusion as to the nature of operations research — its purpose, potential, and limitations — with resultant disillusionment when clearly implementable results were not apparent.

The purpose of this discussion is to introduce the reader to operations research as a valuable technique for the study of problems involving decision-making in the health services. Emphasis will necessarily be placed on the history and philosophy of operations research, the conceptual framework of various approaches to decision problems, recurrent system phenomena, and the appropriate models. The general aim is to familiarize the reader sufficiently so as to enable him to recognize those instances wherein the application of operations research might be of assistance in decision-making — whether the reader is an administrator or someone engaged in research. This discussion, however, does not come without caveat; in the interests of ideational clarity no assumptions are made as to mathematical sophistication. This means that both models and examples necessarily are unrealistically simplified and cannot, therefore, represent fully the kinds of analytical efforts applicable to any real-world problem.

OPERATIONS RESEARCH

Definition

Defining operations research is not an easy matter. This is especially so when such terms as management science, administrative science, systems analysis, or systems engineering are often used interchangeably with operations research. Indeed one discovers rather quickly that definitions are as ubiquitous as practitioners and tend to vary with the background and experience of the particular practitioner. Operations researchers are often looked on as industrial engineers, statisticians, applied mathematicians, computerniks, and on occasion, social scientists — an assignment that includes economists and social organization theorists. Although operations research is, in fact, none of the foregoing as such, nevertheless the discipline to some degree includes all of them and more, as will become apparent.

Since a formal definition at this point is desirable, a reasonably well-accepted one is: "Operations research is the rigorous application of quantitative scientific techniques, by persons from a variety of disciplinary backgrounds, to the study of the basic laws governing the operation of a human organization or system. Its purpose is to provide a basis for predicting quantitatively the results of actions taken under given sets of variable conditions, thereby enabling the prescription of decisions leading to optimal operational effectiveness."

Perhaps the two most significant words in this definition are "operations" and "decisions." Operations research, as opposed to most physical, biological, or behavioral research, focuses on decision-making in the operation of human organizations. The primary reason for conducting operations research is to bring about the more efficient and effective management of an organization while achieving its goals and objectives. The activity is motivated by the fact that decisions must be made, i.e., courses of action must be selected from among many alternatives. These decisions, moreover, must often be made under conditions of uncertainty or risk and with every likelihood of conflicting outcomes. The problem, essentially, is to seek the best or optimal course of action by using available and appropriate scientific methodology to evaluate alternative decisions and their outcomes.

Another very real distinction implied in the definition of operations research is the use of the methodology for prescriptive rather than for merely descriptive or even predictive research. As will become clear later in this discussion, many of the models developed by the operations research analyst to study a system are capable of being manipulated so as to indicate explicitly the decisions to be made.

Finally, to avoid any residual misunderstanding it becomes useful to examine more closely some of the other names frequently applied to operations research. As noted earlier, they are often used interchangeably and sometimes incorrectly, although one may question whether or not any serious harm is done. If distinctions are to be made, systems analysis is usually thought of as an activity largely concerned with the study of physical systems, despite the fact that human components may be involved. Examples include aerospace systems or complex computer information storage and retrieval systems. Systems engineering is closely associated with systems analysis but tends to emphasize the actual design and development of a predominantly hardware system.

Operations research, on the other hand, focuses primarily on the human component in the systems studied and relies heavily on theoretical or mathematical analysis as a basis for decision and control. Similarly management science and administrative science depend largely on quantitative approaches to human organizations and their operations — but with significant behavioral science aspects. As a concrete example, the development of a health-services management—information computer system might require the efforts of systems analysts or systems engineers, whereas the decision-making framework within which the information system is to operate and the synthesis of the flow of information into forms that prescribe action to be taken is the concern of the operations analyst. These distinctions are, obviously, not hard and fast and tend to become fuzzy as disciplinary lines are crossed in practical applications.

Characteristics

Rather than to try to define operations research more specifically, it may be of greater value and interest to examine briefly some of the characteristics of the activity — characteristics that are simultaneously similar to and yet different from other kinds of research.

As noted earlier, operations research is concerned with the analysis and synthesis of large organizations and systems. The research emphasis tends to be placed on the operation of the total system, in so far as possible, and the manner in which the goals and objectives of the system are achieved. This means that the research must take into account the often-conflicting aims of the various functional subdivisions of an organization. One may, of course, approach complex organizational problems by first studying components of the system, as, e.g., has been done in studying nursing-unit staffing in hospitals, admissions procedures, or clinic operations. Prescriptive action in such instances may be termed "suboptimal" in that maximizing effectiveness for a component of a system may not necessarily improve the effectiveness of the organization as a whole. In other words suboptimization occurs when the objectives of the total system have not been taken explicitly into account.

In general, however, one is interested ultimately in the manner in which the actions taken by the components affect the operation of the overall system. Optimization is the term often applied when total organizational effectiveness is maximized, it being recognized that when this is done, component effectiveness may not necessarily be maximized. In practice, optimization is rarely achieved. Difficulties related to the determination of objectives, availability of data, incomplete knowledge of possible alternatives, and political constraints enable, at best, the selection of courses of action that lead to operational improvements but seldom to a complete textbook-like solution of a problem.

A second major characteristic of operations research is the use of the multidisciplinary team approach. Although this concept is no longer novel and has indeed been somewhat traditional in health research, operations research, as opposed to many other kinds of research, early recognized that organizational problems are necessarily broad. Such problems clearly involve physical, behavioral, economic, and probabilistic aspects. They therefore demand the efforts of a mixed team, each member bringing his own discipline and background to bear. Until recently the majority of operations research practitioners were trained in disciplines other than operations research. This accounts for the diverse definitions that are currently extant; definitions tend to reflect the team-member's particular background and those aspects of research problems with which he is concerned. However, over the years operations research has drawn upon methodologies, theory, and quantitative techniques from many different disciplines. These have been modified, reshaped, and added to, thereby extending theoretical frontiers toward a discipline in its own right.

A third major characteristic of operations research is the orientation toward determining the significant underlying phenomena governing the operation of a system. Once they are identified, an attempt is made to abstract the operation of a system in the form of a model. Many different kinds of models may be used, depending on the problems being studied. The least frequently used, perhaps, are iconic models, which include pictures, sculpture, or scale models; such models closely resemble what they represent. More often an operations researcher employs an analogue model, which includes maps, graphs, charts, and most importantly computer simulations. Here, the original system is represented by substituting a transformation according to rigorous rules. Finally symbolic models may be used in which the operational effectiveness of a system is usually given in terms of one or more mathematical equations.

There is little doubt that symbolic models have proven to be the most powerful analytical tool in conducting operations research. Predominantly human systems are influenced strongly by natural laws that are known to produce almost identical behavior in systems of inert material, and many of the mathematical equations used to describe physical phenomena can also be used to describe organizational phenomena. It follows that one is frequently able to abstract the essence of the operations of a system in the form of a mathematical model. Symbolically it becomes possible to express the effectiveness of an operation as a function of both controllable and uncontrollable variables, e.g., $E = f(X, Y, Z)$, where E represents some measure of effectiveness and X, Y, and Z represent variables and parameters that in some manner influence E.

Given this functional relationship, which incidently may be extremely complex and difficult to derive, controllable variables can be manipulated in a manner such that those values which maximize E are indicated as the optimal course of action. As a very simple example, it can be shown [52] that the average daily census, C, in a hospital or in an individual nursing unit is largely a function of the average daily admission rate, λ, and the average length of stay, t, or $C = f(\lambda, t)$. This implies that control over the census may be achieved by a study of the admissions process or the length of stay of patients; these are factors well known to those engaged in utilization studies.

Again, it should be pointed out that the functional relationships alluded to may frequently be too complex for ease in obtaining analytical solutions. When this happens, it may become necessary to resort to computer simulation or other analogue models of a system as a means for evaluating alternative courses of action. Finally it may happen that in either case a unique analytical solution cannot be found — nor may it be required if sufficient insight is gained so as to indicate the decisions to be made.

HISTORY OF OPERATIONS RESEARCH

Military Origins

One can argue that operations research is as old as the basic sciences, with roots in the various traditional disciplines. From this point of view operations research may be considered to be a somewhat "eclectic" activity, engaged in the synthesis and the application of knowledge and methodologies drawn from such areas as engineering, economics, statistics and probability theory, and the behavioral sciences. Operations research has, however, during the last decade developed to the point where many investigators now consider it to be a distinct area for scholarship and training. Indeed substantial numbers of academicians in the field are occupied solely with theoretical and basic research rather than with the application of known techniques.

Actually the beginnings of operations research as such are often and somewhat arbitrarily traced to the United Kingdom during World War II, when groups of scientists were asked to work on a number of complex military operational problems that had previously defied objective solution. Although the groups were interdisciplinary, they consisted largely of physicists, mathematicians, and engineers, with a curious sprinkling of historians and philosophers. These operational research groups, as they were called, were concerned with such problems as the optimal utilization of radar, then newly developed; the effectiveness of mine laying and bombing patterns; submarine search techniques; and the evaluation of invasion plans. The research activities were soon enlarged to include the effects of the introduction of new weapons systems on organization and manpower, logistics, fire-power effectiveness, and ultimately tactics and strategies to be employed in conducting the war.

Today a number of organizations such as the RAND Corporation, the Institute for Defense Analyses, the Research Analysis Corporation, and a multitude of others are conducting research for various components of the defense establishment on such problems as defense posture, nuclear strategy, weapons systems, and the allocation of military resources.

Soon after the early 1940s the use of operations research spread to industry where it has usually been associated with industrial engineering and accounting activities. The basic approaches that had by now been developed were ideally suited for problems related to resource allocation, competitive strategies, product flow, and general operational decision making. Few large corporations today are without an operations research or management science activity.

Growth in Health Services

It is instructive for this discussion to look more closely at the growth of operations research in the health services. A somewhat recent development, it was made possible by the passage of the Hill-Burton Act in 1946 — which while providing government funds for the construction of hospitals also made available additional funds for research on problems of facilities development and utilization, generally in the form of grants to non-profit institutions. The kinds of problems that needed to be solved attracted the attention of operations analysts, although in spite of a number of early attempts, operations research as a clearly identifiable activity did not really emerge until the late 1950s, and then in essentially three phases.

During what might be considered the first phase, 1950–1956, much of the early work was conducted by industrial engineers [20]. Given the dilemma of hospitals confronted with ever-rising costs, shortages of manpower especially in nursing, and the inefficient use of facilities and resources, a number of industrial engineers were motivated to attempt to solve operational problems through the application of traditional techniques that had proved so successful in industry. Emphasis was therefore placed on work simplification and methods improvement with a concentration on the use of disposable supplies, the redesign of equipment, and the analysis of operational procedures in such areas as the laundry, dietary department, and pharmacy. Much of the early industrial engineering work was done by Smalley [39]; today a considerable amount of this kind of research is being done by independent management consulting firms.

The second phase, 1956–1962, was characterized by an intensified interest in administrative decision problems, a growing awareness of the potential of operations research approaches and techniques, and an increasing concern for bringing about significant improvements in staffing, logistics, and the utilization of facilities. Examples of the kinds of work done during this phase include the patient classification and nurse-staffing models of Connor [10–13], Wolfe [47, 48], and Young [53]; the prediction of demand by Flagle [18, 19] and Balintfy [4]; the control of bed utilization by Young, [51, 52]; and a variety of studies of out-patient departments, laboratories, and auxiliary facilities by others [20, 42, 49]. In general the models developed during this period concentrated largely on the solution of problems involving the allocation of scarce resources *within* a health-service facility.

The third phase, extending from 1962 on, reflects a shift in emphasis toward an examination of the *total* health delivery system rather than its components. Interests have been enlarged to include regional manpower allocation studies [37, 38], the development of computerized information systems for both medical and administrative decision-making [50], the evaluation of the care delivery process and the system within which this is carried out, and the investigation of the effects of increased reliance on technology in health [22, 43].

RECURRENT MODELS

Basic Approaches

It can be argued that to a considerable extent operations research, as a basic discipline, is much the same as statistics, probability theory, or mathematics. The fundamental principles of experimental design, regression analysis, and many other such analytical techniques have the inherent property of being applicable to a wide variety of industrial, social, or health problems. In a similar manner many of the approaches of operations research, based as they are on related mathematical concepts, find their applicability in myriad organizations where management decisions are required. For example, problems involving the allocation of resources under constraints are much the same and lead to models that can be structured similarly, whether one is considering industrial production, defense strategies, or the provision of health services.

More specifically models for the allocation of nursing manpower among nursing units are fundamentally the same as those for determining optimal product mix in a manufacturing facility; models of patient flow in an out-patient clinic are conceptually identical with those describing traffic flow on a highway, waiting lines in supermarkets, or aircraft landing patterns. This basic characteristic of operations research holds true in spite of the fact that parameters in any given situation may obviously be different, and the resultant models may display considerable modifications in their complexity.

Nevertheless it is often convenient to identify two fundamental types of operations research approaches frequently employed. These may be labeled a "cognitive" approach and a "normative" approach. The two are not necessarily mutually exclusive, and indeed the cognitive approach is often not accepted as true operations research unless ultimately imbedded in a subsequent normative model.

The cognitive approach is essentially *predictive*. The primary effort is to study the properties of a system and its behavior in order to gain understanding and insight. The aim of such research is largely to describe phenomenological processes and to predict outcomes without passing judgment on their desirability or undesirability. As will be seen, within this class of models may be included regression models, discriminant analysis, and queuing models, all of which explain and predict — but without any attempt at optimization as such.

Normative approaches, on the other hand, are *prescriptive* in that optimization of some sort is involved and decision rules are provided for administrative action. This necessarily implies some changes in the mode of operation with corrective action indicated where required in order to effect improvements.

It becomes helpful therefore to examine in greater detail the kinds of models frequently recurring when the two types of approaches are used, again with the caveat that the discussion here is necessarily oversimplified in order to present basic concepts and easily grasped examples. Real life is never this simple, and rarely can textbook examples be applied without considerable modifications or extensions.

Cognitive Models

STANDARD INDUSTRIAL ENGINEERING TECHNIQUES

Applied operations research relies heavily on data as input to the various model-building efforts. One can, of course, as a scholarly endeavor develop a variety of new potentially useful theoretical models and mathematical techniques, but no meaningful prescriptive decision rules can be provided for ultimate administrative action without quantitative information related to actual system operations. Industrial engineers have long recognized this fact and have developed numerous approaches for collecting data in the analysis of man-machine operations. Among them the most notable are time-and-motion study techniques, work sampling or activity analysis, link analysis, and flow charting.

Perhaps the best known example of the use of such techniques in health-services research is the work done by Connor [10–13], with regard to staffing nursing units within a hospital. Traditionally nursing-unit staffing had been accomplished by using, as a rule of thumb, some fixed amount of nursing hours/patient day, based on historical measures of peak needs. Such procedures did not take into account the highly variable daily demand for care or the chronic shortage of nursing personnel; indeed they were based more on the number of patients to be cared for than on the actual nursing care required by different patients.

Connor, using time-study and work-sampling techniques, measured the frequency and nature of patient demands and nursing services provided. In so doing, he was able to show a fundamental linear relationship between the degree of illness of patients, as reflected by their degree of self-sufficiency, and the nursing services required. An index of care needs was formulated based on daily patient information supplied by the nursing unit. Specifically this index was based on a patient classification system, and, as derived from the time-study data, it anticipates the total hours of direct care to be furnished to a patient population categorized as to the number of total, partial, or self-care patients. Staffing of nursing personnel was then accomplished on the basis of daily expected demand for care rather than on a physical count of bed occupancy. Since the constant shortage of nursing personnel on the nursing units prevented meeting peak needs on all units simultaneously, this index permitted the allocation of available resources where crucial needs were likely to occur.

The pioneering approaches used by Connor to address problems of staff allocation have since been applied with some modifications to a wide variety of situations in which activity analysis permits the determination of demand for services and the distribution of scarce manpower to meet these demands. Levine and Abdellah [29] have provided an excellent summary of the various efforts and the methodologies used to study patient care in a text particularly useful for nursing researchers.

A major concern of Bartscht et al. [6] has been the manpower required for staffing the many logistical functions within a hospital. Standard times, another traditional industrial engineering approach, were determined for laundry, dietary, and pharmacy operations and were used to plan personnel needs in terms of a workload based on daily in-patient bed occupancy. The methodologies used in these studies have been extended to analyze the operation and staffing of admissions offices, x-ray departments, messenger services, and many other ancillary services.

Studies by Smalley and others [39] have focused on the problems of make-or-buy long familiar to industry. Modern industrial production methods have been used to make available a variety of disposable products such as syringes, needles, gloves, and so forth. Human engineering concepts have been combined with work measurement techniques to study in-patient furniture and nursing-unit equipment. Many of these studies have led to rather dramatic improvements in patient care over the past decade.

STATISTICAL TECHNIQUES

In addition to the numerous industrial engineering tools available for data collection and activity analysis, statistics and probability theory provide a substantial underpinning to much of operations research. Although experimental design techniques and associated hypothesis testing are frequently used to determine the significance of operational variables, regression analysis is relied on quite heavily to explain and predict the effects of alternative courses of action. As an example Jelinek [27], in a detailed study that extended the earlier work of Connor, developed an econometric regression model of the total patient-care system on a nursing unit that provided increased understanding of the day-to-day operational aspects of nursing care and a method for periodically examining the effects of changes in organizational, workload, and environmental factors on the outcome of patient care. The model is useful not only for daily allocation of nursing staff but also for long-range planning of organizational and staffing policies. Additional work by Yett [49] has concentrated on the larger problem of overall nursing manpower needs for the future and is based on the application of complex sets of multiple-regression models.

The prediction of demand for and utilization of health-services facilities has been the focus of a number of attempts to apply econometric regression models. Largely the concern of health economists, the models have nevertheless implicitly suggested the cognitive approach of operations research. For example, Feldstein [14] and Rosenthal [36] examined the functional relationships between economic and demographic factors and the expected demand for hospitalization. Beenhakker [7] derived a multiple regression model that uses 117 factors to forecast future demand for hospital beds.

The fundamental concepts of a cognitive approach commonly called queuing theory are extremely useful in the analysis of input-output systems where the stochastic or time-dependent, probabilistic nature of the flow patterns create uncertainty as to the state of the system at any particular moment. For illustrative purposes a queuing system may be regarded as any sort of system in which elements arrive, requiring some kind of service at one or more service channels; when service is completed, each element departs, to be replaced in the service channel by a new element if there is such available from the general population of elements, or from a waiting line or queue that may have formed. Note that if arrivals and services can be completely scheduled, i.e., the system is deterministic, no serious problems are encountered.

For example, if exactly 10 patients arrive at a hospital facility each day and stay exactly ten days, the daily census would be 100 patients, with no variation and thus no uncertainty for the administrator as to expected patient load. The difficulties arise because of the probabilistic or stochastic nature of the arrival and service patterns. Frequently elements may enter the system in rapid succession and with very short interarrival times; occasionally long intervals will pass before the next arrival. Similarly service times may be short and many elements may be processed quickly. But a few long service times may mean that the system will be confronted with waiting elements. In other words the random flow patterns over time create an essential "feast or famine," leading to periods of congestion or of idleness for the service facility.

This kind of queuing problem arises in many different contexts, such as highway tollbooths, aircraft-landing facilities, ship-docking facilities, cafeteria lines, and telephone-trunking systems, to name a few. In the health services it is easy to recognize the potential value of queuing analysis for ambulatory clinics, x-ray departments, in-patient bed facilities, or pharmacy and laboratory services.

The objective, in the application of queuing theory techniques, is to analyze the systems under study so as to determine their behavior under varying conditions, i.e., to study the effects of changes in arrival and service patterns, system configuration, or servicing policy. These effects are often expressed in terms of $P_n(t)$, the probability that the system is in some state, n, at time t, with n denoting the number of elements in the system; $E(n)$, the expected or average state of the system; $Var(n)$, the variation in system state; and $W(t)$, the average waiting time for those elements in the system that must wait for service. Of course many other aspects of the system may also be studied, but the models then become correspondingly more complex.

Queuing models are generally cognitive, i.e., they describe system behavior and predict the consequences of any changes made. Because of this, a number of operations researchers insist that unless these models are embedded in a larger optimization model, the analysis is not truly operations research. It is easy to argue that this must ulti-mately occur in any event for the queuing approach to have any practical value. Consider, e.g., the options open to an administrator dealing with a service system. Depending on arrival patterns and the service-time distribution, he may choose to increase waiting lines and waiting times by reducing available service; by doing so, he decreases idleness in the service facilities. Or he may wish to decrease congestion by expanding service, thereby running the risk of in-creased periods of idleness. His choice of course will depend on the relative costs or utility associated with waiting and possible balking, reneging, or no-show, as opposed to the costs or utility of providing sufficient service and maintaining this service availability during inevitable periods of idleness. In some cases dramatic changes can be made with little increased overall system "cost" merely by chang-ing the scheduling system, rearranging service channel configurations, or changing the flow linkage through the service channels.

By way of illustrating basic concepts, consider the simplest possible queuing system, consisting of a single channel serving one element at a time. It is often assumed that the number of arrivals to the system per unit time is given by the well-known Poisson probability distribution; it immediately follows that the distribution of time intervals between arrivals follows what is known as the negative exponential density function. This assumption is based on the frequently observed natural phenomenon of a very large number of opportunities for an event, such as an arrival, to occur, but on a very small probability that the event will occur at any particular instant. Indeed it can be shown that arrivals to a hospital facility adhere to these concepts; in a large population there are many opportunities for an individual to become ill or have an accident and to require hospitalization, but small probabilities of this actually occurring [3].

Similarly it can be assumed that the distribution of service times in the single channel follows a negative exponential density function. For both arrivals and services this means, as noted earlier, that there will be many short-time intervals but occasional long ones — creating the randomness so often found in actual operations.

For this system a few long-service times, combined with rapid arrivals, tends to build up a waiting line which, theoretically, could become infinite. The system itself, might look as follows:

Arrivals	Waiting Elements	Service Channel	Departures
0——▶	0 0 0 0 0	0	0——▶

Under steady-state conditions (which means that the system has been operating sufficiently long for transient or time-dependent effects to die away — such as may be caused by the initial start up from state zero), the probability that n elements are in the system, i.e., in service and in the waiting line, is given by:

$$P_n = \rho^n (1 - \rho)$$

where

$$\rho = \frac{\lambda}{\mu}$$

and

λ = the average arrival rate in number/time
μ = the average service rate in number/time

The expected state of the system is given by

$$E(n) = \frac{\rho}{1 - \rho}$$

This means that if the average arrival rate is, say, 8/day and the average service rate is, say, 10/day, then $\rho = .8$. The average number in the system would be:

$$E(n) = \frac{.8}{1 - .8} = \frac{.8}{.2} = 4$$

It should be noted that as the arrival rate approaches the service rate, or as ρ approaches 1, the expected number in the system, $E(n)$, approaches infinity, implying a very large waiting line. Also, for $\rho = .8$, the probability of being in state zero, or the proportion of time the facility is idle, is:

$$P_o = (.8)^o (1 - .8) = .20$$

As ρ approaches 1, P_o approaches 0, and there will be no idle time. Simultaneously it can be shown that waiting time increases as ρ increases. This phenomenon is one that must be considered by administrators; if a long waiting line is felt to be undesirable, then excess service capacity must be provided, even though it may result in an occasional idle service facility. All too frequently, in spite of known random effects, service capacity is matched exactly to anticipated arrivals in order to minimize idle time, with resultant anguish over having to deal with inevitable long waiting lines.

The previous example is of course oversimplified. A number of assumptions have been made as to the arrival and service processes so as to enable an analytical solution and convenient equations. In the real world these assumptions may not hold, although it is frequently possible to use the resultant model as a rather close approximation to reality for all practical purposes. The queuing literature over the past decade has become extensive and deals with various multiple-channel system configurations, the effects of priorities, the advantages and disadvantages of scheduling policies for both arrivals and service, queue discipline, and transient behavior.

The work of Young [51, 52, 54] is an example of the application of queuing theory to a multiple-service channel system. The general aim of this study was to improve the stability and predictability of hospital in-patient census through the effective control of waiting lists and elective admissions. Initial investigations identified the existence of both chance and controllable, deterministic factors in the environment influencing bed occupancy. The research effort dealt with these simultaneously in order to provide meaningful decision rules for the hospital administrator.

It had been shown earlier by Bailey [1] that the average daily census is primarily a function of the admission rate and of the length of stay. Data collected in typical hospital in-patient areas revealed that admissions may be regarded in terms of a Poisson input superimposed on various kinds of scheduled inputs; and lengths of stay in terms of what are known as K-Erlang distributions (or modified Gammas) of which the negative exponential is a special case. Limited, parallel-channel queuing models and cybernetic control concepts describe the operation of a typical hospital ward. Two basic alternative systems were examined: one, an "adaptive control system," designates a decision level of B beds such that whenever occupancy dropped below B, a scheduled input was required, sufficient to raise the occupancy level back to B. The other system, "constant rate system," considers a constant scheduled daily input of elective admissions regardless of occupancy levels. Both systems assume a superimposed Poisson non-scheduled input.

Analytical and simulation results provided for the selection of decision rules as to the kind and amount of input, an indication of expected census levels, the number of patients to maintain on a "call list" in order to assure a proper flow of scheduled patients, and the "overflow" likely to be encountered after a unit happens to be filled to capacity. In the final analysis the choice of particular decision rules is shown to be a function of the relative values placed on retaining a high daily census as opposed to the risk of overflow; given the appropriate decision rules, system stability is improved and the more precise prediction of occupancy permits a more rational allocation of resources for patient care.

Similar use of queuing theory has been made in an analysis of congestion in out-patient clinics by Flagle [21] and Soriano [40], in a study of in-patient flow patterns by Balintfy [3], and in a study of the sequential two-stage, operating room—bed occupancy scheduling process by Resh [35]. More recently Gupta has suggested the use of queuing theory to plan hospital manpower needs [23].

Again it should be noted that once the simplifying assumptions of negative exponential distributions for arrival intervals and service times is removed, the mathematics used to study queuing problems tends to become extremely complex. At one time this proved to be an almost insuperable barrier in that the theory which could be handled mathematically did not fit the situations which it was desired to investigate practically. However, the advent of the computer and the subsequent ability to carry out Monte-Carlo type simulations on a massive scale have completely revolutionized the approach to applied queuing problems. Virtually all queuing problems can now be dealt with by simulation techniques, the main difficulty being the collection of meaningful data and the programming of a simulation model that validly reflects the system under study.

OTHER COGNITIVE MODELS

A number of other cognitive approaches of passing interest may be mentioned, although the claim that they are truly operations research is difficult to defend. They are nevertheless frequently used in the study of systems. Cybernetics, or control theory, has been mentioned in connection with queuing models of hospital in-patient units; feedback control based on information as to the state of the system can be used to determine further patient input.

Howland and McDowell have suggested cybernetic concepts to study the nurse-doctor-patient triad and to determine the nature of resources required to maintain desired equilibriums in the patient-care process [25].

Information theory, social dynamics, discriminant analysis, and pattern recognition techniques may also be mentioned as being useful in operations research studies. However, much of their potential value depends on additional quantitative, theoretical developments in these areas, which in turn depends on more widespread practical applications.

Normative Models

ALLOCATION MODELS

Perhaps the most widely applicable and therefore the most useful normative models of operations research are those dealing with resource allocation decision problems. The basic models, although conceptually similar, nevertheless are sufficiently different in their appropriate uses as to be called assignment models, transportation models, transshipment models, network flow models, shortest route models, traveling salesman models, and critical path models — to name just a few. These models are all special cases of linear optimization models or, more popularly, linear programming models, long familiar to economists.

Although mathematical programming models and their solutions may become extremely complex in any real-life situation and may take a variety of specific forms, the overall aim is to specify an objective, examine alternative ways of achieving that objective through the allocation of available resources, and select the optimal alternative while at the same time recognizing a number of constraints relating to the limited resources that may exist.

A very simple example may involve the allocation of various kinds of nurses to a number of clinics or hospital in-patient facilities so as to minimize the overall costs of the assignments. With this objective in mind, one must account for such constraints as the available number of nurses of each type, the differences in costs of particular assignments, and the needs or demands for patient services that must be satisfied. The models developed to study this kind of problem are usually called "assignment" models, if there is a one-to-one allocation of resource units to demand units; on the other hand, if resources from several sources are allocated to a number of facilities demanding these resources, with the objective of minimizing costs or maximizing some measure of gain, then the model may be termed a "transportation" model. Both of these models, nevertheless, are variants of the generic linear programming model.

As a very simple and admittedly somewhat unrealistic illustration of a basic linear programming model, assume that an out-patient facility must deal with two kinds of patients. Let X_1 and X_2 represent the number of each kind of patient seen within a particular planning time frame of, say, one day. Also assume that each patient of either type must pass through two clinics, C_1 and C_2, where C_1 may be a diagnostic or screening clinic and C_2 may be a treatment clinic. Total physician hours available in C_1 are, say, 36 hours/day; in C_2, 54 hours/day. It is known from experience that, on an average, patients of type 1 will require three hours in C_1 and nine hours in C_2, whereas patients of type 2 will require four hours in C_1 and three hours in C_2. This information may be displayed in tabular or matrix form as shown in Table 7-1.

Table 7-1. Example of a Basic Linear Programming Matrix

| | Type of Patient | | Total Hours |
Clinic	X_1	X_2	Available/Day
C_1	3	4	36
C_2	9	3	54

Now assume that some measure of value, perhaps reflecting quality of care or improvement in patient state, has been developed so that for each patient of type 1 passing through the facilities there is a "return in value of 12 units, and for each patient of type 2 a "return" of 10 units.

The overall objective is to determine the number of patients of each type to send through the clinics so as to maximize the total "return" value, while at the same time recognizing the constraints concerning the time required for each patient and the total physician hours available in each clinic. The solution to such a problem is by no means immediately obvious; as will be seen there are many alternatives that are "feasible" or possible, but only one alternative that is "optimal." It should also be noted at this point that since X_1 and X_2 represent "whole" patients expressed as integers, this kind of problem should be solved by using more appropriate integer programming techniques. However, the conceptual nature of the problem and the solution techniques are not significantly altered by adhering to basic linear programming techniques.

The "objective function" to be maximized, and which reflects the overall objective in quantitative terms, may be expressed as

$$\text{Total Value} = T = 12X_1 + 10X_2$$

where again X_1 and X_2 represent the number of patients of each kind seen in the clinics, and the coefficients 12 and 10 represent the units of value or "return"/patient of each kind. The constraints may be expressed as:

$$3X_1 + 4X_2 \leqslant 36$$

$$9X_1 + 3X_2 \leqslant 54$$

These equations simply state that the hours/patient in each clinic times the number of patients of each kind flowing through the clinic must be equal to or less than the total hours available in the clinic. Note that $X_1 = 2$ and $X_2 = 3$ satisfy each of the equations by using only 18 hours in C_1 and 27 hours in C_2. However, since the capacities of the clinics permit a greater patient load, these numbers of patients of each type constitute a feasible but not optimal solution. Indeed any values of X_1 and X_2 that satisfy the constraint equation are feasible; the task is, however, to find the particular values that maximize the objective function.

A problem this simple may be solved graphically. This will be done here to demonstrate the basic solution concepts. A more complex problem, however, involves many more constraint equations with many more variables and requires the use of the computer and an algorithm based on what is known as the "simplex method" for the solution of simultaneous equations. (An algorithm may be defined as a simplified solution technique, or a set of rules or procedures to follow, for standardized models so as to enable a solution without the necessity for rigorous and more lengthy analytical procedures.)

Graphically the situation just described is shown in Figure 7-1. In the graph are plotted the lines $9X_1 + 3X_2 = 54$ and $3X_1 + 4X_2 = 36$. These lines represent the upper bounds of the constraints, since whatever mix of X_1 and X_2 is chosen, the values must be such that the point on the graph representing the choices must be below the lines on the origin side of the graph. Furthermore, since the values of X_1 and X_2 must satisfy both constraints simultaneously, feasible solutions must be within the shaded portion of the graph. The objective then is to choose those values that will maximize the value return and still remain in the shaded polyhedron bounded by the constraint lines.

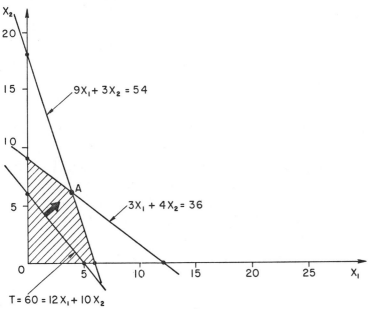

Fig. 7-1. Constraint equations with feasibility space.

The line $T = 12X_1 + 10X_2$ is also plotted on the graph for an arbitrary value of $T = 60$, since the exact position of this line will depend on the value of T. For $T = 0$ the line will intersect the origin; as T is increased, the line will move upward and to the right, while retaining the same slope. It should be noted that the values of X_1 and X_2 chosen must now satisfy the equation $T = 12X_1 + 10X_2$ and must lie within the shaded constraint space. Given the slope of the objective function line, the maximum value of T, in this instance, is obtained at the point A when $X_1 = 4$ and $X_2 = 6$ and $T = 108$. Since no other feasible values of X_1 and X_2 will provide a larger T, an optimal solution has been found.

Much more complex formulations than the preceding have been used to study the allocation of nursing skills to in-patient units in hospitals [30, 46], to provide an optimal mix of foods and nutrients in dietary services [2, 5], to determine the scheduling of patients into operating rooms and hospital beds [35], and to study the appropriate mix of health manpower within regions [37, 38].

The work of Wolfe serves as an excellent example. Although the patient classification system and the controlled variable staffing procedures developed by Connor [4, 13] provided an excellent basis for quantitatively staffing a nursing unit, they did not deal with the more qualitative aspects of nurse allocation. Wolfe [46, 48] applied integer linear programming techniques to refine the basic approach of Connor; within the framework of a multiple assignment model he attempted to match available personnel and individual skills to specific task complexes demanded by a variety of patients. This model yields information for the nursing service administrator not only as to the quantitative needs of any particular in-patient unit but also to the qualitative demands, i.e., what kinds or levels of nursing personnel are needed to meet varying nursing-care requirements of particular patients.

The formulation uses as its measure of effectiveness, expressed in terms of an objective function similar to the one discussed earlier, a cost that is based on a combination of physical and psychological value measures. This enables the allocation of personnel recommended by the model to be optimal for both the number of individuals necessary for the satisfaction of patient needs and for the qualifications that each of these individuals should possess.

Specific problems of logistical distribution and flow in such areas as dietary services have received considerable attention. Balintfy has employed linear programming techniques to study the economic planning of menus for hospital patients [2, 5]. Computer programs have been developed that will provide the dietitian with the proper mix and purchase quantities of food items, recognizing nutritional constraints, medical restrictions, and the need to minimize the overall costs of food service operations.

Shuman formulated an analytical framework for health-services planning that provides a more quantitative and a more logical basis for the planning process than present methods in use [37, 38]. The framework is essentially in the form of four mathematical programming models. Two of the models are concerned with regional health planning and focus on the relationships between manpower, technology, and production. More specifically the objective of the models is to minimize the total cost to a community for providing health services, subject to constraints imposed by quality requirements, available manpower and technology, demands for services, and limited funds. The objective function that has been developed attempts to balance the costs of providing indicated services against the economic loss associated with not furnishing the services. The remaining two models consider the effects of increasing productivity through the direct substitution of various personnel classes. One of these models has as its objective the minimization of the cost of assignment policies; the other, the maximization of the total quality level of the health services provided, with quality assumed to be a utility function of the personnel class providing a particular service and the average service time allotted.

Fetter and Thompson have for a decade been engaged in extensive simulation of a number of hospital subsystems, including maternity, out-patient, and surgical services [15, 16]. A major portion of this research has relied on queuing theory concepts for assessing the flow of patients through the subsystems and the resources required in response to this flow. The intent was to integrate the individual subsystem simulation models into a total hospital-systems model; responses to needs were to be aggregated over the entire hospital system so as to prescribe optimal allocation procedures for available resources. Unfortunately it was found that such an integrated simulation quickly becomes impossibly complex and unwieldy.

More significantly it was found that conclusions derived from the simulation model were often relatively insensitive to the vast detail included. As a result, current efforts have been redirected toward the development of macromodels of the total system that employ mathematical programming techniques. These models would essentially maximize utilization subject to cost and demand constraints and would include stochastic effects, non-linear resource limitations, and value judgments as to quality of services provided. Insights obtained from the earlier simulation efforts are of course expected to play a large role in shaping the new models, and relevant processes will be embedded in the analyses. Hopefully the flexibility of the models will enable extension to regional systems of health-care delivery.

The allocation of resources under constraint at whatever level in the health system is a perennial problem; programming models are proving to be extremely useful in approaching such problems. It is necessary, however, to express a caveat that is certain to have become apparent to the reader. Although the mathematical techniques and the algorithms for dealing with programming models, once they have been clearly formulated, are well established albeit complex, the development of the objective function and the delineation of the associated costs or value return for particular alternatives remain most difficult tasks for anyone attempting to apply these kinds of approaches.

GAME THEORY

Game theory seeks to deal with any human decision-making situation that involves conflict of interest. The methodology has proved useful to economists, political scientists, sociologists, industrial managers, and military strategists. It can be applied in any conflict situation where decisions must be made or a course of action or strategy must be selected from among many alternatives, and the opponent decision-makers may be viewed as competitive corporations, opposing armies, or a physician and nature. The distinctive feature of game theory is that the outcome, or payoff, of a decision may be uncertain and strongly influenced by the strategy chosen by a real or hypothetical rational opponent.

As a simple example, assume two decision-makers, P_1 and P_2, who are in conflict and who each has available three courses of action. The payoff matrix for the situation is displayed in Table 7-2. The numbers in the cells represent some payoff value to P_1 accord-

Table 7-2. Example of a Game Theory Payoff Matrix with "Saddle-Point"

		P_2 Alternatives			
		1	2	3	Min
P_1 Alternatives	1	4	3	6	③ max min
	2	2	1	3	1
	3	6	2	1	1
	Max	6	③	6	
			min max		

ing to his choice of action and P_2's simultaneous choice of action. If P_1 chooses alternative 2, e.g., and P_2 chooses alternative 3, then the payoff to P_1 is three units. Such a game is known as a "zero-sum" game in that no value is added to or subtracted from the game, i.e., what P_2 loses, P_1 must gain. This game of course is hardly fair for P_2, since he loses no matter what he does, but it is convenient for illustrative purposes in that negative values, which would indicate a payoff from P_1 to P_2 and which would complicate matters somewhat, can be neglected without detracting from basic concepts.

Obviously P_1 will wish to maximize his payoff and may therefore be tempted to choose alternative 3, hoping to receive six units if P_2 plays alternative 1. On the other hand, P_2, whose objective is to minimize his losses, will recognize that P_1 may be tempted to choose alternative 3 and may therefore select his own alternative 3 so as to reduce the payoff to 1 unit. Yet P_1 may reason that P_2 will follow this logic and select alternative 1 so as to gain six units. Such reasoning may go on endlessly and ultimately result in critical catatonia for both players; the basic question arises: What is the appropriate or optimal way to play the game, recognizing the objectives of each of the players?

Although a variety of approaches have been suggested [33], a useful and perhaps the most well-known one is the "minmax" approach, which offers a way toward a solution albeit with a somewhat pessimistic viewpoint. This approach requires that P_1 examine each alternative for the worst or minimum payoff that can occur. For alternative 1 this is three units, for alternative 2 this is one unit, and for alternative 3 this is one unit. Therefore if P_1 chooses alternative 1, he can assure himself of at least a three-unit payoff if P_2 chooses wisely, and more if P_2 does not. This is called the *maxmin* payoff for P_1 and, as can be seen, reflects a rather conservative decision-making attitude that may not be to the liking of those willing to take greater risks.

Note now that if one assumes P_2 is a rational decision-maker and equally conservative, he will examine each of his alternatives for the worst, or in this case the maximum payoff that can occur. For alternative 1 this is six units, for alternative 2 this is 3 units, and for alternative 3 this is six units. Therefore if P_2 chooses alternative 2, he can be certain that, regardless of what P_1 does, he will never have to pay more than three units and possibly less. This is known as the *minmax* payoff for P_2.

Acting rationally, neither player can do better; a "fixed strategy" is employed that selects a single or "pure" alternative, and since the maxmin = minmax, this game is said to have a "saddle-point" from which there will be no motivation to depart. Consider, however, the payoff matrix shown in Table 7-3.

Table 7-3. Example of a Game Theory Payoff Matrix without "Saddle-Point"

		P_2 Alternatives			
		1	2	3	Min
P_1 Alternatives	1	2	3	6	② max min
	2	2	1	3	1
	3	6	2	1	1
	Max	6	③	6	
			min max		

Here the maxmin is not equal to the minmax, and an examination of the matrix will show that no fixed strategies can be selected. If P_1 chooses alternative 1 so as to gain a maxmin payoff of at least two units, P_2 may anticipate this and switch from his minmax strategy to choose alternative 1 which assures this minimum payoff – a payoff less than the minmax payoff. But P_1 may reason that P_2 may do this and select alternative 3 for a payoff of six units. On the other hand, P_2, looking further ahead, might attempt to anticipate P_1's action and choose alternative 3 so as to reduce the payoff to one unit – which is less than P_1's maxmin. A continuation of this kind of search for a rational alternative will lead to the realization that no fixed strategies are available and there is no saddle-point.

It can be shown that P_1 and P_2 must make their selection on the basis of probabilities. Specifically each player can be provided with a "mixed" strategy that prescribes the proportion of time each alternative should be chosen if the game is played repetitively; or the particular alternative to be employed, using random number selection procedures if the game is a so-called one-shot affair. The determination of appropriate strategies can become very complex even for simple games such as the two described. A further discussion of techniques for doing so cannot be presented conveniently here. Rather the interested reader is referred to the voluminous literature for theoretical extensions in various kinds of situations [31, 45].

Suffice it to say that if the proper mixed strategies are employed by both players, a game "value" or expected payoff will be found that lies between the maxmin and the minmax. If it happens that this value is equal to zero, then the game is considered a "fair" game. If it is positive, as it will be in the game previously described, it is biased in favor of P_1; if negative, in favor of P_2.

Although widely used for industrial and military problems, especially in conjunction with computer-assisted simulations, meaningful game theory applications in the health services have not yet been evident. Nevertheless, of unique significance to health are the games against nature, derived from statistical decision theory, which may be simplified as follows: Assume two states of nature indicated by Θ_1, which represents the presence of a disease, and Θ_2 which represents the absence of a disease. Furthermore assume that a physician has available two courses of action — A_1, which is to treat and A_2, which is not to treat. Assume a payoff matrix as shown in Table 7-4, which now represents a value cost to the patient or to society for the states of nature and the actions taken.

Table 7-4. Example of a Game against Nature

		State of Nature	
		Disease	No Disease
Action		Θ_1	Θ_2
Treat	A_1	2	3
Don't treat	A_2	10	1

If one knows the specific state of nature, then a specific course of action can easily be selected. For example, if Θ_1 exists, which means the disease is present, then A_1 should obviously be chosen so as to minimize costs to two units. Such a game is known as decision-making under *certainty*.

On the other hand, if the specific state of nature is not known, but nature's strategies are known, i.e., from experience it is known, e.g., that Θ_1 occurs one-tenth of the time and Θ_2 occurs nine-tenths of the time, then the "expected" or average cost for each action can be computed as:

$$A_1 = 2(.1) + 3(.9) = 2.9$$

$$A_2 = 10(.1) + 1(.9) = 1.9$$

The minimum average cost of 1.9 occurs for A_2, and this is the appropriate action to be taken. Such a game is known as decision-making under *risk*.

If nature's strategies are completely unknown, then nature may be treated as a rational opponent, and the minmax approach may be applied to yield fixed or mixed strategies. Such a game is known as decision-making under *uncertainty*. Complete ignorance of nature's strategies is rarely the case; usually some information, however imprecise, is available that can improve the expected payoff.

A more complex approach would be to construct tests for the states of nature and to base the selection of a course of action on the results of such tests. If the test outcomes are probabilistic, or imperfect, much more extensive techniques must be used than can be described here. Such games, however, have been found to be useful for problems related to diagnosis and therapy, especially now that computers are available to assist in the mathematical manipulations of data required for solutions. Flagle, e.g., has cast the entire process of diagnosis and therapy into the format of a game against nature [17], recognizing that this kind of approach requires a set of probabilities relating symptoms to a disease; values or cost of outcomes of actions taken, which may be quite difficult to assess; and a rational process, not necessarily the minmax, for combining probabilities and values to arrive at an optimal decision.

A related model, similar to that of decision-making under risk, is one based on Churchman's so-called approximate measure of value [9]. This approach, used by Stimson [41] for regional public health planning and by Hellman [24] for evaluation of NIH research expenditures combines elements of game theory, the well-known Delphi technique, and probability theory for the evaluation of alternative courses of administrative action.

As a rather simple example, however unrealistic, assume that one is evaluating alternative public-health programs for dealing with a particular disease. Assume further that one is confronted with multiple objectives such as: O_1: to reduce the incidence of the disease, O_2: to minimize the cost of the program, and O_3: to minimize the time required for results.

These objectives may conflict in the sense that some alternatives may reduce incidence rather strikingly but at an almost unacceptable cost. Another alternative may reduce incidence adequately and may be relatively inexpensive but may require too long to implement. In any event suppose that by means of Delphi techniques, or any other sociological or psychological measuring and scaling techniques, the three objectives just noted have been selected as the most significant, and, moreover, that they have been assigned normalized relative values based on rank order of preference as given: $O_1 = .55$, $O_2 = .35$, and $O_3 = .10$.

The situation may be displayed in the matrix shown in Table 7-5. A_1, A_2, and A_3 represent alternative programs, and the numbers in

Table 7-5. Example of Relationship of Objectives and Alternatives

		Objectives		
		O_1	O_2	O_3
Relative Value		.55	.35	.10
	A_1	1	.1	.4
Alternatives	A_2	.3	1	1
	A_3	.5	.2	.6

the cells represent the probability that the particular alternative will achieve a given objective. Needless to say, these probabilities and for that matter the relative values of the objectives may be very difficult to obtain in any practical situation.

The three alternative programs may now be evaluated much like the strategies for games under risk, using expected values, i.e.:

Effectiveness of $A_1 = .55(1) + .35(.1) + .10(.4) = .625$
Effectiveness of $A_2 = .55(.3) + .35(1) + .10(1) = .615$
Effectiveness of $A_3 = .55(.5) + .35(.2) + .10(.6) = .405$

Since the computed expected effectiveness of A_1 is the greatest, this alternative emerges as the optimal course of action. Several deficiencies in this approach, however, should appear obvious. If, e.g., three alternative programs are being evaluated rather than three alternatives for a single program, the approach just described represents an all-or-nothing action which is rarely the case. One may construe the relative effectiveness measures as an indication of the apportionment of effort, but not without at least further assignment of relative values to the three programs. Also public-health planning is not a static decision-making process. Over a period of time objectives may change, the degree of success of a particular alternative may require reevaluation, shifts in available resources may constrain efforts, and the political climate may force modification of program directions. The model, as it stands, requires much more complex extension in order to convert it into a dynamic optimization framework. Theoretical efforts along these lines are extensive, but they have as yet yielded little that can be conveniently applied in any meaningful health-services situation. Hopefully, usable models will become available in the near future.

INVENTORY THEORY

Inventory theory, as the name suggests, was originally developed largely to deal with problems relating to industrial and military stocking policies, wherein sometimes even small changes in policy can be translated into enormous reductions in costs. As will be seen, however, inventory theory models are not restricted to inventory problems as such; rather they can be applied to a variety of input-output situations in which, as opposed to the usually cognitive nature of queuing theory, some optimization of flow is sought. Indeed it is frequently the case that queuing theory models are imbedded in a larger inventory model in order to achieve a prescription for action to be taken. It should also be noted that inventory models, derived as they are from the basic mathematics of electronic circuit theory, can easily be modified to deal with feedback systems, wherein some measure of administrative control is desired.

The main elements of fundamental inventory problems are the costs that result from various stocking policies. Carrying stock such as drugs in a pharmacy service, e.g., incurs costs owing to inventory investment, storage facilities, handling, and perhaps spoilage or obsolescence. Nevertheless such costs are often tolerated in order to avoid even greater costs, tangible and intangible, that might arise from shortages. Additional costs might also result from frequent reordering or replenishment of supplies. The primary objective of inventory theory is to seek a policy that balances these various costs in such a manner that the overall costs are minimized.

Simple inventory problems usually focus on three costs, namely, C_1 as the carrying cost/unit for a given length of time, C_2 as the shortage cost/unit for the length of time that the shortage exists, and C_3 as the cost of replenishment each time this occurs. If I_1 is the average inventory carried, I_2 the average shortage incurred, and N the number of times stock is replenished, then ETC = $I_1 C_1$ + $I_2 C_2 + NC_3$ is the "expected total cost" of the inventory policy for the time period under consideration. Obviously increasing the amount of inventory reduces the shortage costs and the number of times that replenishment must occur. But this will also increase carrying costs. Depending on the relative costs, surplus must be balanced against shortages; if replenishment costs are small, frequent replenishment can avoid either a large inventory or shortages. The problem then is to determine the amount of inventory to be carried and the frequency of replenishment so as to minimize the overall costs of the supply operation.

As a very simple example, assume that the optimal inventory level of a particular drug is to be determined. Assume also that the shortage costs are infinite, which implies that having the drug on hand is sufficiently crucial so that no shortages are permitted. To further simplify the problem for illustrative purposes, assume that q is the quantity of the drug ordered each time that an order is placed, T the total time for which the inventory policy is to be determined, t the interval between placing orders, and r the usage rate of the drug during each t. A pictorial model of the situation is given in Figure 7-2.

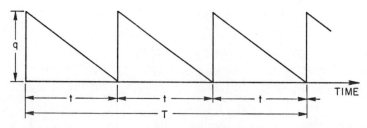

Fig. 7-2. Determining optimal inventory level when no shortages are permitted.

The pictorial model, it should be noted, assumes a uniform usage rate during each interval, t, and also assumes that inventory is replaced instantaneously. This means that the rate of use of the drug within the replenishment scheduling period t is given as $r = q/t$. The average inventory carried over T, by geometry, may be determined as $q/2$. If T is taken as some unit time period, then the number of times stock is replenished, N, is given by $1/t = r/q$. The expected total inventory cost of this system, then, is:

$$\text{ETC} = \frac{qC_1}{2} + \frac{rC_3}{q}$$

i.e., the sum of the average carrying costs plus the replenishment costs. The objective now is to determine the optimal inventory level, q_o, so as to minimize the expected total costs of the system.

Another way of looking at the problem is shown in Figure 7-3. Here the average inventory costs, $qC_1/2$ can be seen to increase linearly with q, whereas the replenishment costs, rC_3/q decrease with q. The expected total cost, ETC, is the sum of each of these costs for each q and has a minimum point at q_o. Mathematically the equation for ETC represents an objective function without constraints; as such the easiest way to determine the minimum ETC is to use straightforward techniques of the calculus and differentiate

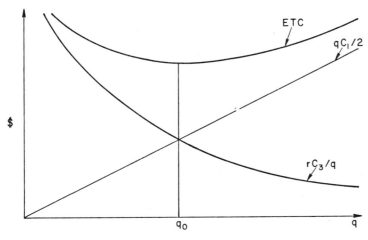

Fig. 7-3. Relationship of inventory costs to inventory level.

the preceding equation with respect to q, set the derivative equal to zero, and solve for what then will be q_o. If this is done, the solution is found to be:

$$q_o = \left[\frac{2rC_3}{C_1} \right]^{\frac{1}{2}}$$

which will be recognized as the standard lot size formula often used in industry. The optimal reorder period, t_o, may be determined by $t_o = q_o/r$ and the minimum expected total cost by:

$$ETC_o = \frac{q_o C_1}{2} + \frac{rC_3}{q_o}$$

More complex models consider the effects of shortages. If the cost of shortage is not too severe compared to carrying costs, the optimal solution for minimum total costs may suggest permitting a certain amount of shortage during each time period. It should be noted that most elementary inventory models consider mainly the three costs already discussed, recognizing that these costs can represent a combination of a variety of specific individual costs. If other kinds of costs enter the picture, they can be dealt with, but of course the models that need to be developed become increasingly complex. Realistic models, which are inevitably more complex than simple textbook examples, must consider variable demand or usage rates, substitutability of items in the event of shortage, variable reorder periods, lead times, discount or price breaks, multiple-item reordering, and so on. In many instances actual problems may lead to intractable mathematical models, and one must resort to computer simulation for solutions.

As implied earlier, inventory models have found widespread usage, especially in industry and the military, for the solution of many different kinds of problems related to supplies. There have been some applications in the health field as well. Middelhoven, e.g., studied the correlation between the demand for nursing-unit supplies and measures of the care needs of individual patients, taking into account the stochastic nature of illness [32]. His ultimate aim was to develop administrative mechanisms for determining optimal inventory levels for central supply items that would provide both adequate supply and indications of departures from expected usage. The effectiveness of an automatic supply delivery system was evaluated in terms of anticipated shortages and the cost of delays. Guides were provided for use in determining the appropriate items to be stored on a nursing unit and their inventory levels, based on an analysis of usage rates and the storage space available.

Reed proposed procedures for improved economic control of general hospital inventories; emphasis is placed on optimal reorder points and purchase quantities [34]. Hsieh [26] designed a linen distribution system that is responsive to fluctuations in daily needs of a nursing unit caused by changes in the characteristics of a patient population as measured by Connor's classification system [13]. Jennings proposed an inventory theory as a means of controlling whole blood in a hospital blood bank [28].

In a broader context inventory theory models may be applied in many different situations in which the chief concern is with estimating the level of resources to have available over time, and in which a cost of maintaining this level must be balanced against a cost of shortage. Young imbedded the queuing models developed for studying in-patient bed utilization into a modified inventory model in order to designate optimal decision rules for admitting elective patients [54]; essentially the positive value of maintaining a desirable census level was balanced against the negative value of shortage represented by overflow. In addition he showed how inventory theory concepts could be applied to determine the optimal number of beds within units; here the costs of providing the beds and their occasional underutilization are balanced against the costs of shortage when demanded and not available.

Inventory theory models are also of value for estimating the number of clinics to have available in a given facility and the manpower required to staff them. Again the costs of providing the resources must be compared with the risk of shortage. Finally the approaches are applicable to the analysis of manpower problems, when the costs of training and maintaining a variety of skills are considered relative to the costs of shortages that might occur over time.

The approaches that have been discussed here are perhaps the most well known in operations research and are potentially the most useful for application to health-services problems. A number of other approaches may be mentioned, however, as a matter of some interest. A more detailed discussion can easily be found in any standard text on operations research [44].

Deterioration and obsolescence cause replacement problems. Some things, such as a physical facility, may deteriorate or become obsolete slowly and may permit more or less long-range planning for replacement. Other things, such as electronic equipment, may become inoperative without warning. The problem facing an administrator is to make decisions that balance the costs of preventive maintenance or of anticipating replacement against the risks and the associated costs of operational failures.

Preventive maintenance of equipment is a problem common to every organization. Replacement models have been developed that show, e.g., that the mass replacement of light bulbs in a manufacturing plant area is less costly than individual replacement as bulbs burn out. The same concepts have been applied to the replacement of electronic gear in aircraft or ships.

Although somewhat tenuous and requiring considerable additional research, similar approaches may be applied to problems of preventive care. Functional breakdown in patients may be viewed in terms of a replacement model, i.e., one would attempt to balance the costs of preventive care with the costs of breakdown that might occur with or without such preventive care. This would lead to some level of preventive care that would serve to minimize the total costs of the care delivery system.

Search problems arise when there are limited resources, such as time or skills, to use in detection. Sophisticated mathematical techniques for such problems were developed during World War II in the search for enemy submarines or for mines in a minefield. These techniques have since been applied to the exploration for oil and other minerals and are now being considered for use in the detection of disease. Examples include the search for diseases that can be detected by blood tests or the detection of patterns in x-rays.

Sequencing or scheduling models are concerned with elements waiting to be processed at a series of facilities of some sort where a decision must be made as to the order in which they should be handled. The objective is to minimize the idle time of the facilities; an alternative objective might be to maximize the throughput of elements. It is clear that such models are applicable for clinic scheduling, in-patient admissions procedures, laboratory testing sequences, and operating-room scheduling, as examples. Although the theoretical models are complex and their usefulness has been somewhat limited, nevertheless the underlying concepts have been of inestimable value when combined with simulation techniques. Indeed the familiar Gantt charts, the Program Evaluation and Review Techniques (PERT), and the Critical Path Method (CPM) are all based on fundamental sequencing notions.

COMMENT

A number of concluding comments are in order. Some of them relate to the rather considerable current research attention being directed toward the creation of what are variously called health-, hospital-, or regional-information systems. Associated with ongoing or proposed research efforts is the almost ritualistic assertion that the "systems analysis approach" is being applied to the design of future automated processes for the improvement of the quality of care. Many of the current efforts reflect a growing and desirable interest in the area of information flow, i.e., the creation, acquisition, storage, and retrieval of pertinent data within health systems for use in medical and administrative decision-making.

A rather disturbing characteristic of contemporary research, however, has been the lack of regard for the total decision framework within which the developing information systems are to operate. A viable system must be capable of decision and control as well as communication; the flow of data is of limited usefulness as a management tool unless it is synthesized into a form that prescribes action to be taken. If a health-services system is viewed as a communications network, with its functional components as information network nodes, then the kinds of approaches discussed here are necessary for building decision rules into the system at every node. When combined with the concurrent flow of data reflecting the state of the system at any given time, these decision rules enable a more dynamic response in the allocation of nursing services and logistical resources, the utilization of facilities, and the selection of therapeutic strategies.

The potential for operations research in the health services is considerable. Although many of the applications to date have concentrated largely on what may be considered administrative decision problems, increasing amounts of study have shifted toward such areas as the logic of screening and diagnosis, and the decisions required for therapy. The quality of patient care is another matter that has been the object of rather more subjective discussion than prescriptive quantification — future research obviously calls for the application of such techniques as discriminant analysis combined with linear or dynamic programming techniques similar to those proposed by Burroughs [8] and Liebman [30].

Another important development is the notion of comprehensive patient care and the creation of health-maintenance organizations. The hospital is no longer thought of as an isolated institution but as a member of a set of health services that include home care, rehabilitation, extended care, and multiphasic screening. Here again there is need to synthesize new systems, to estimate human and physical resources required for a myriad of new demands. The techniques of operations analysis are clearly called for to convert qualitative concepts of health services into effective working systems.

Let no one be persuaded, however, that operations research offers magical solutions to complex problems. Indeed one can argue that to date operations research has not led to any significant or profound changes in health-care delivery, even when the extensive applications in nursing care are considered. To some extent the argument is valid — although operations research has proved to be immensely useful to defense and to industry, its impact on health is not yet so evident. There are several reasons why this may be so. First, there are relatively few high-quality operations research practitioners in health, with many of the best still being absorbed in military and industrial problems. Second, operations research is still not as well understood or accepted by the health professionals. Finally and perhaps most importantly, the problems and objectives in the military and industry have been more readily identified; in health this has not yet been done and all indications are that they will prove much more difficult and elusive.

This discussion has emphasized some of the more important fundamental aspects of operations research and has indicated a number of well-known instances in which the techniques have been applied in the health services. The models that have been presented and the applications referred to can hardly be regarded as exhaustive; indeed one can easily argue that they are rather inadequate. In the interests of clarity regarding basic concepts, oversimplification has been the rule. Spatial constraints do not permit the kind of detailed examination of approaches and techniques that is obviously desirable. Similarly it would prove to be an enormous task to attempt to list the growing variety of research efforts in the health services during the last few years that have utilized operations research methodologies. Hopefully, however, sufficient interest in the potential of operations research for improving health-care delivery has been stimulated so as to motivate further inquiry and understanding.

REFERENCES

1. Bailey, N. T. J. Statistics in hospital planning and design. *Journal of the Royal Statistical Society: Applied Statistics* 5(3):146–157, November, 1956.
2. Balintfy, J. L. Menu planning by computer. *Communications of the ACM,* 7(4):225–259, April, 1964.
3. Balintfy, J. L. Mathematical Models and Analysis of Certain Stochastic Processes in General Hospitals. Doctoral dissertation, The Johns Hopkins University, 1962.
4. Balintfy, J. L. A stochastic model for the analysis and prediction of admissions and discharges in hospitals. In C. W. Churchman and M. Verhulst (Eds.), *Management Sciences: Models and Techniques,* vol. II. New York: Pergamon Press, 1960.
5. Balintfy, J. L., and Prekopka, A. Nature of random variation in nutrient composition of meals. *Health Services Research* 1:141–169, Fall, 1966.
6. Bartscht, K. G., et al. The Development of an Effective Method for Determining Staffing Requirements in Hospitals. *Project Report, Hospital Systems Research Group,* University of Michigan, February, 1965.
7. Beenhakker, H. L. Multiple correlation: A technique for prediction of future hospital bed needs. *Operations Research* 11(5):824–839, September-October, 1963.

8. Burroughs, M. O. Quantitative Measures for Quality of Nursing Care. Master's essay, The Johns Hopkins University, 1967.

9. Churchman, C. W., Ackoff, R. L., and Arnoff, E. L. *Introduction to Operations Research.* New York: Wiley and Sons, 1957.

10. Connor, R. J. Hospital work sampling with associated measures of production. *Journal of Industrial Engineering* 11(2):105–107, March–April, 1961.

11. Connor, R. J. A work sampling study of variations in nursing work load. *Hospitals* (Chicago) 35(9):40–41, May, 1961.

12. Connor, R. J., et al. Effective use of nursing resources: A research report. *Hospitals* (Chicago) 35(9):30–39, May, 1961.

13. Connor, R. J., et al. A Hospital Inpatient Classification System. Doctoral dissertation, The Johns Hopkins University, 1960.

14. Feldstein, P. J., and German, J. J. Predicting hospital utilization: An evaluation of three approaches. *Inquiry* 2(1):13–36, June, 1965.

15. Fetter, R. B., and Thompson, J. D. A decision model for the design and operation of a progressive patient care hospital. *Medical Care* 7(6):450–462, November–December, 1969.

16. Fetter, R. B., and Thompson, J. D. The simulation of hospital systems. *Operations Research* 13(5):689–711, September–October, 1965.

17. Flagle, C. D. A Decision Theoretical Comparison of Three Methods of Screening for a Single Disease. *Proceedings of the 5th Berkeley Symposium on Mathematical Statistics and Probability,* 1965.

18. Flagle, C. D. Operations research in the health services. *Operations Research* 10(5):591–603, September-October, 1962.

19. Flagle, C. D. The problem of organization for hospital inpatient care. In C. W. Churchman and M. Verhulst (Eds.), *Management Science: Models and Techniques,* vol. II. New York: Pergamon Press, 1960.

20. Flagle, C. D., and Young, J. P. Application of operations research and industrial engineering to problems of health services, hospitals, and public health. *Journal of Industrial Engineering* 17(11):609–614, November, 1966.

21. Flagle, C. D., et al. Analysis of Congestion in an Outpatient Clinic. *Final Report, USPHS Grant W-96.*

22. Gabrieli, E. R., et al. The use of data mechanization and computers in clinical medicine. *Annals of the New York Academy of Sciences* 161:37–830, September, 1969.

23. Gupta, I., Zoreda, J., and Kramer, N. Hospital manpower planning by use of queuing theory. *Health Services Research* 6(1):76–82, Spring, 1971.

24. Hellman, L. P. A Value Measure for Selecting Proposals for Research Grant Support. Doctoral dissertation, The Johns Hopkins University, 1967.

25. Howland, D., and McDowell, W. E. The measurement of patient care: A conceptual framework. *Nursing Research* 13(4):4–7, Winter, 1964.

26. Hsieh, R. K. C. A Study of Linear Processing and Distribution in a Hospital. Master's essay, The Johns Hopkins University, 1961.

27. Jelinek, R. C. A structural model for the patient care operation. *Health Services Research* 2:226–242, Fall-Winter, 1967.
28. Jennings, J. B. Hospital Blood Bank Whole Blood Inventory Control. *Technical Report #27,* Operations Research Center, MIT. December, 1967.
29. Levine, E., and Abdellah, F. G. *Better Patient Care Through Nursing Research.* New York: Macmillan, 1965.
30. Liebman, J. S. The Development and Application of a Mathematical Programming Model of Personnel Allocation in an Extended Care Unit. Doctoral dissertation, The Johns Hopkins University, 1971.
31. Luce, R. D., and Raiffa, H. *Games and Decisions.* New York: Wiley & Sons, 1958.
32. Middelhoven, W. Analysis and Reorganization of a Central Supply Delivery System. Master's essay, The Johns Hopkins University, 1964.
33. Miller, D. W., and Starr, M. K. *The Structure of Human Decisions.* Englewood Cliffs: Prentice-Hall, 1967.
34. Reed, R., Jr., and Stanley, W. Optimizing control of hospital inventories. *The Journal of Industrial Engineering* 16(1):48–51, January–February, 1965.
35. Resh, M. Mathematical Programming of Admissions Scheduling in Hospitals. Doctoral dissertation, The Johns Hopkins University, 1967.
36. Rosenthal, G. D. Factors affecting the utilization of short-term general hospitals. *American Journal of Public Health* 55(11):1734–1740, November, 1965.
37. Shuman, L. J. Mathematical Models for Health Manpower Planning. Doctoral dissertation, The Johns Hopkins University, 1969.
38. Shuman, L. J., Young, J. P., and Naddor, E. Manpower mix for health services: A prescriptive regional planning model. *Health Services Research* 6(2):103–119, Summer, 1971.
39. Smalley, H. E., and Freeman, J. R. *Hospital Industrial Engineering.* New York: Reinhold, 1966.
40. Soriano, A. A Comparative Study of Block and Individual Appointment Systems in the Outpatient Department. *Progress Report, USPHA GRANT W-167.*
41. Stimson, D. H. Decision-Making and Resource Allocation in a Public Health Agency. Doctoral dissertation, University of California, Berkeley, 1965.
42. Stimson, D. H., and Stimson, R. H. Operations Research and Systems Analysis in Hospital Administration. *Working Paper No. 147.* University of California, Berkeley: Institute of Urban and Regional Development, 1971.
43. Technology and Health Services. *Proceedings of the IEEE,* 57(11), November, 1969.
44. Wagner, H. M. *Principles of Operations Research.* Englewood Cliffs: Prentice-Hall, 1969.
45. Williams, J. D. *The Compleat Strategyst.* New York: McGraw-Hill, 1954.
46. Wolfe, H. A Multiple Assignment Model for Staffing Nursing Units. Doctoral dissertation, The Johns Hopkins University, 1964.

47. Wolfe, H., and Young, J. P. Staffing the nursing unit, part I: Controlled variable staffing. *Nursing Research* 14(3):236–243, Summer, 1965.
48. Wolfe, H., and Young, J. P. Staffing the nursing unit, part II: The multiple assignment technique. *Nursing Research* 14(4):299–303, Fall, 1965.
49. Yett, D. E. The supply of nurses: An economist's view. *Hospital Progress* 46:88–102, February, 1965.
50. Young, J. P. A conceptual framework for hospital administrative decision systems. *Health Services Research* 3(2):79–95, Summer, 1968.
51. Young, J. P. Administrative control of multiple channel queuing systems with parallel input streams. *Operations Research* 14(1):145–156, January–February, 1966.
52. Young, J. P. Stabilization of inpatient bed occupancy through control of admissions. *Hospitals* (Chicago) 39(19):41–48, October, 1965.
53. Young, J. P. A Method for Allocation of Nursing Personnel to Meet Inpatient Care Needs. *Report on USPHS Grant, GM 005537-05,* October, 1962.
54. Young, J. P. A Queuing Theory Approach to the Control of Hospital Inpatient Census. Doctoral dissertation, The Johns Hopkins University, 1962.

Index